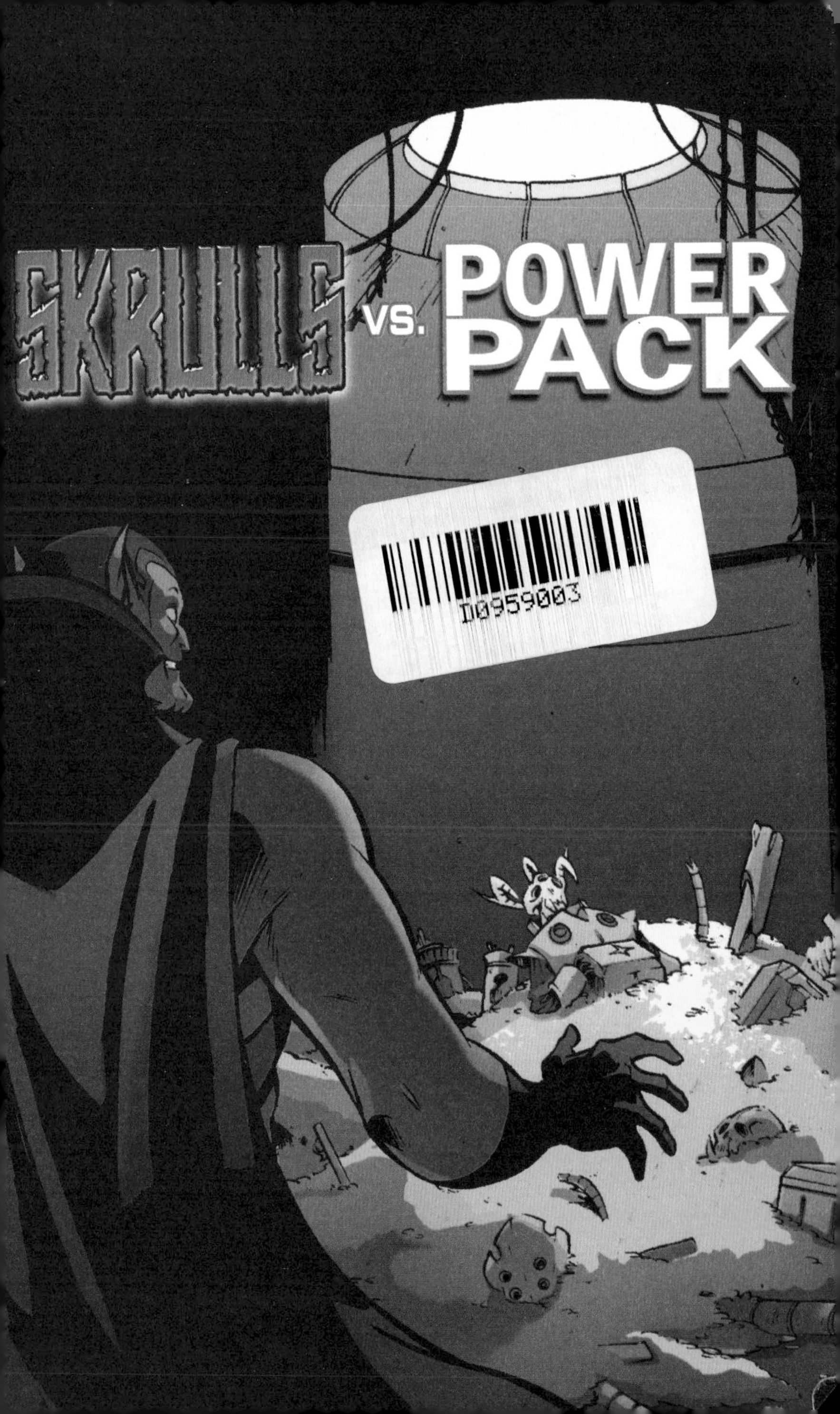
SKRULLS vs. POWER PACK

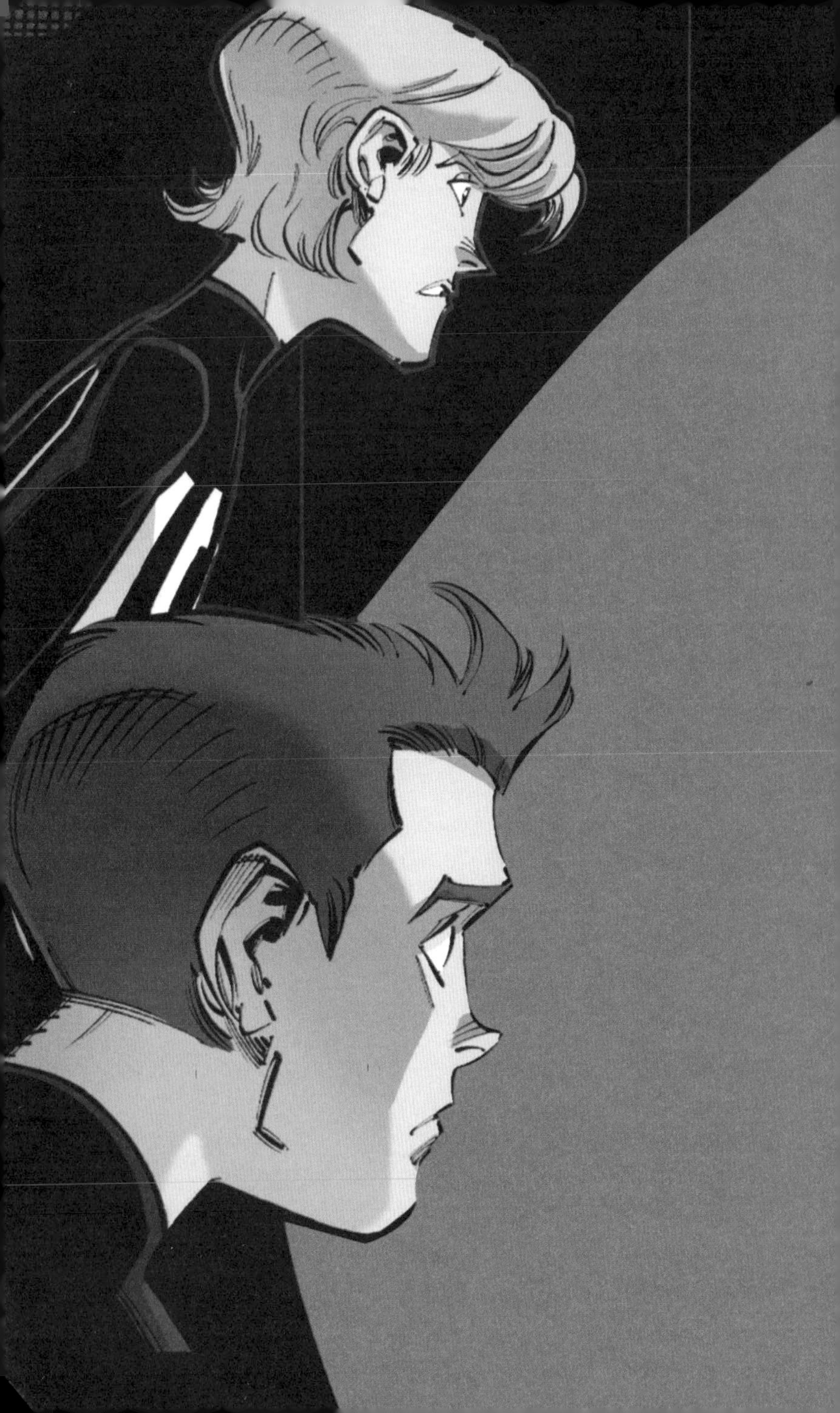

SKRULLS VS. POWER PACK

Writer: Fred Van Lente
Pencilers: Cory Hamscher
with Jacopo Camagni & Gurihiru
Inkers: Cory Hamscher
with Norman Lee & Gurihiru
Colorist: Gurihiru with Wil Quintana
Letterer: Dave Sharpe
Cover Art: Gurihiru
Consulting Editor: Mark Paniccia
Editor: Nathan Cosby

Collection Editor: Jennifer Grünwald
Editorial Assistant: Alex Starbuck
Assistant Editors: Cory Levine & John Denning
Editor, Special Projects: Mark D. Beazley
Senior Editor, Special Projects: Jeff Youngquist
Senior Vice President of Sales: David Gabriel
Book Designer: Carrie Beadle

Editor in Chief: Joe Quesada
Publisher: Dan Buckley

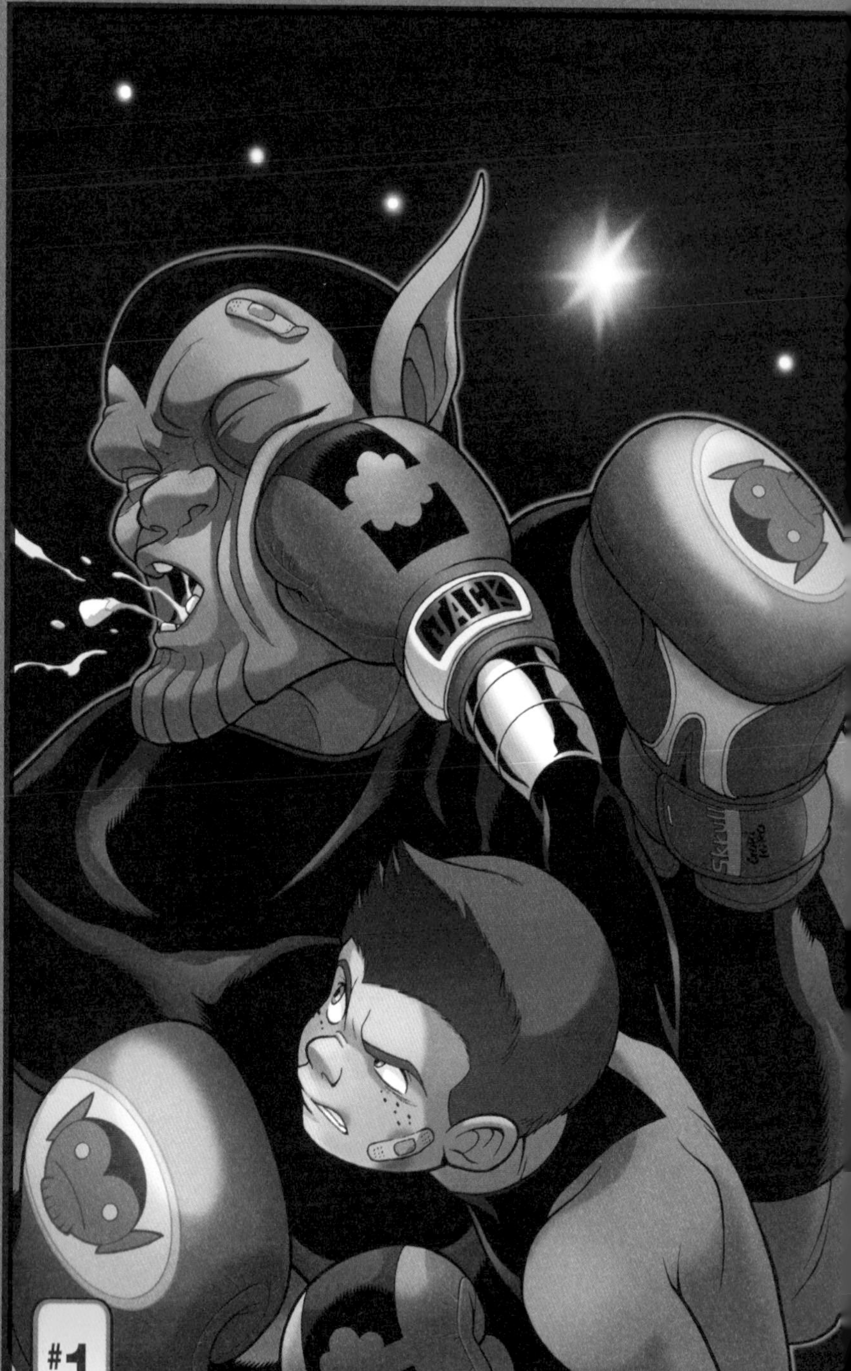
JACK
Skrull

#1

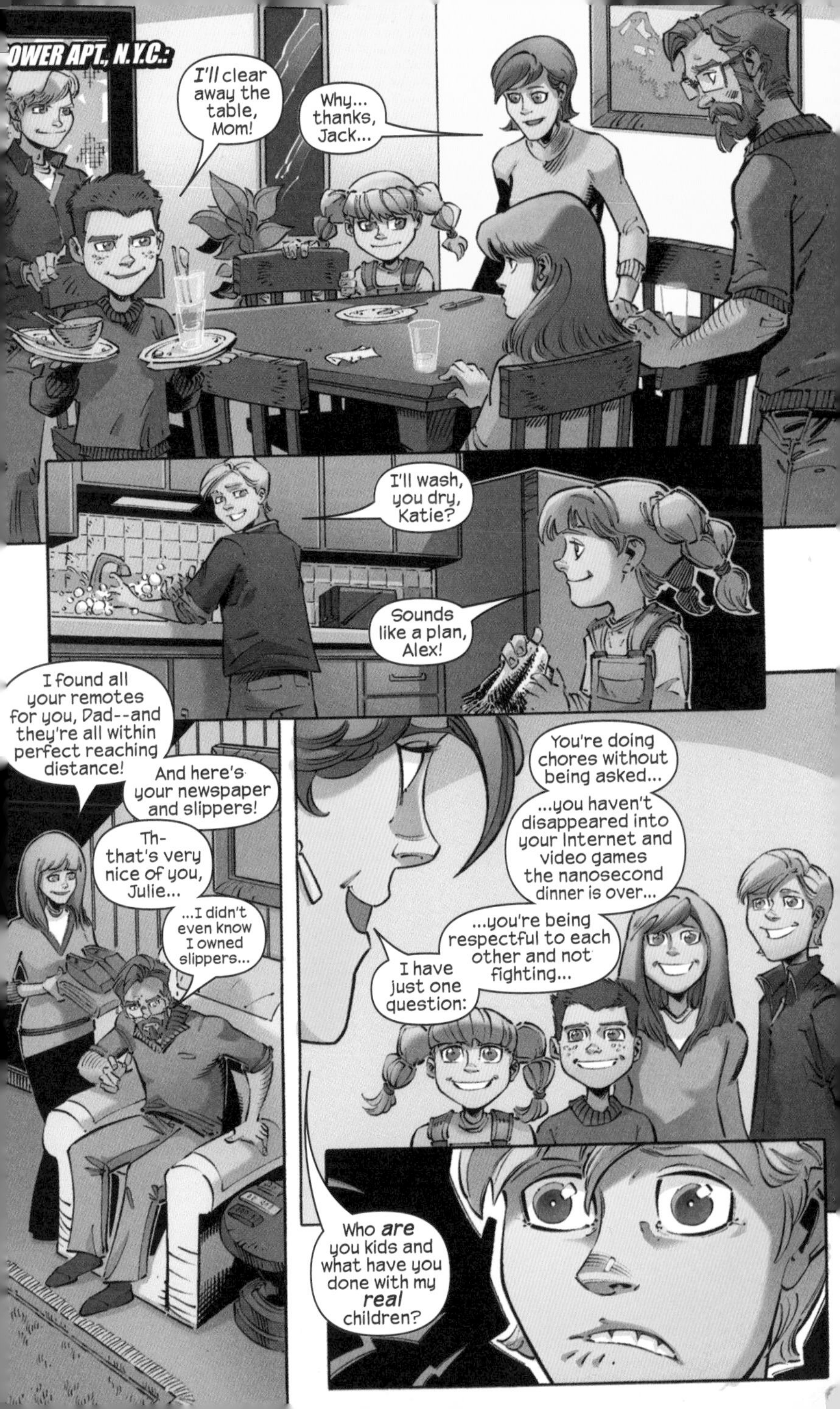

OWER APT., N.Y.C.:
I'll clear away the table, Mom!
Why... thanks, Jack...
I'll wash, you dry, Katie?
Sounds like a plan, Alex!
I found all your remotes for you, Dad--and they're all within perfect reaching distance!
And here's your newspaper and slippers!
Th- that's very nice of you, Julie...
...I didn't even know I owned slippers...
You're doing chores without being asked...
...you haven't disappeared into your Internet and video games the nanosecond dinner is over...
...you're being respectful to each other and not fighting...
I have just one question:
Who are you kids and what have you done with my real children?

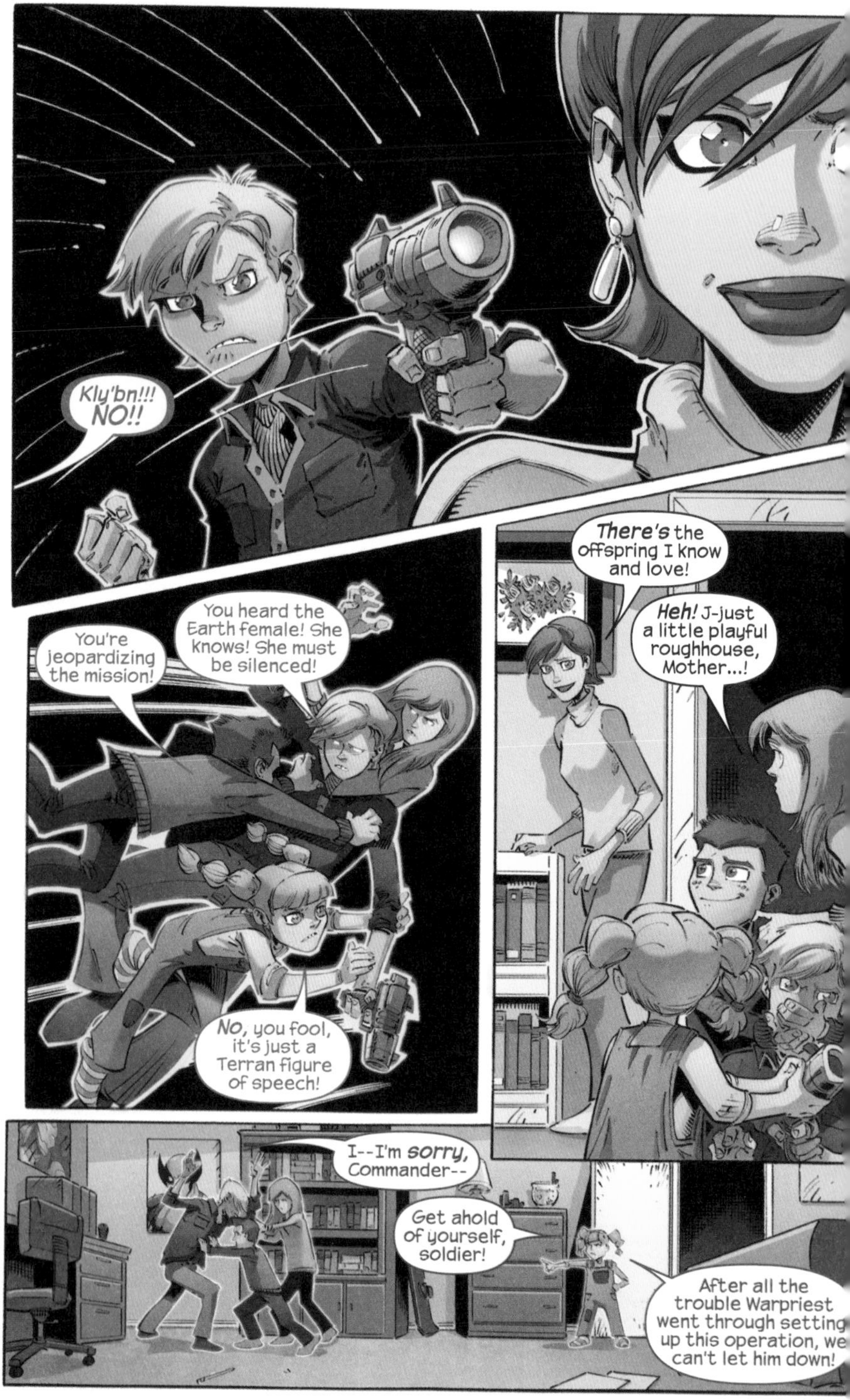
Kly'bn!!! NO!!
You're jeopardizing the mission!
You heard the Earth female! She knows! She must be silenced!
No, you fool, it's just a Terran figure of speech!
There's the offspring I know and love!
Heh! J-just a little playful roughhouse, Mother...!
I--I'm sorry, Commander--
Get ahold of yourself, soldier!
After all the trouble Warpriest went through setting up this operation, we can't let him down!

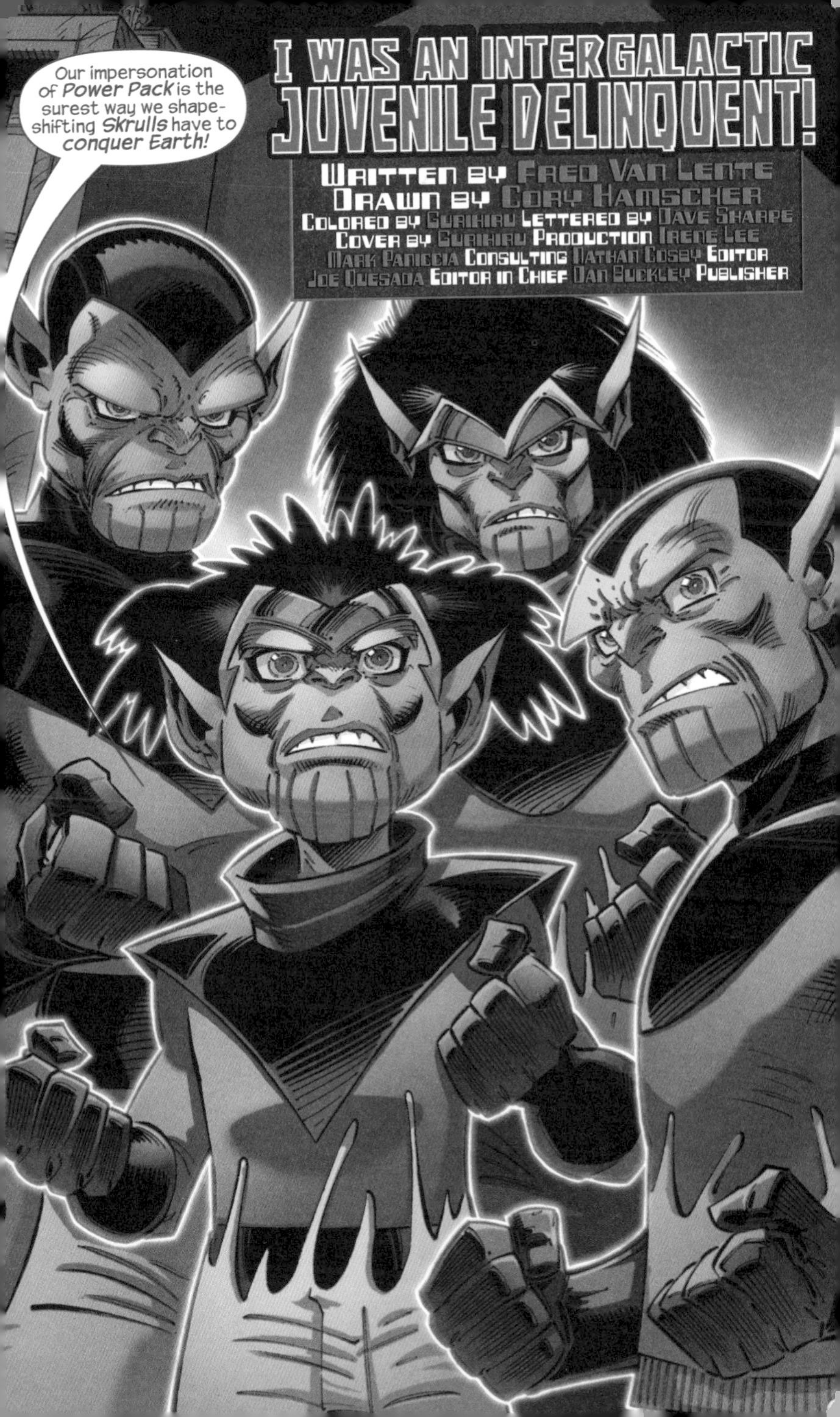

Our impersonation of Power Pack is the surest way we shape-shifting Skrulls have to conquer Earth!
I WAS AN INTERGALACTIC JUVENILE DELINQUENT!
WRITTEN BY FRED VAN LENTE
DRAWN BY CORY HAMSCHER
COLORED BY GURIHIRU LETTERED BY DAVE SHARPE
COVER BY GURIHIRU PRODUCTION IRENE LEE
MARK PANICCIA CONSULTING NATHAN COSBY EDITOR
JOE QUESADA EDITOR IN CHIEF DAN BUCKLEY PUBLISHER

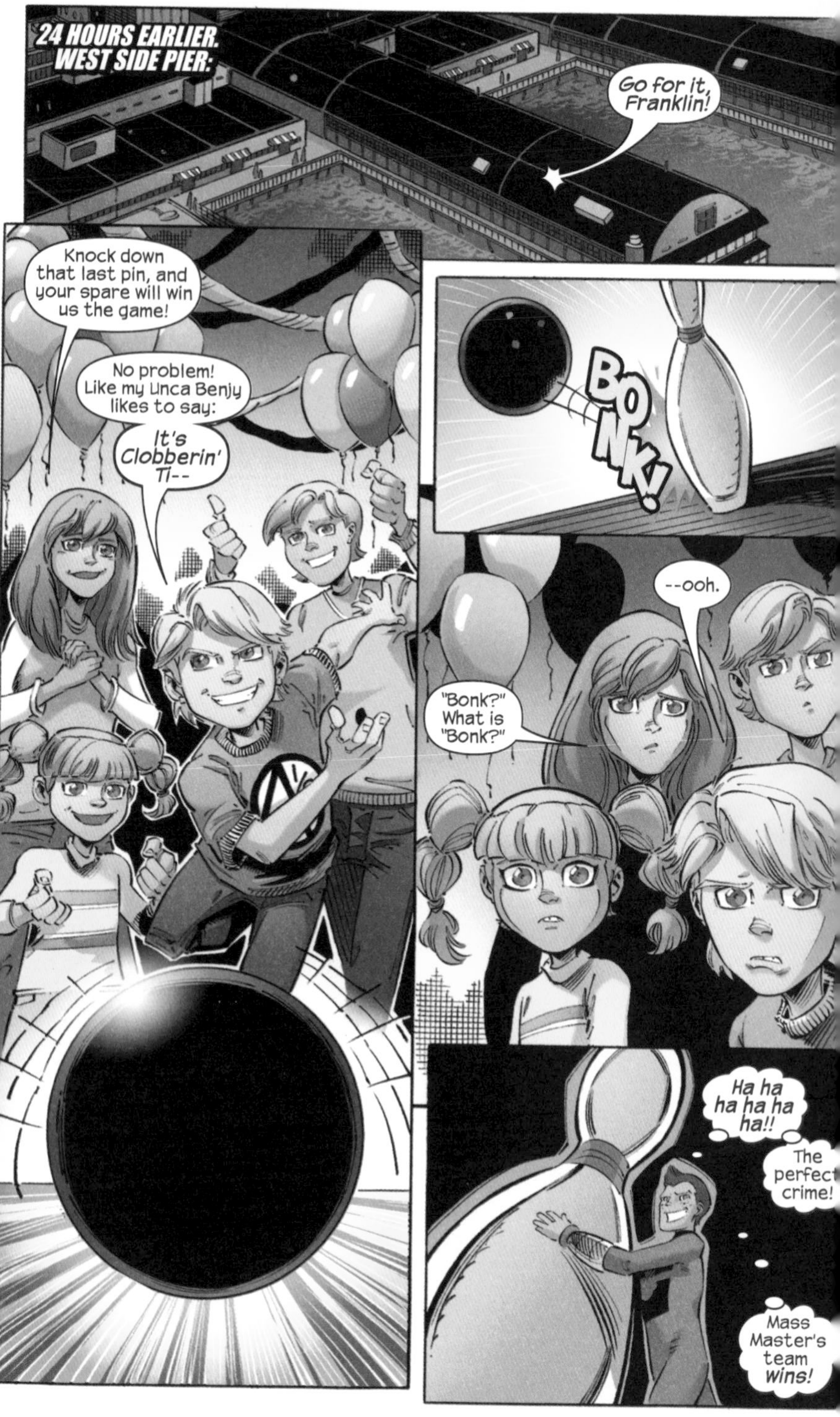

24 HOURS EARLIER. WEST SIDE PIER:
Go for it, Franklin!
Knock down that last pin, and your spare will win us the game!
No problem! Like my Unca Benjy likes to say:
It's Clobberin' Ti--
BONK!
--ooh.
"Bonk?" What is "Bonk?"
Ha ha ha ha ha ha!!
The perfect crime!
Mass Master's team wins!

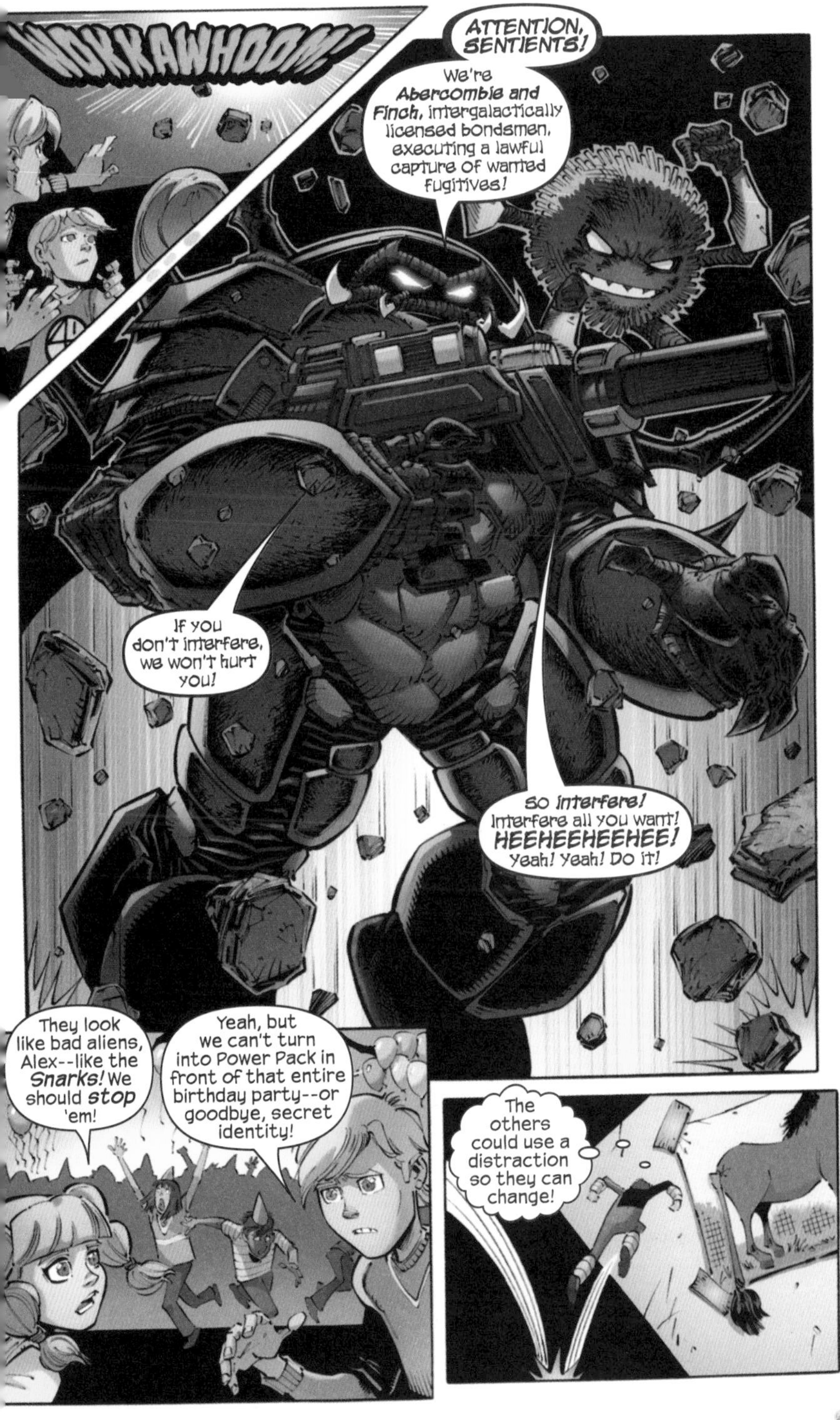
ATTENTION, SENTIENTS!
We're Abercombie and Finch, intergalactically licensed bondsmen, executing a lawful capture of wanted fugitives!
If you don't interfere, we won't hurt you!
So interfere! Interfere all you want! HEEHEEHEEHEE! Yeah! Yeah! Do it!
They look like bad aliens, Alex--like the Snarks! We should stop 'em!
Yeah, but we can't turn into Power Pack in front of that entire birthday party--or goodbye, secret identity!
The others could use a distraction so they can change!

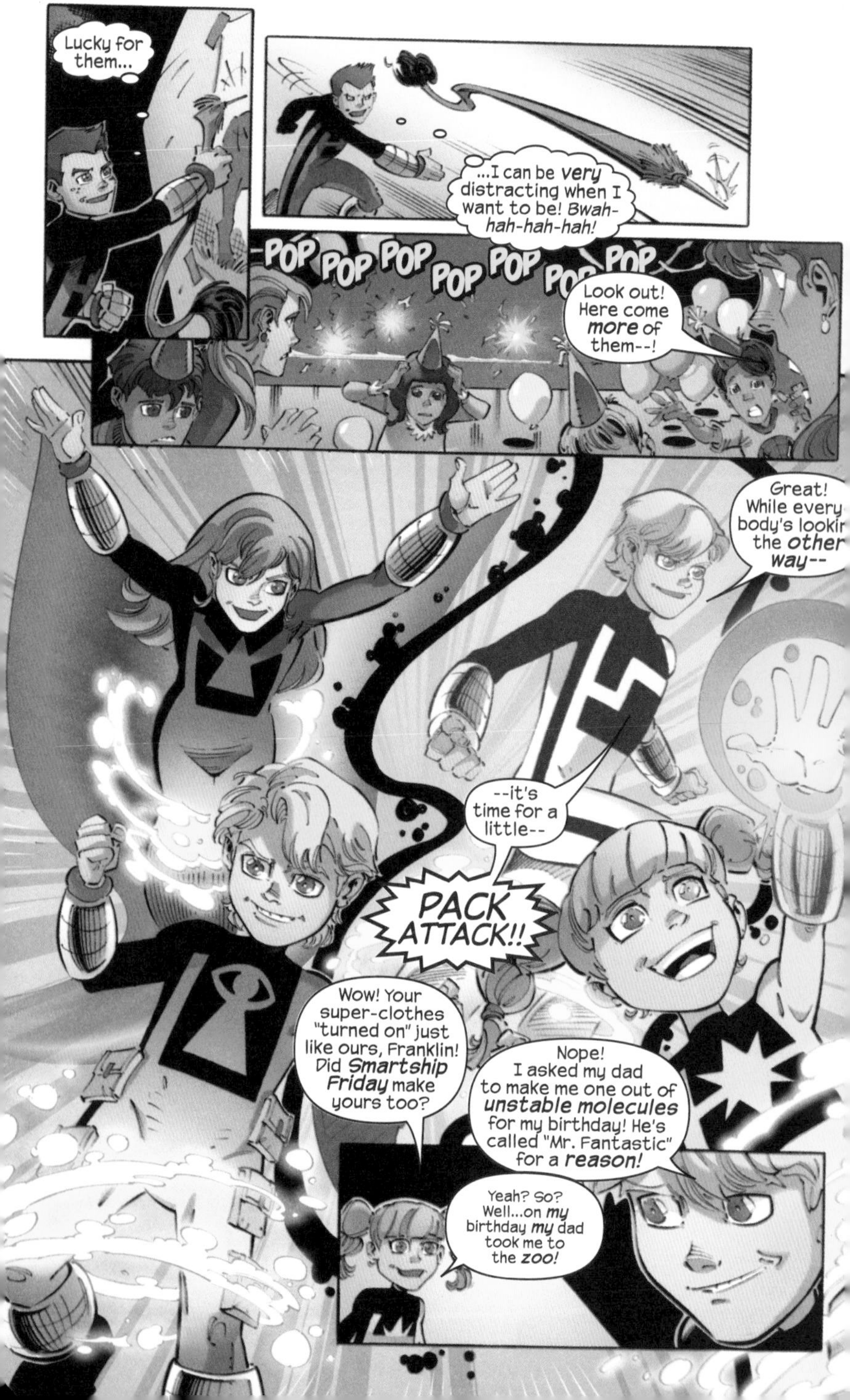

Lucky for them...
...I can be very distracting when I want to be! Bwah-hah-hah-hah!
POP POP POP POP POP POP POP
Look out! Here come more of them--!
Great! While every body's lookir the other way--
--it's time for a little--
PACK ATTACK!!
Wow! Your super-clothes "turned on" just like ours, Franklin! Did Smartship Friday make yours too?
Nope! I asked my dad to make me one out of unstable molecules for my birthday! He's called "Mr. Fantastic" for a reason!
Yeah? So? Well...on my birthday my dad took me to the zoo!

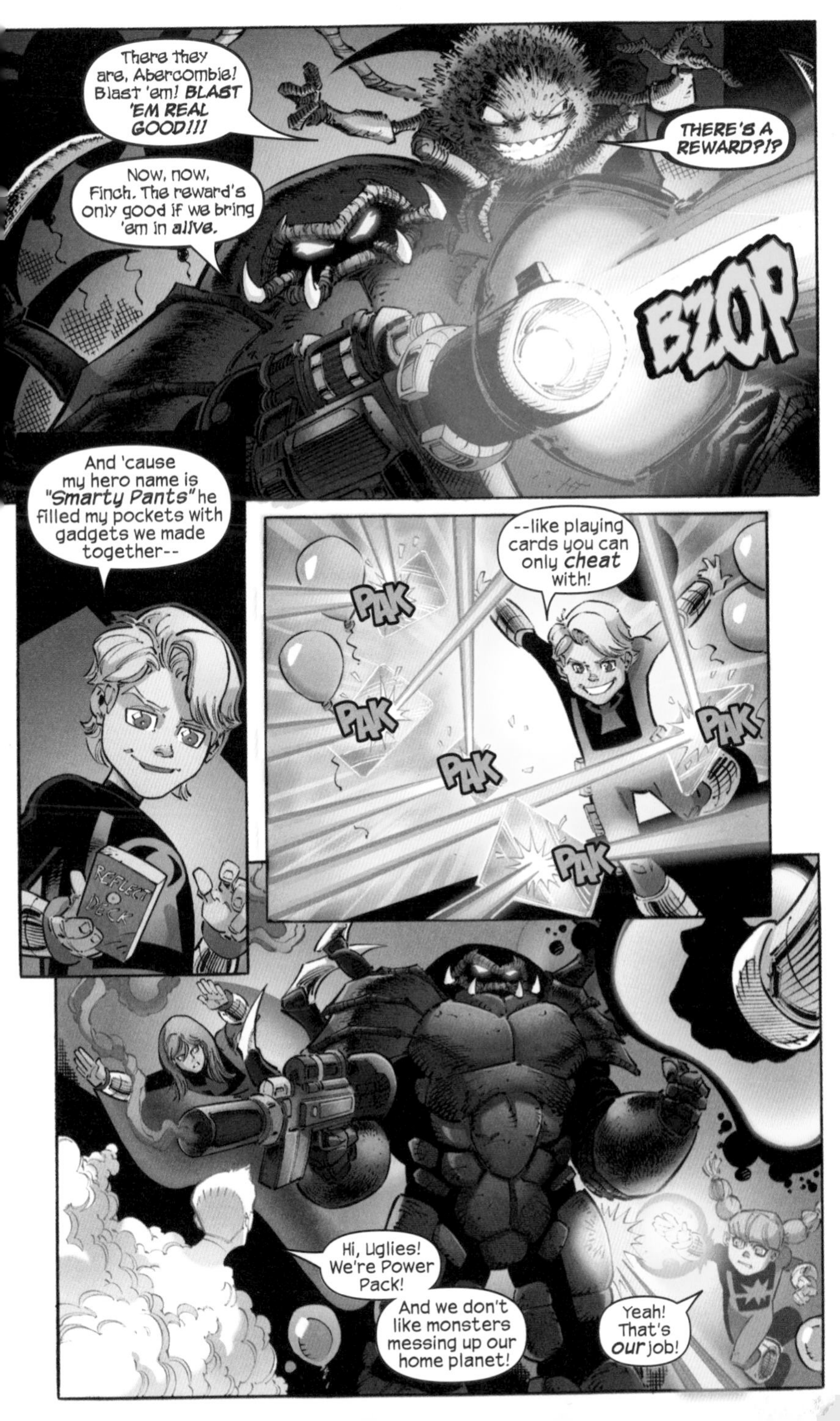
There they are, Abercombie! Blast 'em! BLAST 'EM REAL GOOD!!!
THERE'S A REWARD?!?
Now, now, Finch. The reward's only good if we bring 'em in alive.
BZOP
And 'cause my hero name is "Smarty Pants" he filled my pockets with gadgets we made together--
REFLECT O DECK
--like playing cards you can only cheat with!
PAK
PAK
PAK
PAK
PAK
Hi, Uglies! We're Power Pack!
And we don't like monsters messing up our home planet!
Yeah! That's our job!

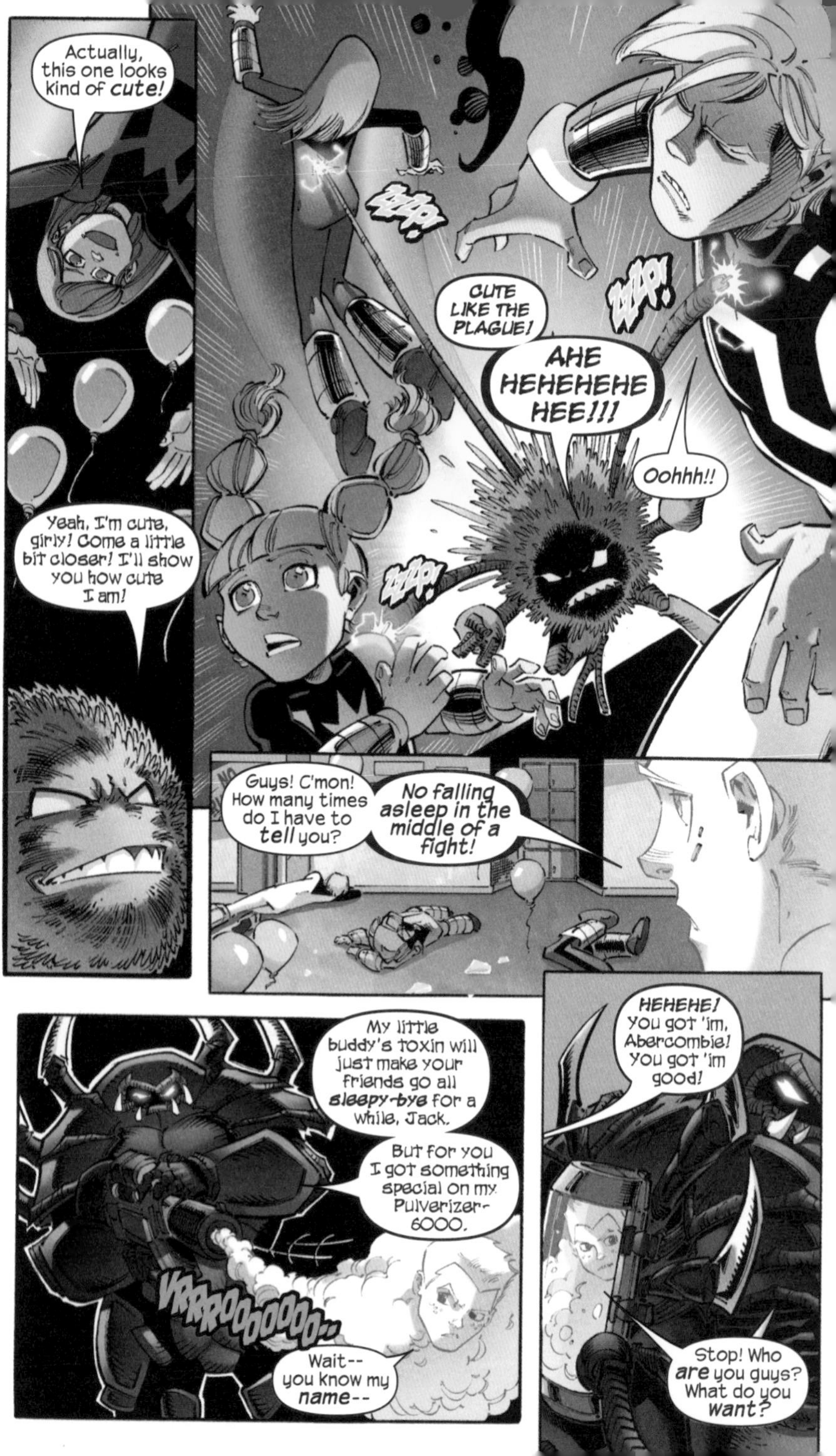
Actually, this one looks kind of cute!
Yeah, I'm cute, girly! Come a little bit closer! I'll show you how cute I am!
ZZZAP!
CUTE LIKE THE PLAGUE!
ZZZAP!
AHE HEHEHEHE HEE!!!
Oohhh!!
ZZZAP!
Guys! C'mon! How many times do I have to tell you?
No falling asleep in the middle of a fight!
My little buddy's toxin will just make your friends go all sleepy-bye for a while, Jack.
But for you I got something special on my Pulverizer-6000.
VRRROOOOOOO--
Wait-- you know my name--
HEHEHE! You got 'im, Abercombie! You got 'im good!
Stop! Who are you guys? What do you want?

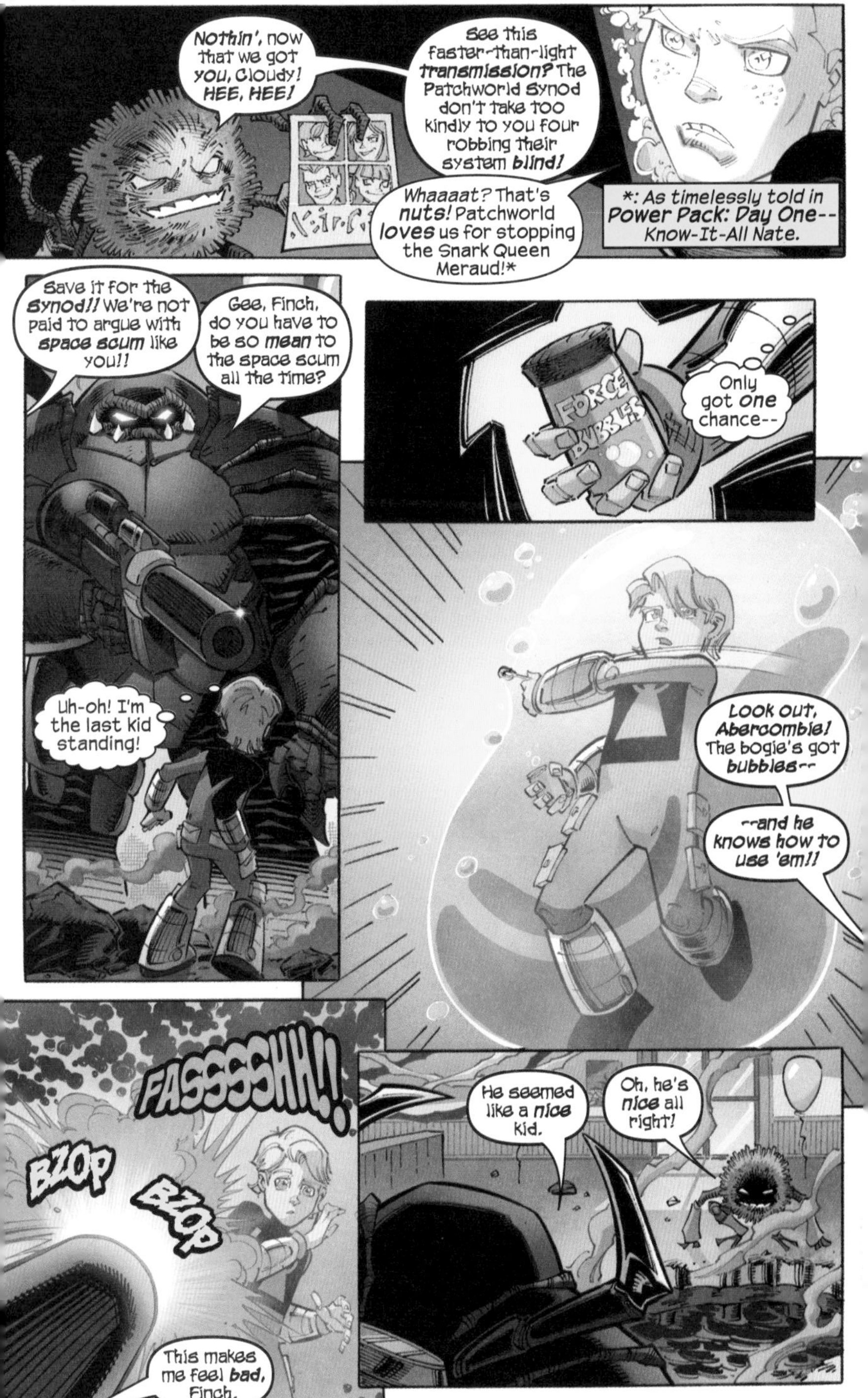

Nothin', now that we got you, Cloudy! HEE, HEE!
See this faster-than-light transmission? The Patchworld Synod don't take too kindly to you four robbing their system blind!
Whaaaat? That's nuts! Patchworld loves us for stopping the Snark Queen Meraud!*
*: As timelessly told in Power Pack: Day One-- Know-It-All Nate.
Save it for the Synod!! We're not paid to argue with space scum like you!!
Gee, Finch, do you have to be so mean to the space scum all the time?
Uh-oh! I'm the last kid standing!
FORCE BUBBLES
Only got one chance--
Look out, Abercombie! The bogie's got bubbles--
--and he knows how to use 'em!!
FASSSSHH!!
BZOP
BZOP
This makes me feel bad, Finch.
He seemed like a nice kid.
Oh, he's nice all right!

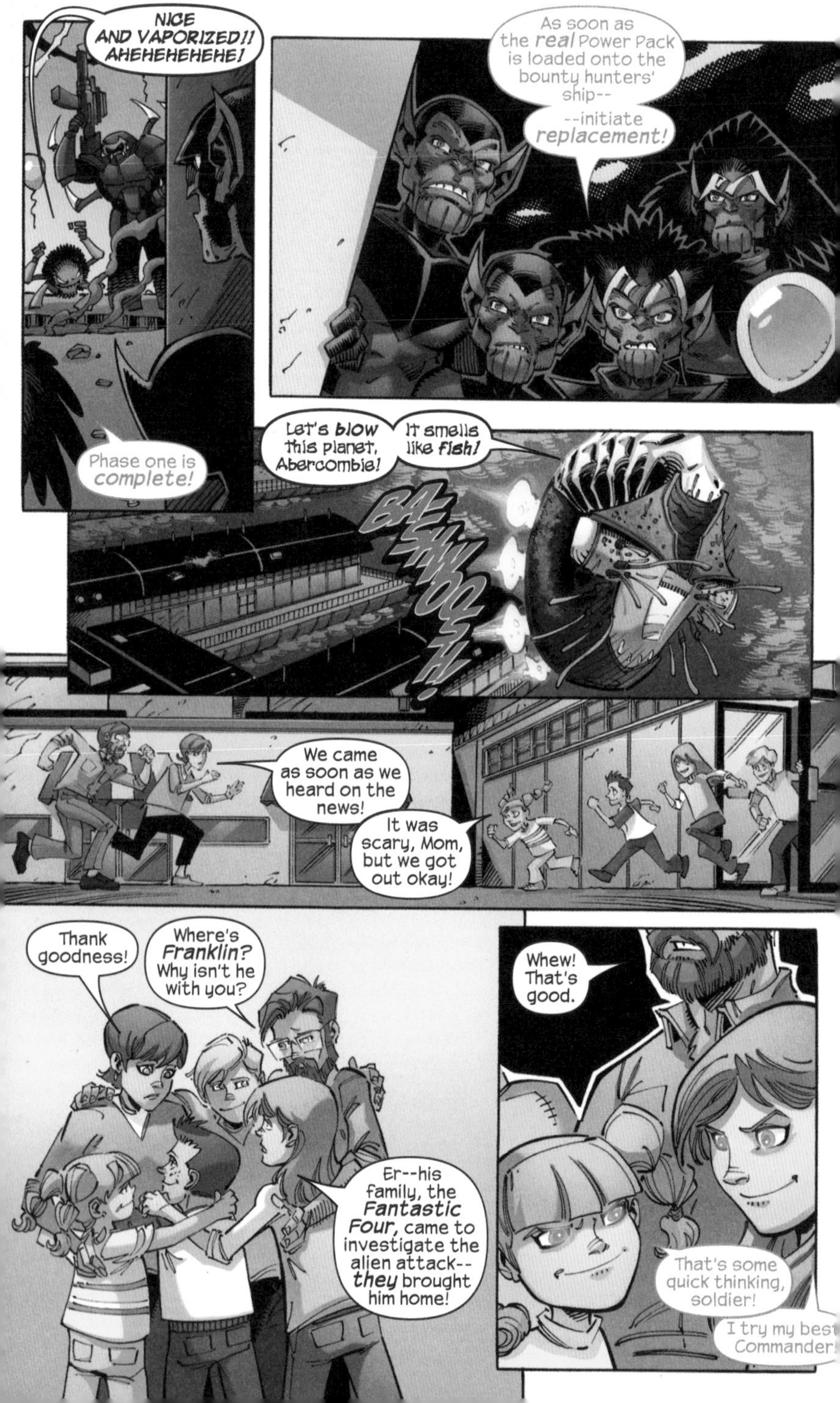
NICE AND VAPORIZED!! AHEHEHEHEHE!
As soon as the real Power Pack is loaded onto the bounty hunters' ship--
--initiate replacement!
Phase one is complete!
Let's blow this planet, Abercombie!
It smells like fish!
BA-SHWOOSH!
We came as soon as we heard on the news!
It was scary, Mom, but we got out okay!
Thank goodness!
Where's Franklin? Why isn't he with you?
Er--his family, the Fantastic Four, came to investigate the alien attack--they brought him home!
Whew! That's good.
That's some quick thinking, soldier!
I try my best Commander!

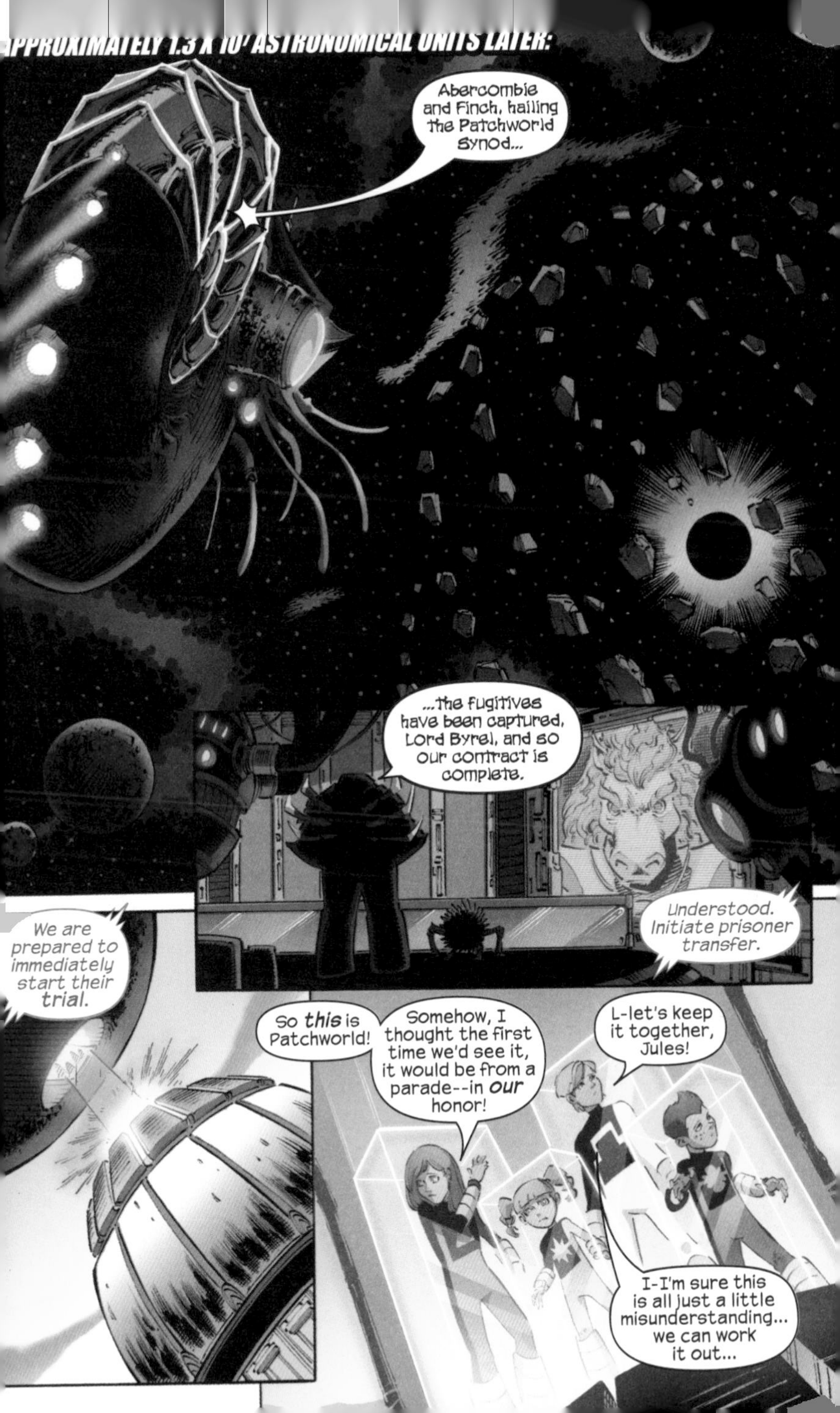
APPROXIMATELY 1.3 X 10⁷ ASTRONOMICAL UNITS LATER:
Abercombie and Finch, hailing the Patchworld Synod...
...the fugitives have been captured, Lord Byrel, and so our contract is complete.
Understood. Initiate prisoner transfer.
We are prepared to immediately start their trial.
So this is Patchworld!
Somehow, I thought the first time we'd see it, it would be from a parade--in our honor!
L-let's keep it together, Jules!
I-I'm sure this is all just a little misunderstanding... we can work it out...

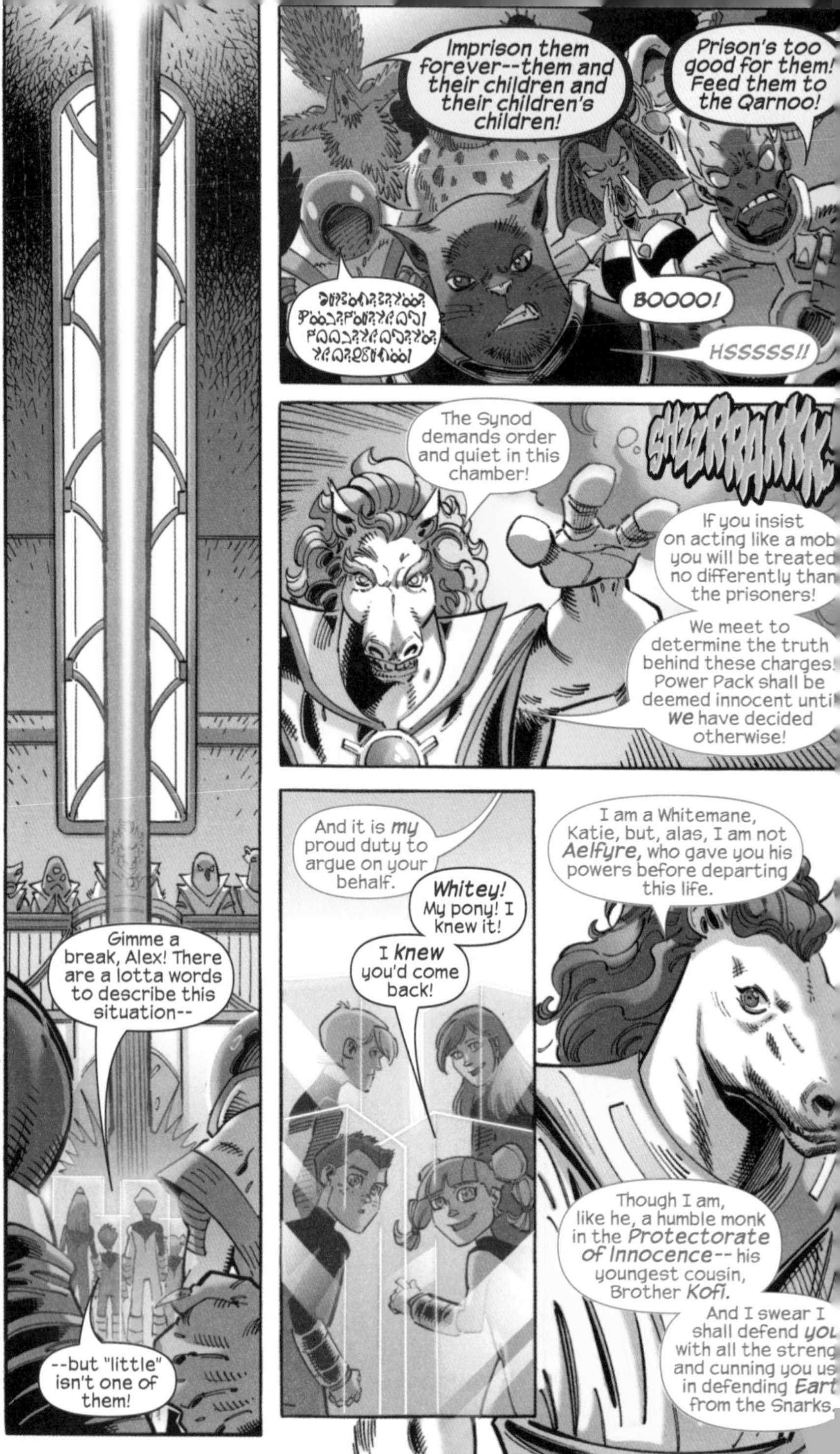
Imprison them forever--them and their children and their children's children!
Prison's too good for them! Feed them to the Qarnoo!
BOOOO!
HSSSSS!!
The Synod demands order and quiet in this chamber!
SHZZRRAKKK
If you insist on acting like a mob you will be treated no differently than the prisoners!
We meet to determine the truth behind these charges. Power Pack shall be deemed innocent until we have decided otherwise!
Gimme a break, Alex! There are a lotta words to describe this situation--
--but "little" isn't one of them!
And it is my proud duty to argue on your behalf.
Whitey! My pony! I knew it!
I knew you'd come back!
I am a Whitemane, Katie, but, alas, I am not Aelfyre, who gave you his powers before departing this life.
Though I am, like he, a humble monk in the Protectorate of Innocence-- his youngest cousin, Brother Kofi.
And I swear I shall defend you with all the streng and cunning you us in defending Eart from the Snarks.

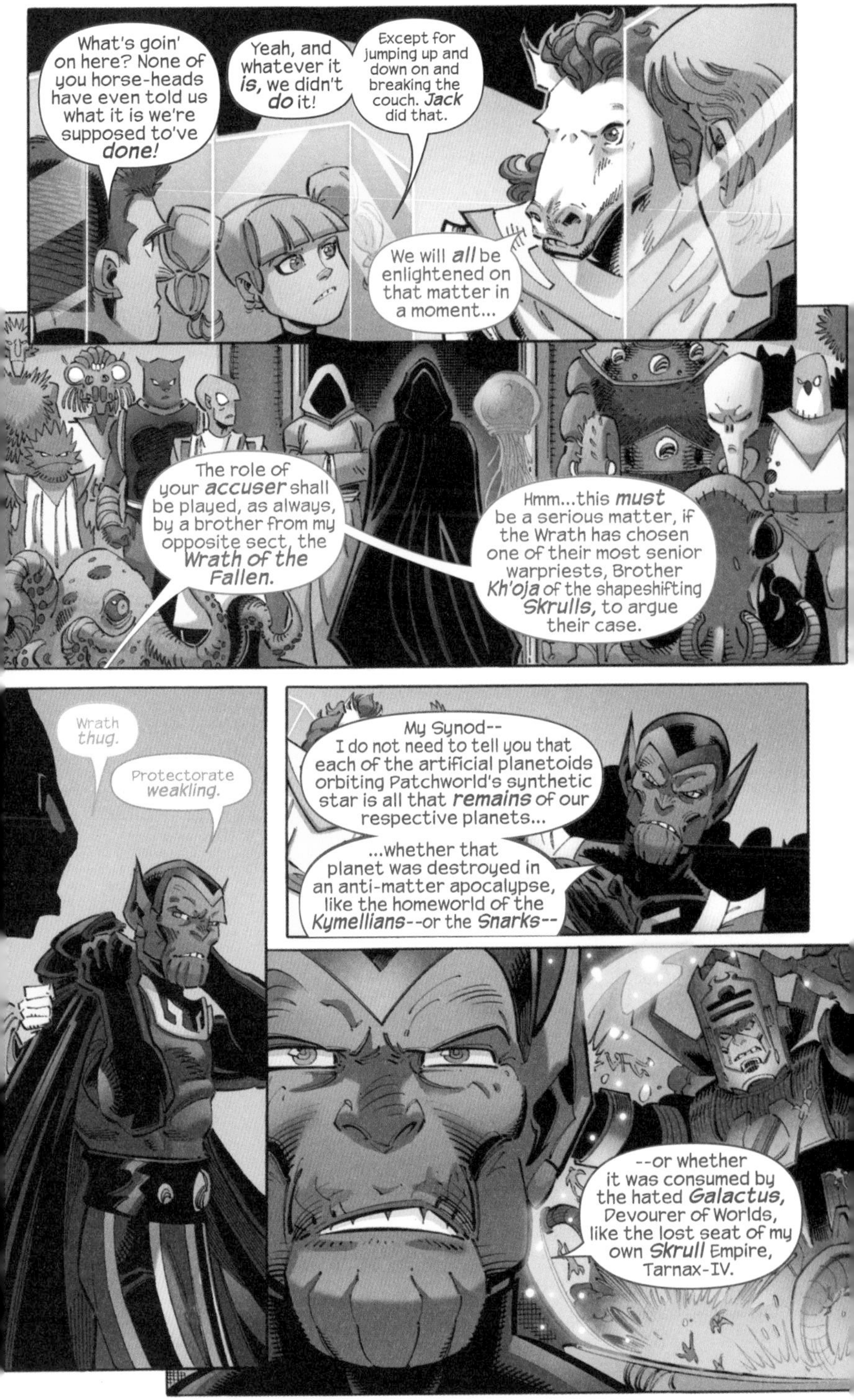
What's goin' on here? None of you horse-heads have even told us what it is we're supposed to've done!
Yeah, and whatever it is, we didn't do it!
Except for jumping up and down on and breaking the couch. Jack did that.
We will all be enlightened on that matter in a moment...
The role of your accuser shall be played, as always, by a brother from my opposite sect, the Wrath of the Fallen.
Hmm...this must be a serious matter, if the Wrath has chosen one of their most senior warpriests, Brother Kh'oja of the shapeshifting Skrulls, to argue their case.
Wrath thug.
Protectorate weakling.
My Synod-- I do not need to tell you that each of the artificial planetoids orbiting Patchworld's synthetic star is all that remains of our respective planets...
...whether that planet was destroyed in an anti-matter apocalypse, like the homeworld of the Kymellians--or the Snarks--
--or whether it was consumed by the hated Galactus, Devourer of Worlds, like the lost seat of my own Skrull Empire, Tarnax-IV.

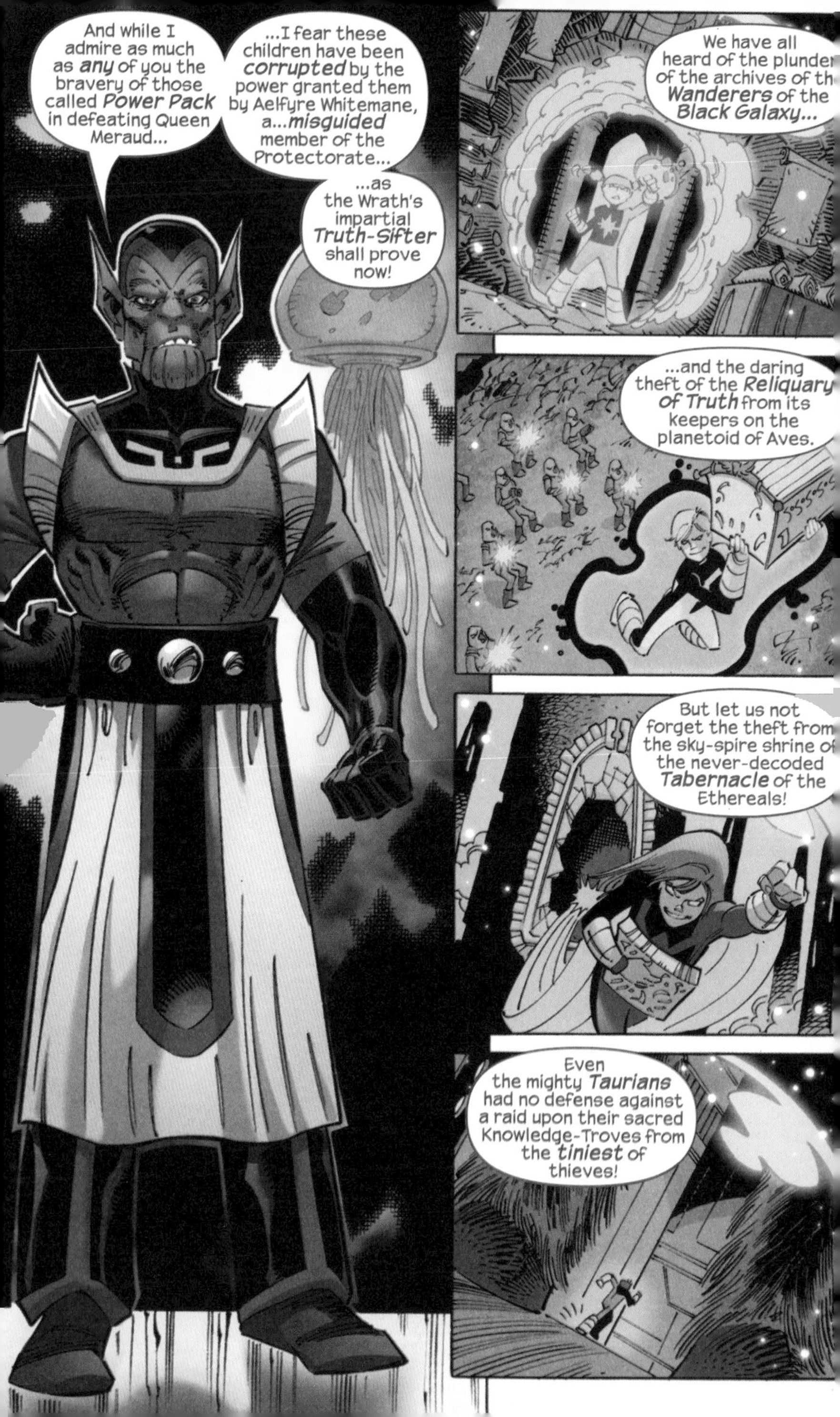

And while I admire as much as *any* of you the bravery of those called *Power Pack* in defeating Queen Meraud...
...I fear these children have been *corrupted* by the power granted them by Aelfyre Whitemane, a...*misguided* member of the Protectorate...
...as the Wrath's impartial *Truth-Sifter* shall prove now!
We have all heard of the plunder of the archives of the *Wanderers* of the *Black Galaxy*...
...and the daring theft of the *Reliquary of Truth* from its keepers on the planetoid of Aves.
But let us not forget the theft from the sky-spire shrine of the never-decoded *Tabernacle* of the Ethereals!
Even the mighty *Taurians* had no defense against a raid upon their sacred Knowledge-Troves from the *tiniest* of thieves!

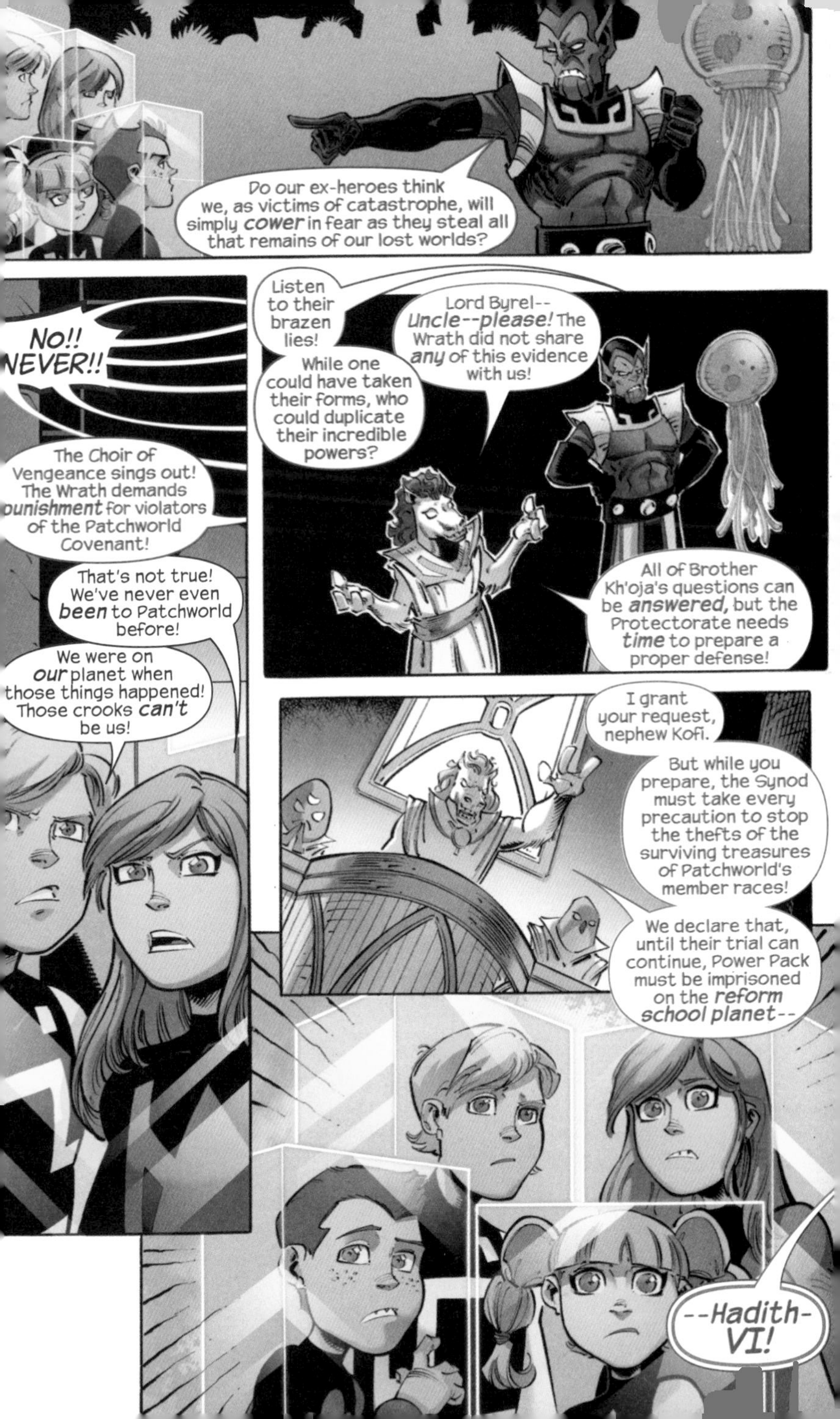

Do our ex-heroes think we, as victims of catastrophe, will simply cower in fear as they steal all that remains of our lost worlds?
NO!! NEVER!!
The Choir of Vengeance sings out! The Wrath demands punishment for violators of the Patchworld Covenant!
That's not true! We've never even been to Patchworld before!
We were on our planet when those things happened! Those crooks can't be us!
Listen to their brazen lies!
While one could have taken their forms, who could duplicate their incredible powers?
Lord Byrel-- Uncle--please! The Wrath did not share any of this evidence with us!
All of Brother Kh'oja's questions can be answered, but the Protectorate needs time to prepare a proper defense!
I grant your request, nephew Kofi.
But while you prepare, the Synod must take every precaution to stop the thefts of the surviving treasures of Patchworld's member races!
We declare that, until their trial can continue, Power Pack must be imprisoned on the reform school planet--
--Hadith-VI!

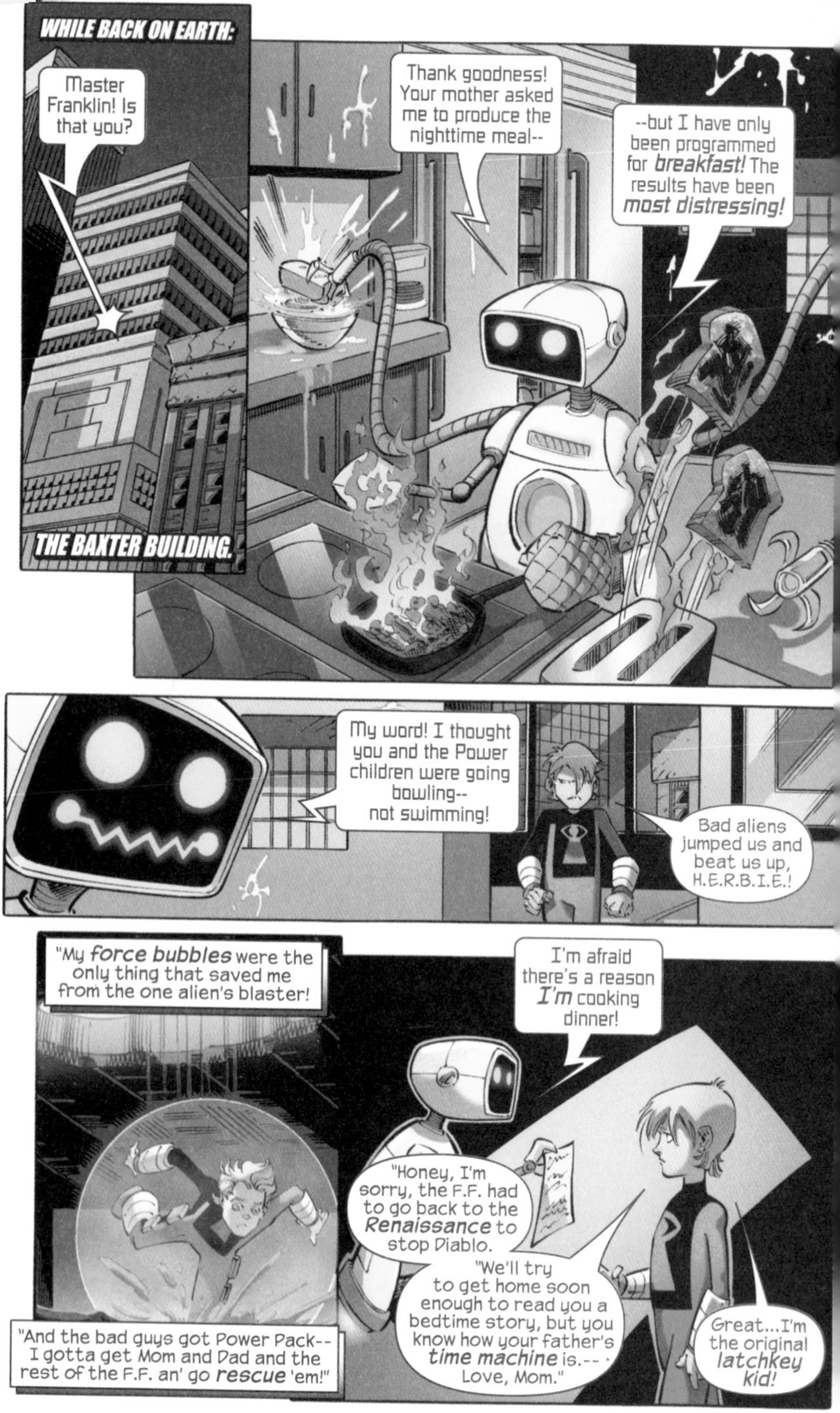

WHILE BACK ON EARTH:
Master Franklin! Is that you?
THE BAXTER BUILDING.
Thank goodness! Your mother asked me to produce the nighttime meal--
--but I have only been programmed for breakfast! The results have been most distressing!
My word! I thought you and the Power children were going bowling-- not swimming!
Bad aliens jumped us and beat us up, H.E.R.B.I.E.!
"My force bubbles were the only thing that saved me from the one alien's blaster!
"And the bad guys got Power Pack-- I gotta get Mom and Dad and the rest of the F.F. an' go rescue 'em!"
I'm afraid there's a reason I'm cooking dinner!
"Honey, I'm sorry, the F.F. had to go back to the Renaissance to stop Diablo.
"We'll try to get home soon enough to read you a bedtime story, but you know how your father's time machine is.-- Love, Mom."
Great...I'm the original latchkey kid!

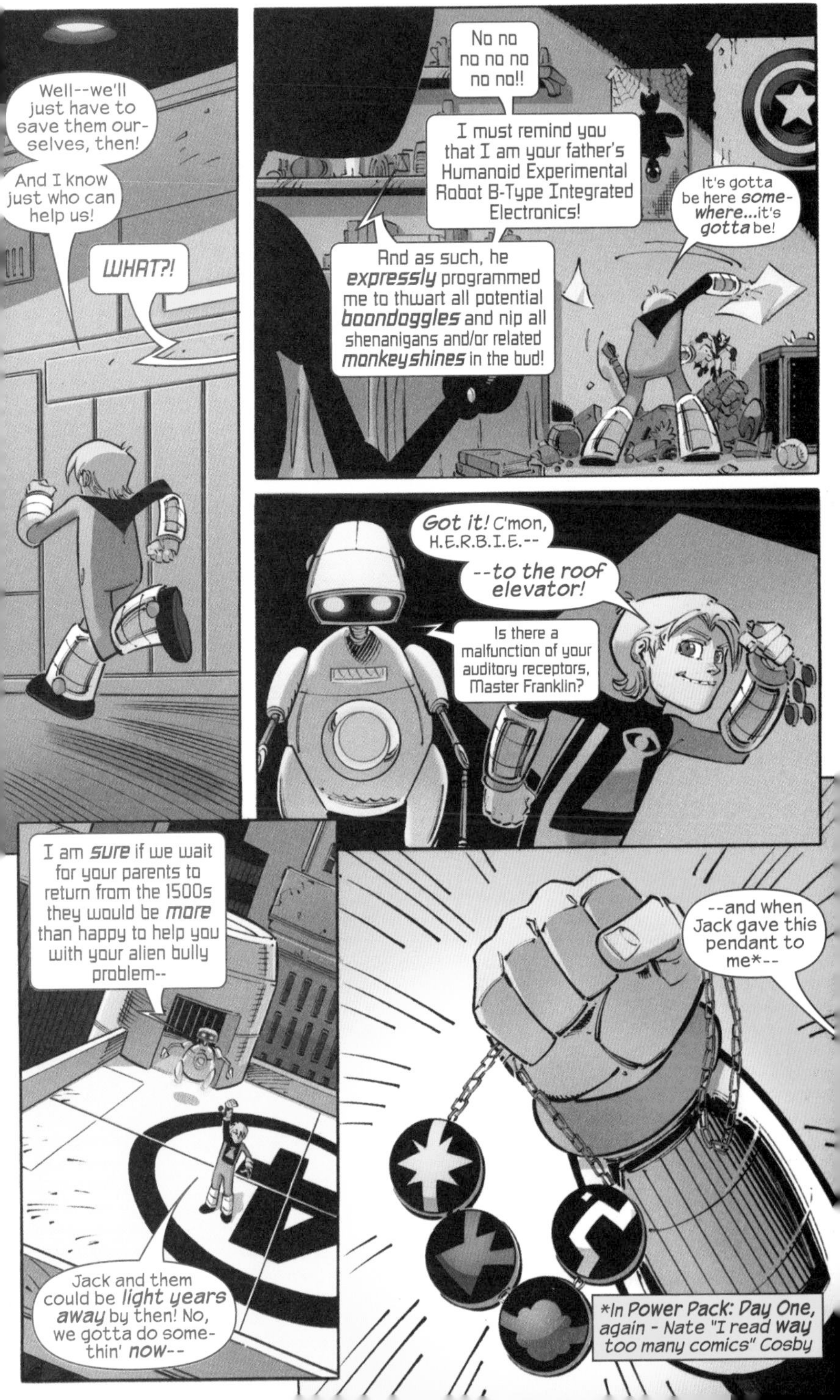
Well--we'll just have to save them our-selves, then!
And I know just who can help us!
WHAT?!
No no no no no no no!!
I must remind you that I am your father's Humanoid Experimental Robot B-Type Integrated Electronics!
And as such, he expressly programmed me to thwart all potential boondoggles and nip all shenanigans and/or related monkeyshines in the bud!
It's gotta be here some-where...it's gotta be!
Got it! C'mon, H.E.R.B.I.E.--
--to the roof elevator!
Is there a malfunction of your auditory receptors, Master Franklin?
I am sure if we wait for your parents to return from the 1500s they would be more than happy to help you with your alien bully problem--
Jack and them could be light years away by then! No, we gotta do some-thin' now--
--and when Jack gave this pendant to me*--
*In Power Pack: Day One, again - Nate "I read way too many comics" Cosby

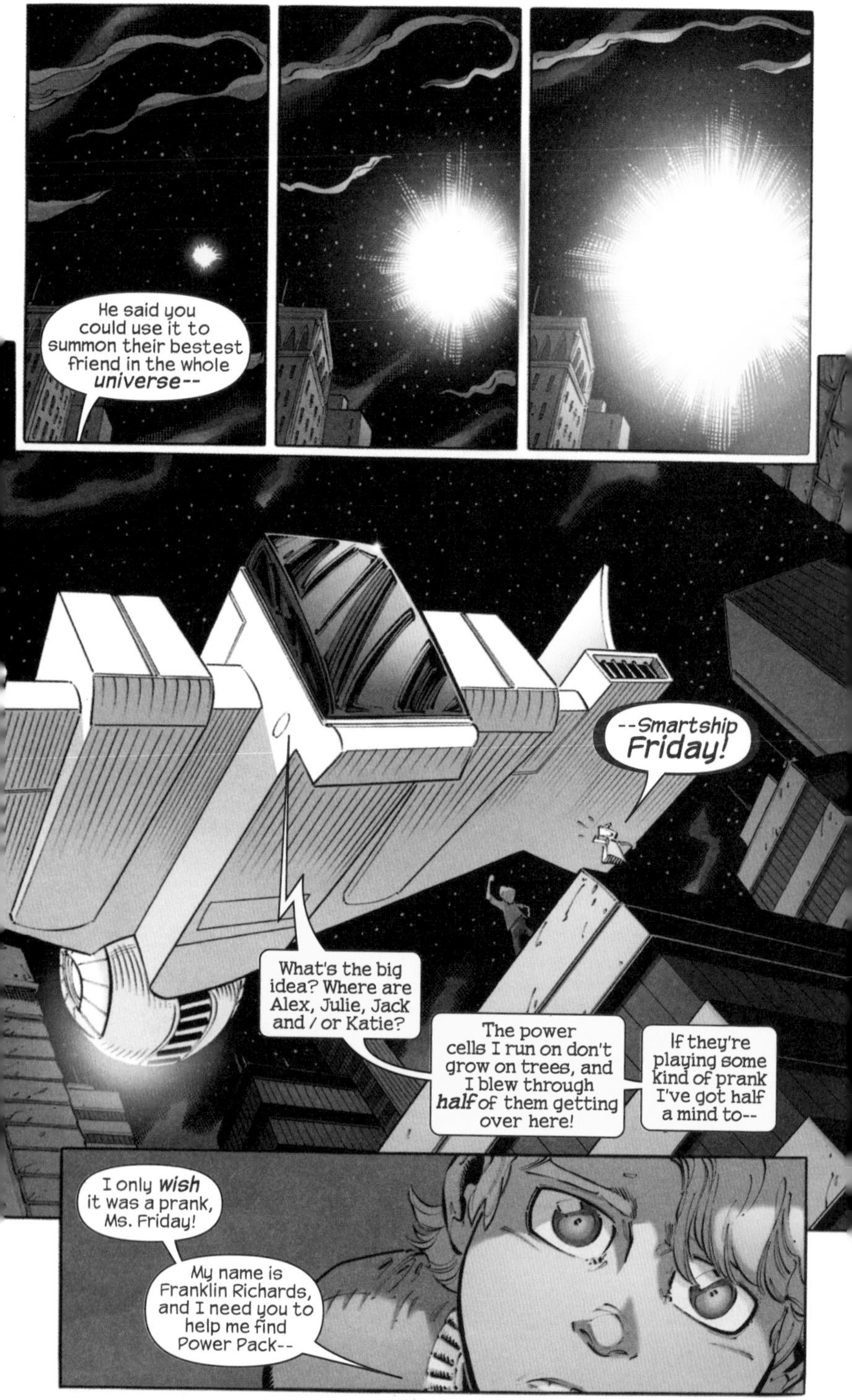

He said you could use it to summon their bestest friend in the whole *universe*--
--Smartship Friday!
What's the big idea? Where are Alex, Julie, Jack and / or Katie?
The power cells I run on don't grow on trees, and I blew through *half* of them getting over here!
If they're playing some kind of prank I've got half a mind to--
I only *wish* it was a prank, Ms. Friday!
My name is Franklin Richards, and I need you to help me find Power Pack--

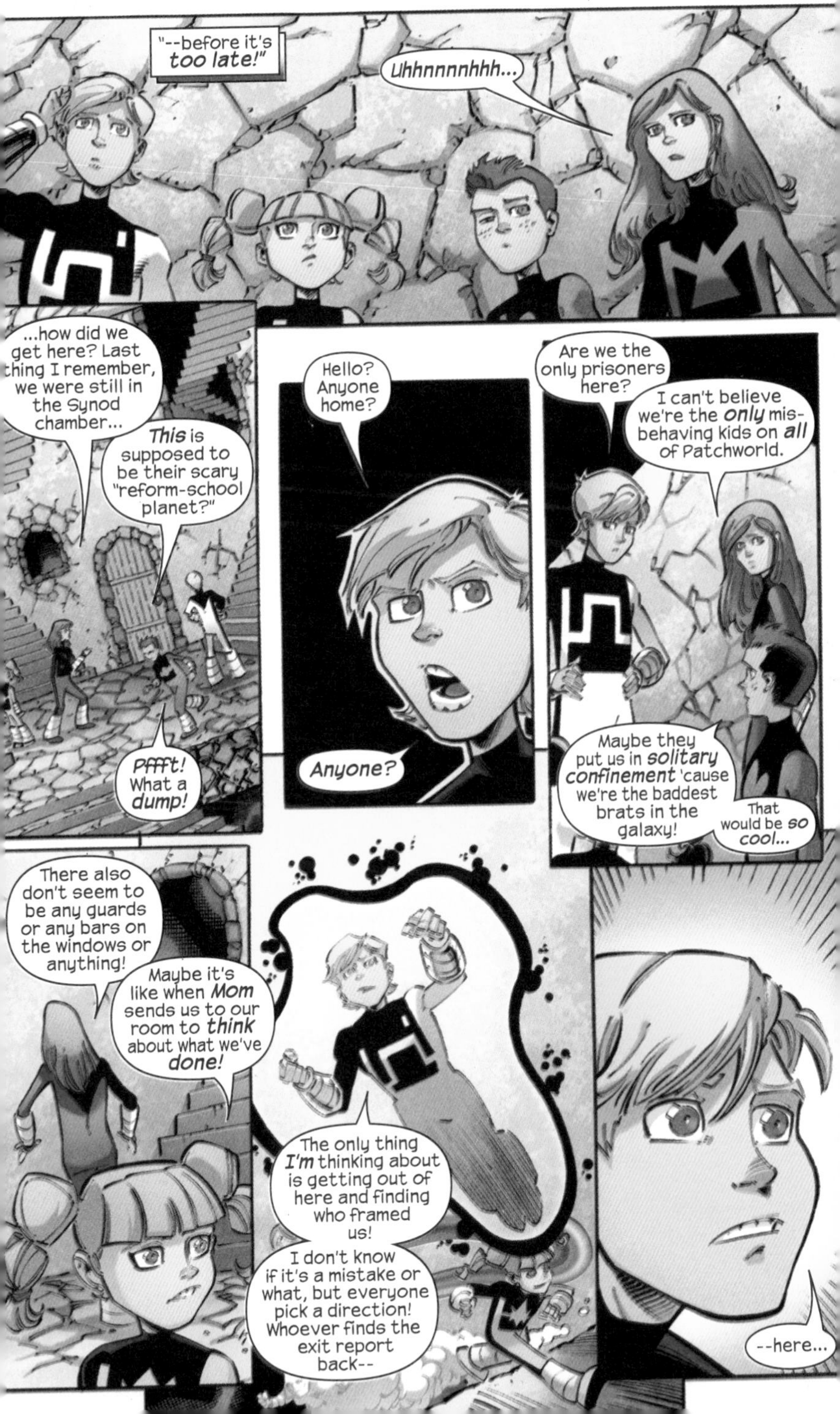
"--before it's too late!"
Uhhnnnnhhh...
...how did we get here? Last thing I remember, we were still in the Synod chamber...
This is supposed to be their scary "reform-school planet?"
Pffft! What a dump!
Hello? Anyone home?
Anyone?
Are we the only prisoners here?
I can't believe we're the only mis-behaving kids on all of Patchworld.
Maybe they put us in solitary confinement 'cause we're the baddest brats in the galaxy!
That would be so cool...
There also don't seem to be any guards or any bars on the windows or anything!
Maybe it's like when Mom sends us to our room to think about what we've done!
The only thing I'm thinking about is getting out of here and finding who framed us!
I don't know if it's a mistake or what, but everyone pick a direction! Whoever finds the exit report back--
--here...

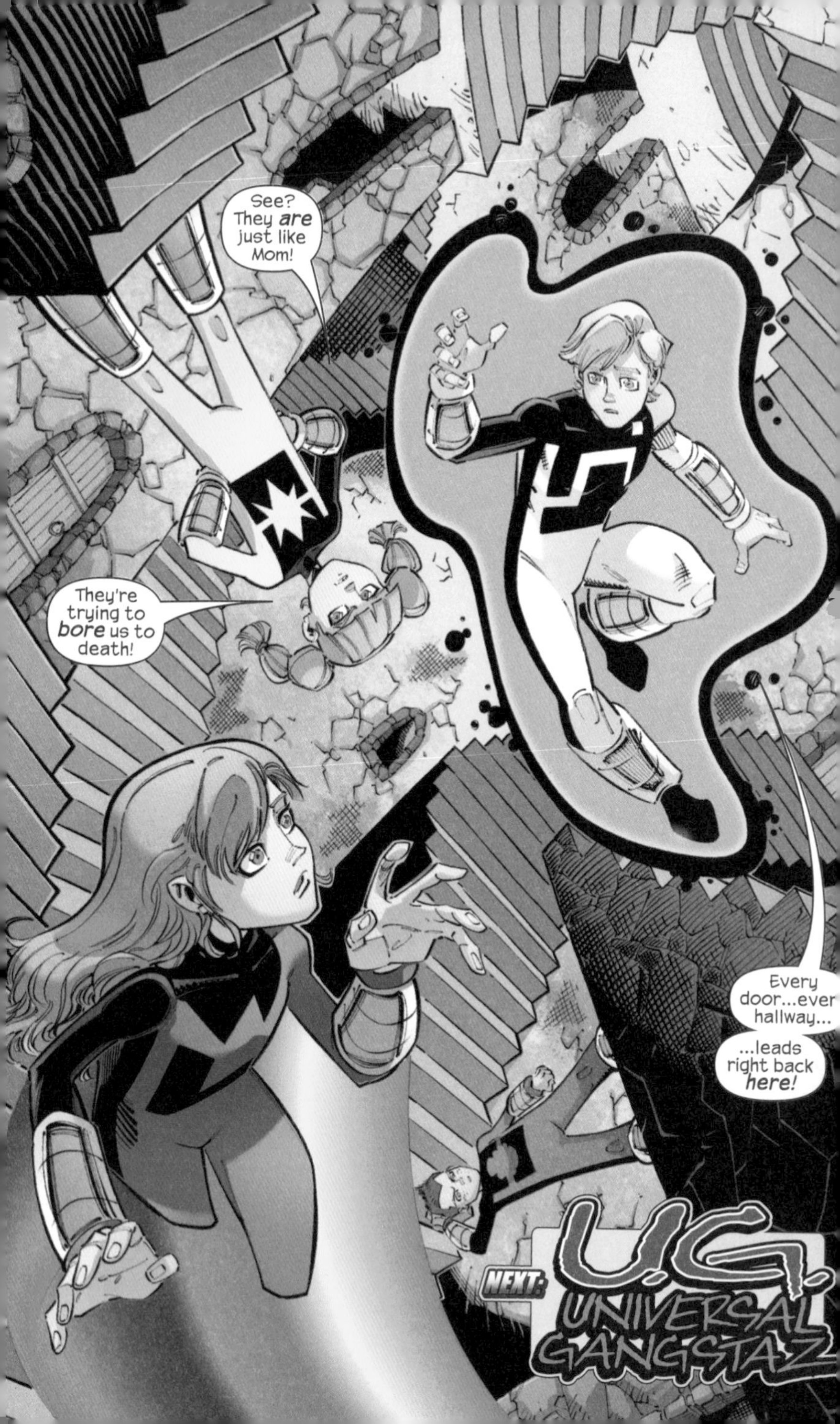

See? They *are* just like Mom!
They're trying to *bore* us to death!
Every door...ever hallway...
...leads right back *here!*
NEXT: U.G. UNIVERSAL GANGSTAZ

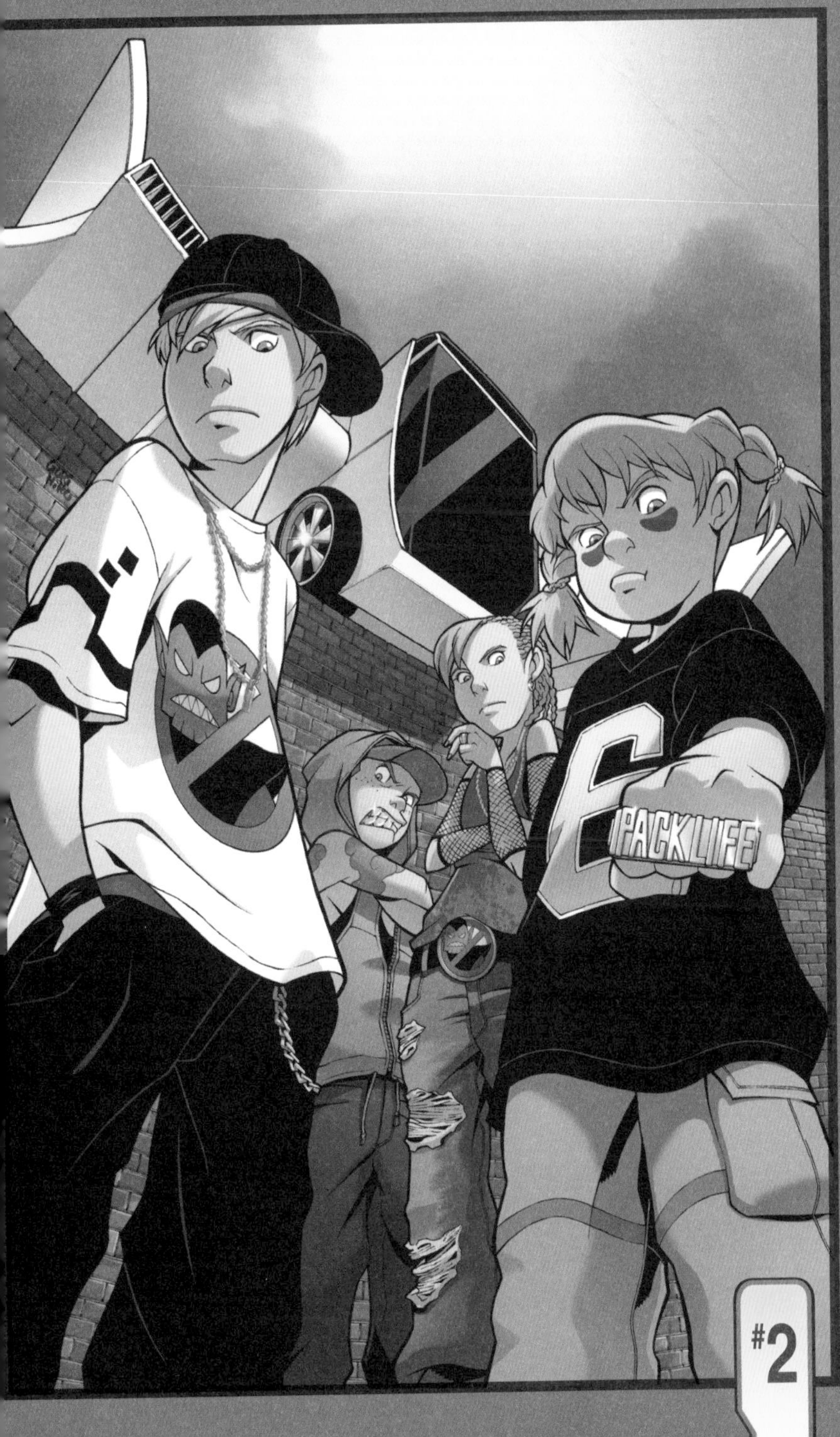
PACK LIFE
#2

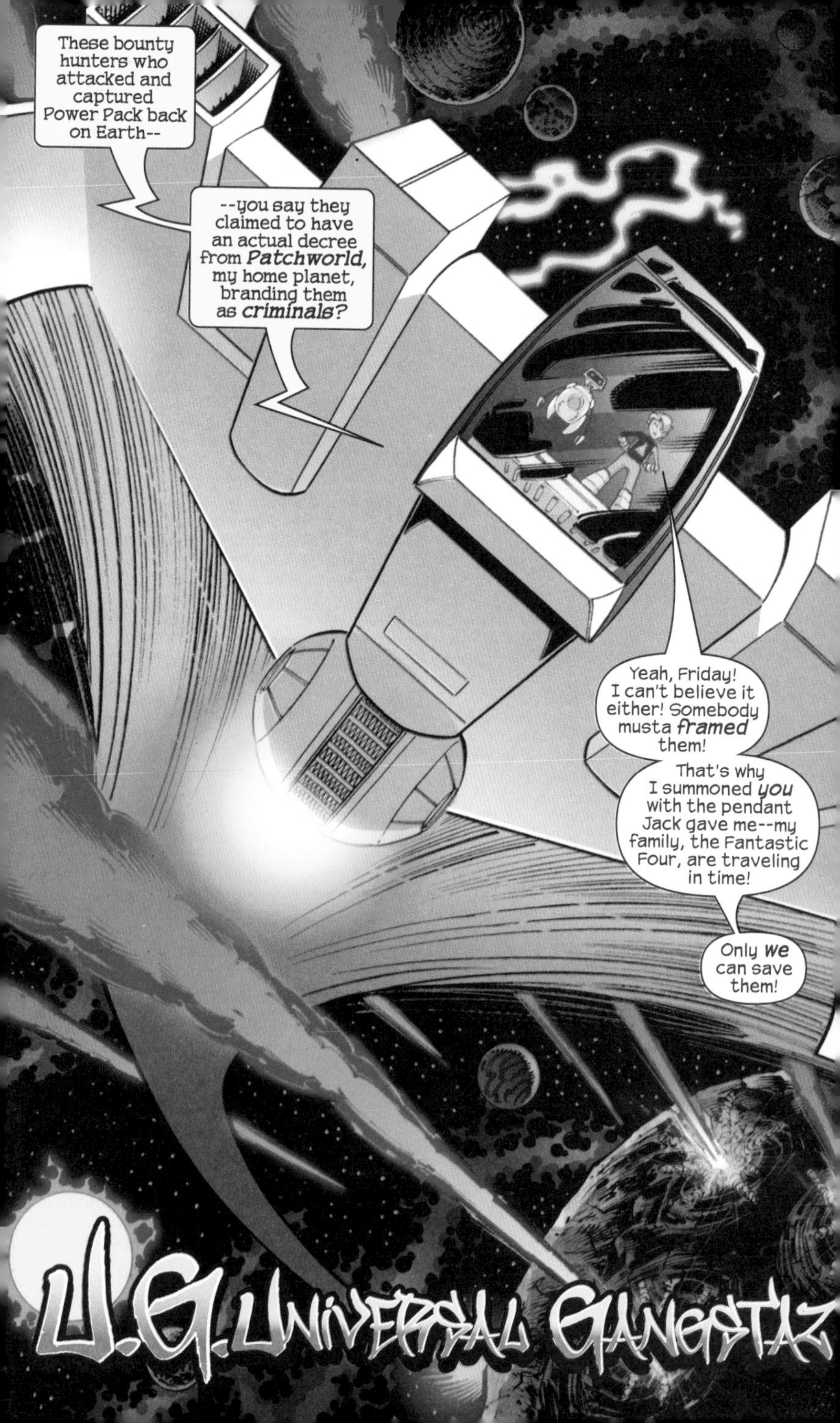
These bounty hunters who attacked and captured Power Pack back on Earth--
--you say they claimed to have an actual decree from Patchworld, my home planet, branding them as criminals?
Yeah, Friday! I can't believe it either! Somebody musta framed them!
That's why I summoned you with the pendant Jack gave me--my family, the Fantastic Four, are traveling in time!
Only we can save them!
U.G. UNIVERSAL GANGSTAZ

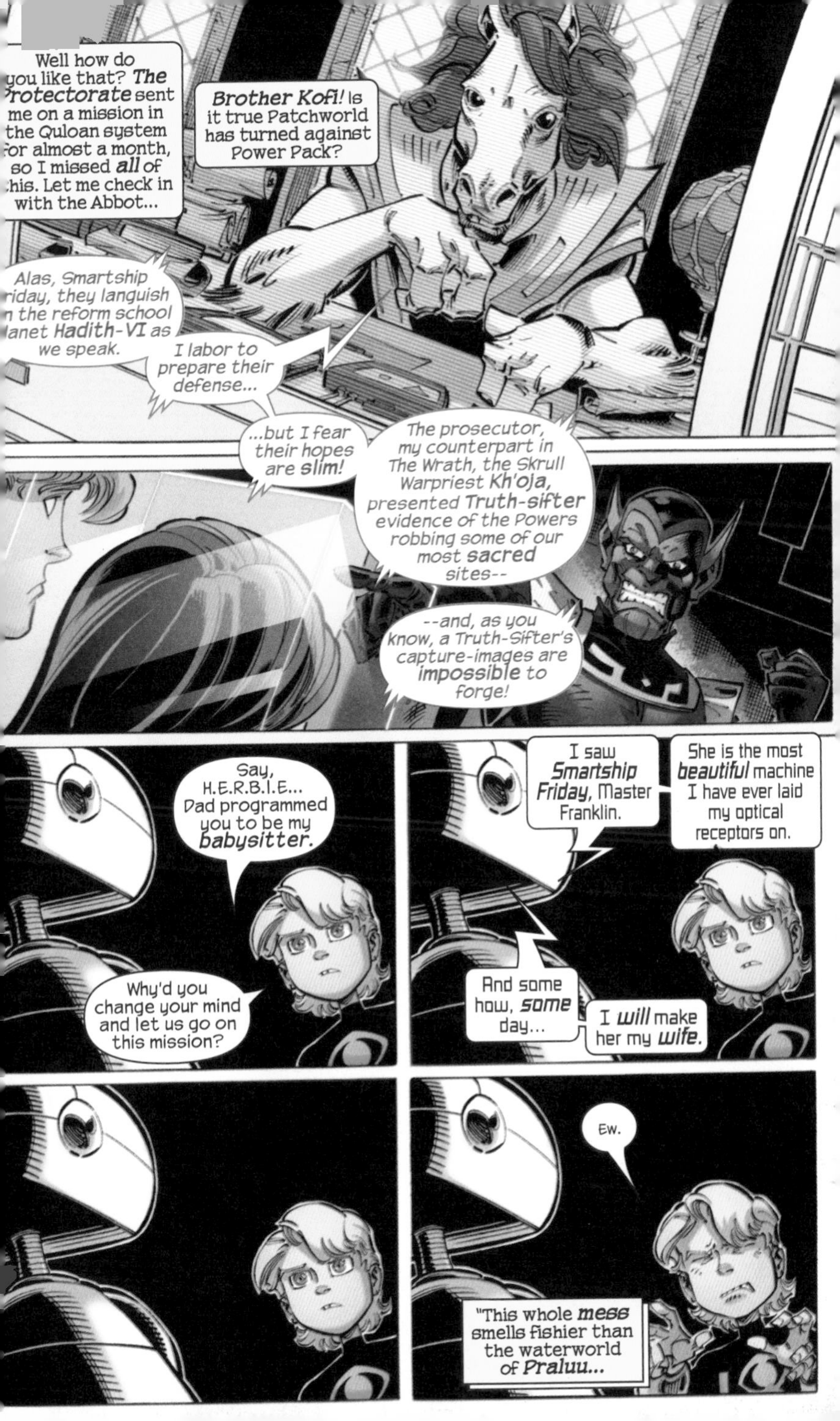
Well how do you like that? The Protectorate sent me on a mission in the Quloan system for almost a month, so I missed all of this. Let me check in with the Abbot...
Brother Kofi! Is it true Patchworld has turned against Power Pack?
Alas, Smartship Friday, they languish in the reform school planet Hadith-VI as we speak.
I labor to prepare their defense...
...but I fear their hopes are slim!
The prosecutor, my counterpart in The Wrath, the Skrull Warpriest Kh'oja, presented Truth-sifter evidence of the Powers robbing some of our most sacred sites--
--and, as you know, a Truth-Sifter's capture-images are impossible to forge!
Say, H.E.R.B.I.E... Dad programmed you to be my babysitter.
Why'd you change your mind and let us go on this mission?
I saw Smartship Friday, Master Franklin.
She is the most beautiful machine I have ever laid my optical receptors on.
And some how, some day...
I will make her my wife.
Ew.
"This whole mess smells fishier than the waterworld of Praluu...

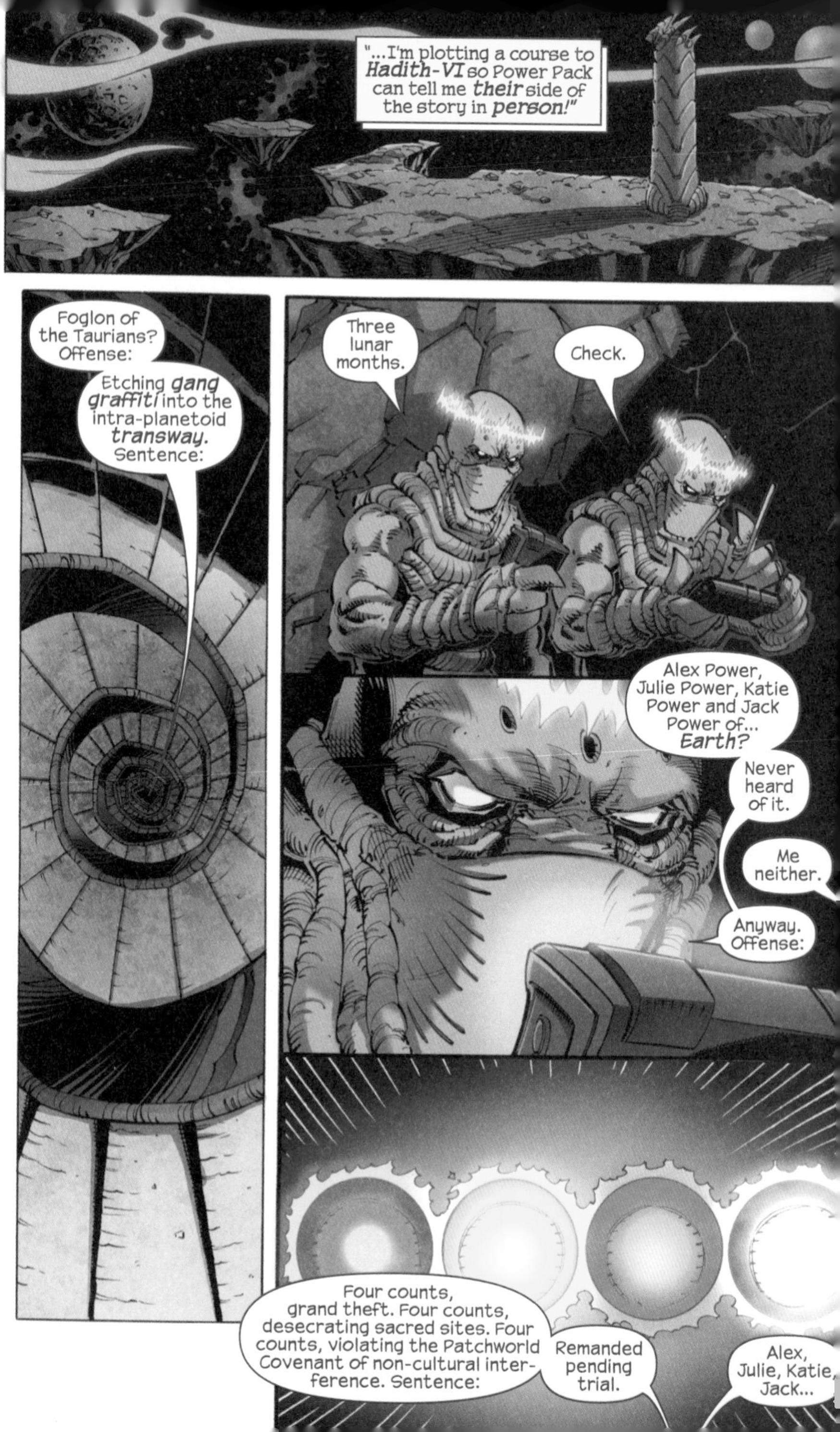
"...I'm plotting a course to Hadith-VI so Power Pack can tell me their side of the story in person!"
Foglon of the Taurians? Offense:
Etching gang graffiti into the intra-planetoid transway. Sentence:
Three lunar months.
Check.
Alex Power, Julie Power, Katie Power and Jack Power of... Earth?
Never heard of it.
Me neither.
Anyway. Offense:
Four counts, grand theft. Four counts, desecrating sacred sites. Four counts, violating the Patchworld Covenant of non-cultural interference. Sentence:
Remanded pending trial.
Alex, Julie, Katie, Jack...

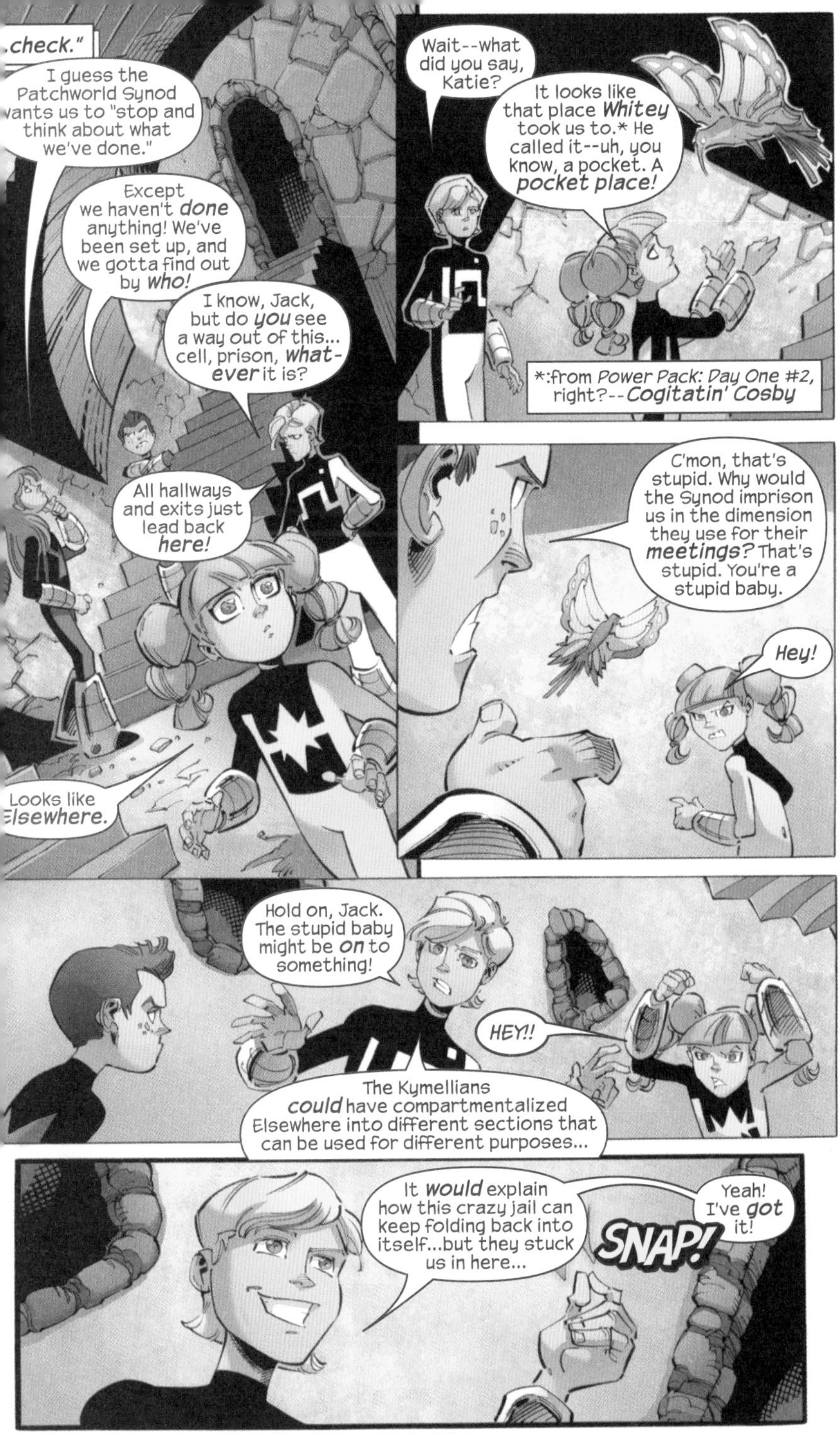

...check."
I guess the Patchworld Synod wants us to "stop and think about what we've done."
Except we haven't done anything! We've been set up, and we gotta find out by who!
I know, Jack, but do you see a way out of this... cell, prison, whatever it is?
All hallways and exits just lead back here!
Looks like Elsewhere.
Wait--what did you say, Katie?
It looks like that place Whitey took us to.* He called it--uh, you know, a pocket. A pocket place!
*:from Power Pack: Day One #2, right?--Cogitatin' Cosby
C'mon, that's stupid. Why would the Synod imprison us in the dimension they use for their meetings? That's stupid. You're a stupid baby.
Hey!
Hold on, Jack. The stupid baby might be on to something!
HEY!!
The Kymellians could have compartmentalized Elsewhere into different sections that can be used for different purposes...
It would explain how this crazy jail can keep folding back into itself...but they stuck us in here...
Yeah! I've got it!
SNAP!

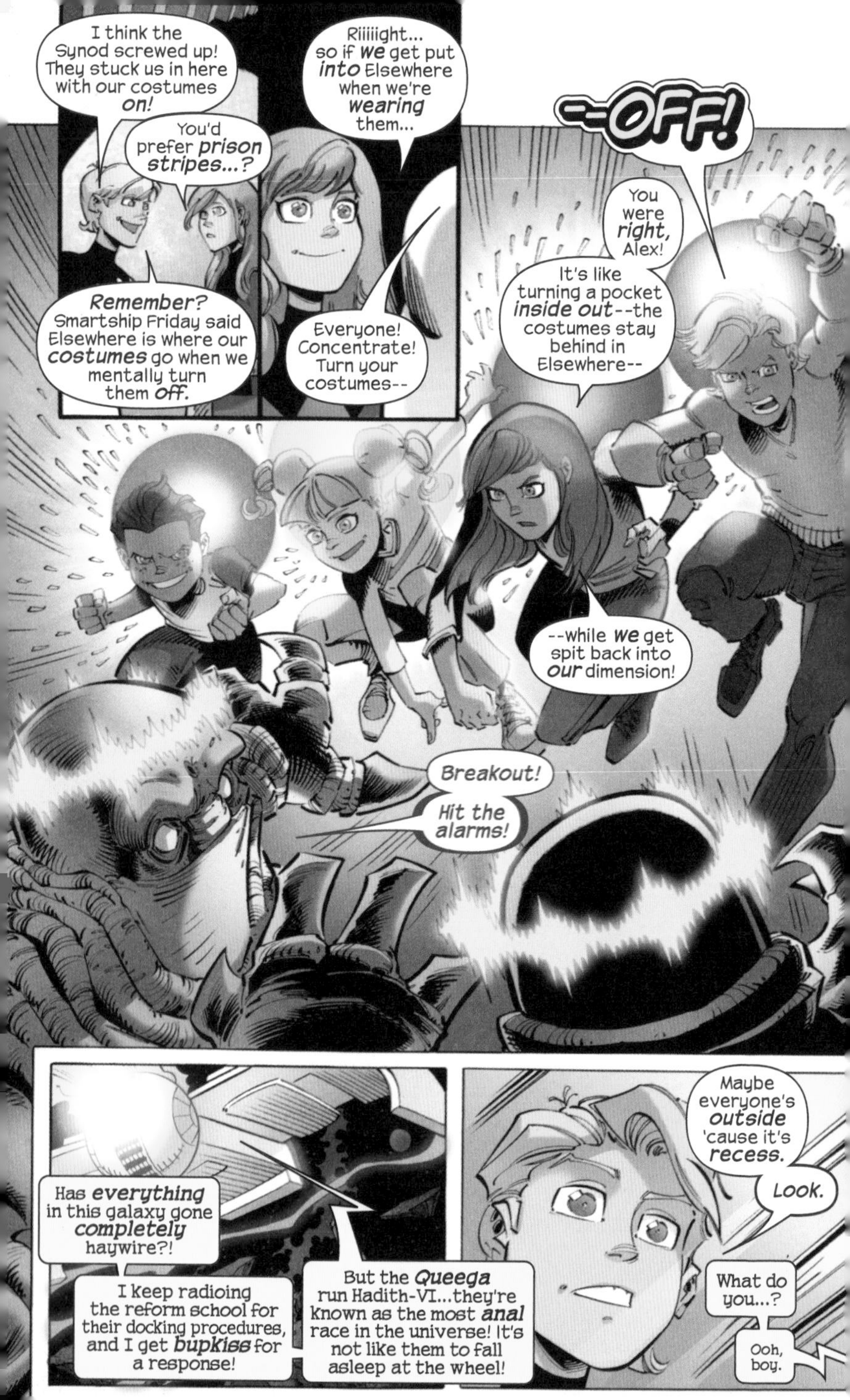
I think the Synod screwed up! They stuck us in here with our costumes on!
You'd prefer prison stripes...?
Remember? Smartship Friday said Elsewhere is where our costumes go when we mentally turn them off.
Riiiiight... so if we get put into Elsewhere when we're wearing them...
Everyone! Concentrate! Turn your costumes--
--OFF!
You were right, Alex!
It's like turning a pocket inside out--the costumes stay behind in Elsewhere--
--while we get spit back into our dimension!
Breakout!
Hit the alarms!
Has everything in this galaxy gone completely haywire?!
I keep radioing the reform school for their docking procedures, and I get bupkiss for a response!
But the Queega run Hadith-VI...they're known as the most anal race in the universe! It's not like them to fall asleep at the wheel!
Maybe everyone's outside 'cause it's recess.
Look.
What do you...?
Ooh, boy.

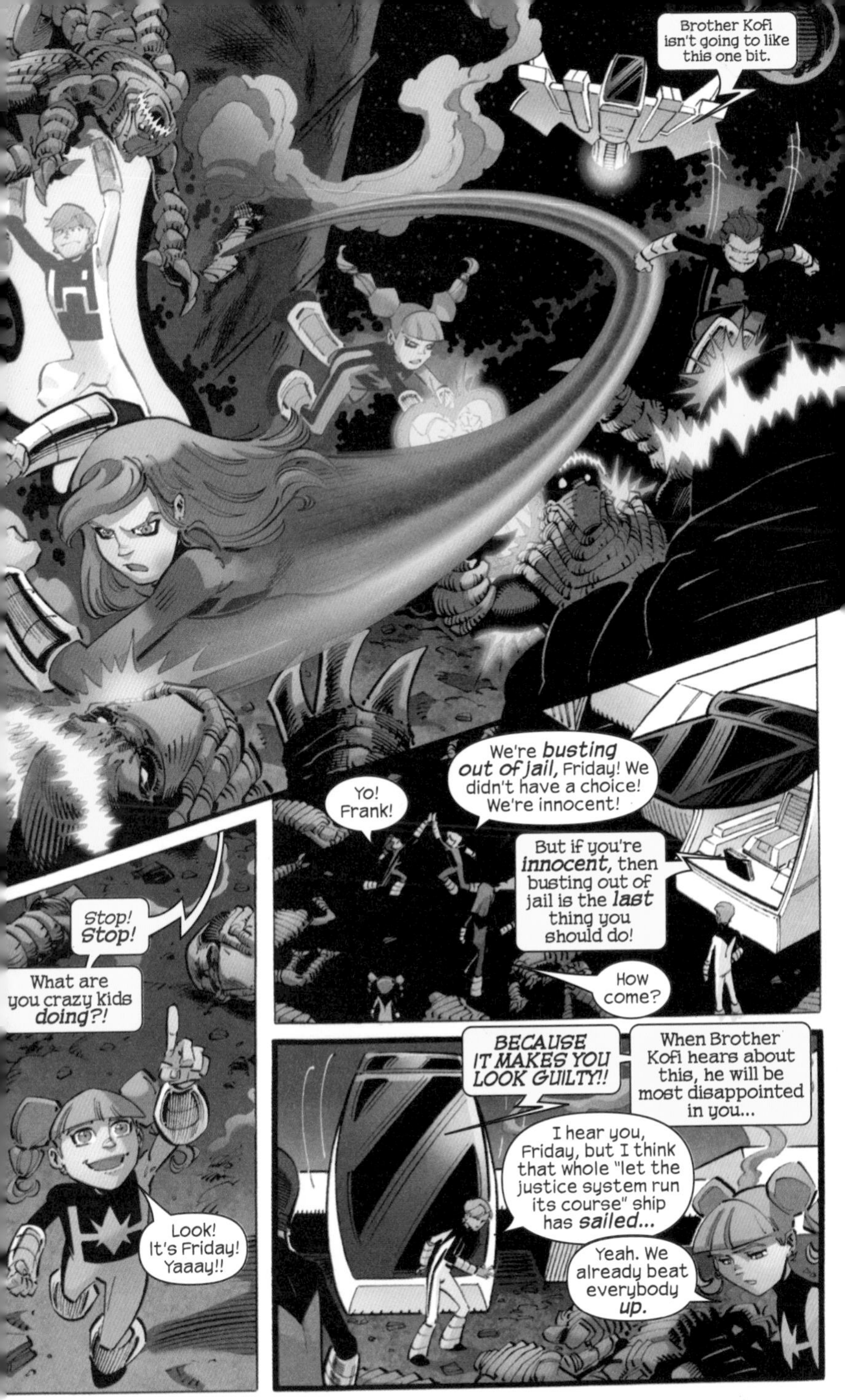
Brother Kofi isn't going to like this one bit.
Yo! Frank!
We're *busting out of jail*, Friday! We didn't have a choice! We're innocent!
But if you're *innocent*, then busting out of jail is the *last* thing you should do!
How come?
Stop! *Stop!*
What are you crazy kids *doing*?!
Look! It's Friday! Yaaay!!
BECAUSE IT MAKES YOU LOOK GUILTY!!
When Brother Kofi hears about this, he will be most disappointed in you...
I hear you, Friday, but I think that whole "let the justice system run its course" ship has *sailed*...
Yeah. We already beat everybody *up*.

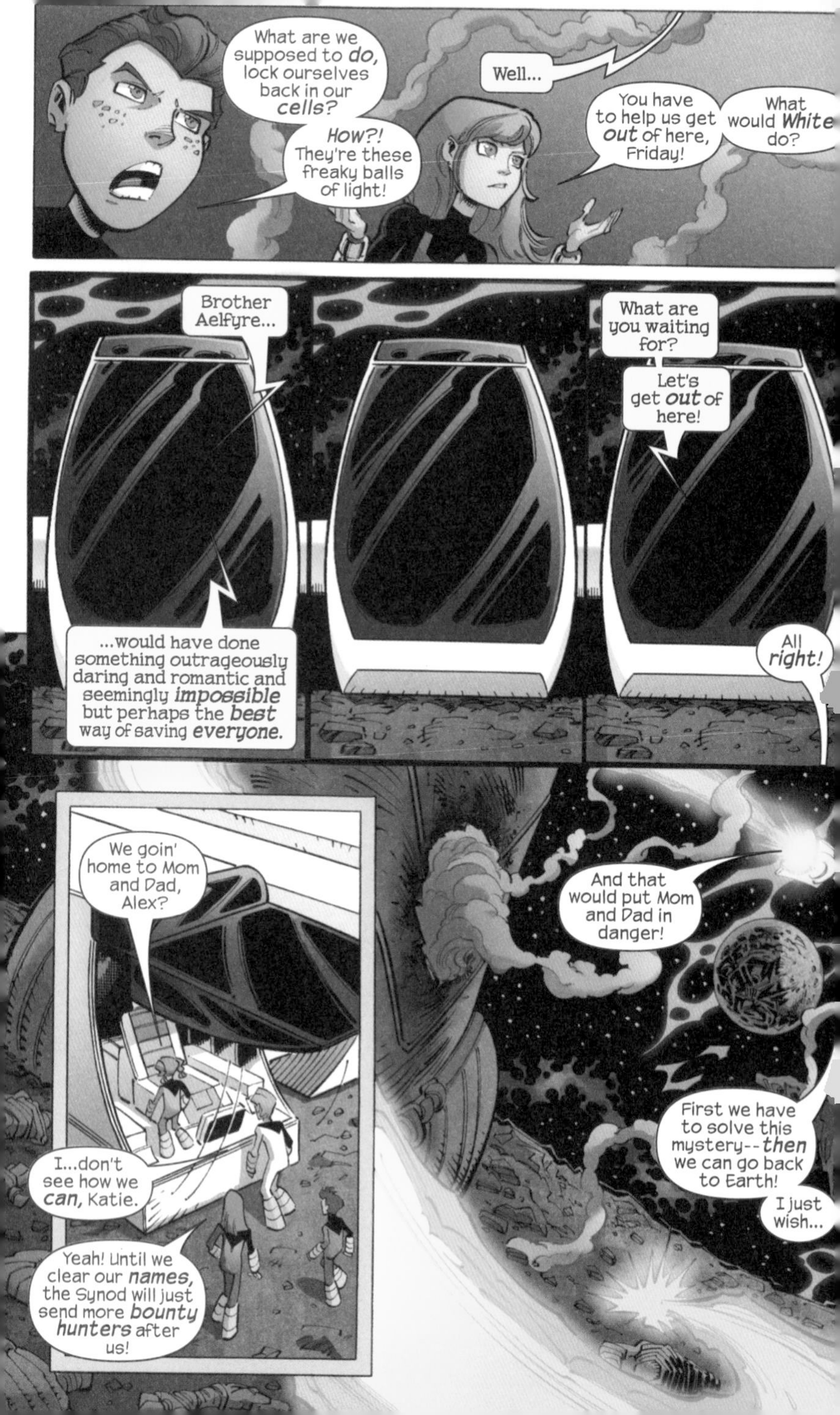
What are we supposed to do, lock ourselves back in our cells?
How?! They're these freaky balls of light!
Well...
You have to help us get out of here, Friday!
What would White do?
Brother Aelfyre...
...would have done something outrageously daring and romantic and seemingly impossible but perhaps the best way of saving everyone.
What are you waiting for?
Let's get out of here!
All right!
We goin' home to Mom and Dad, Alex?
I...don't see how we can, Katie.
Yeah! Until we clear our names, the Synod will just send more bounty hunters after us!
And that would put Mom and Dad in danger!
First we have to solve this mystery--then we can go back to Earth!
I just wish...

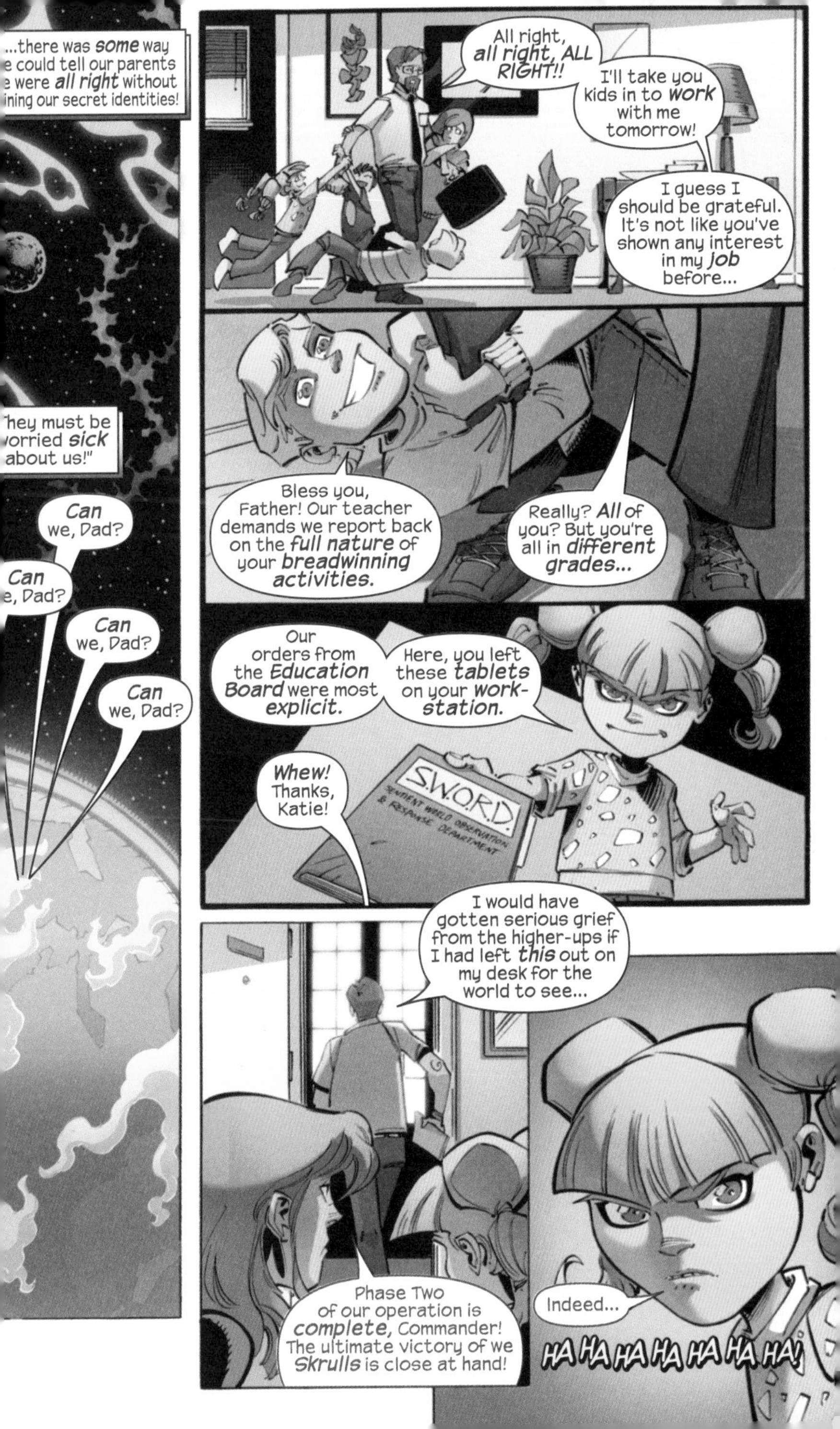
...there was some way
e could tell our parents
e were all right without
ining our secret identities!
hey must be
vorried sick
about us!"
Can
we, Dad?
Can
e, Dad?
Can
we, Dad?
Can
we, Dad?
All right, all right, ALL RIGHT!!
I'll take you kids in to work with me tomorrow!
I guess I should be grateful. It's not like you've shown any interest in my job before...
Bless you, Father! Our teacher demands we report back on the full nature of your breadwinning activities.
Really? All of you? But you're all in different grades...
Our orders from the Education Board were most explicit.
Here, you left these tablets on your work-station.
S.W.O.R.D.
Whew! Thanks, Katie!
I would have gotten serious grief from the higher-ups if I had left this out on my desk for the world to see...
Phase Two of our operation is complete, Commander! The ultimate victory of we Skrulls is close at hand!
Indeed...
HA HA HA HA HA HA HA!

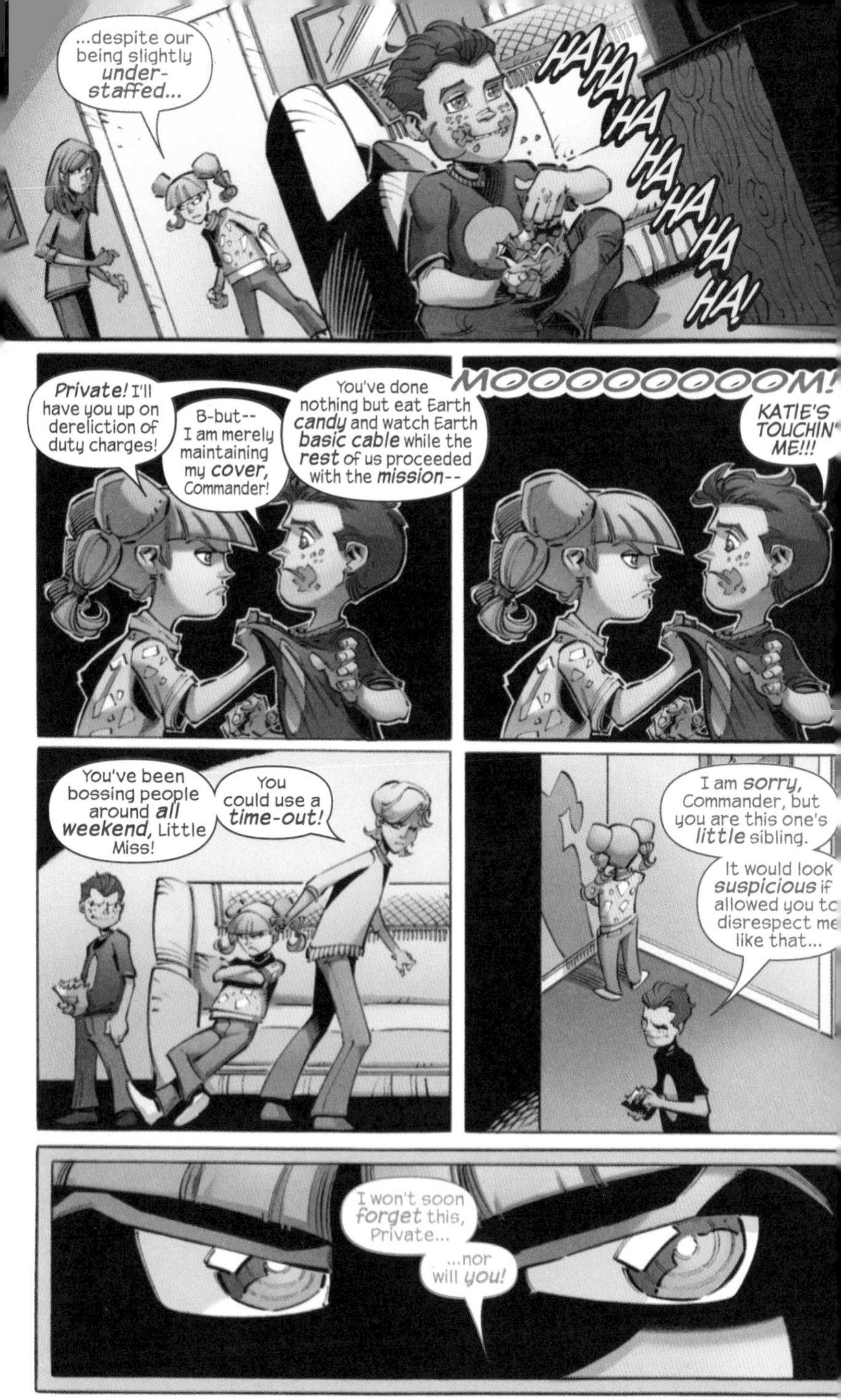
...despite our being slightly under-staffed...
HAHAHAHAHAHAHA!
Private! I'll have you up on dereliction of duty charges!
B-but-- I am merely maintaining my cover, Commander!
You've done nothing but eat Earth candy and watch Earth basic cable while the rest of us proceeded with the mission--
MOOOOOOOOOOM!
KATIE'S TOUCHIN' ME!!!
You've been bossing people around all weekend, Little Miss!
You could use a time-out!
I am sorry, Commander, but you are this one's little sibling.
It would look suspicious if allowed you to disrespect me like that...
I won't soon forget this, Private...
...nor will you!

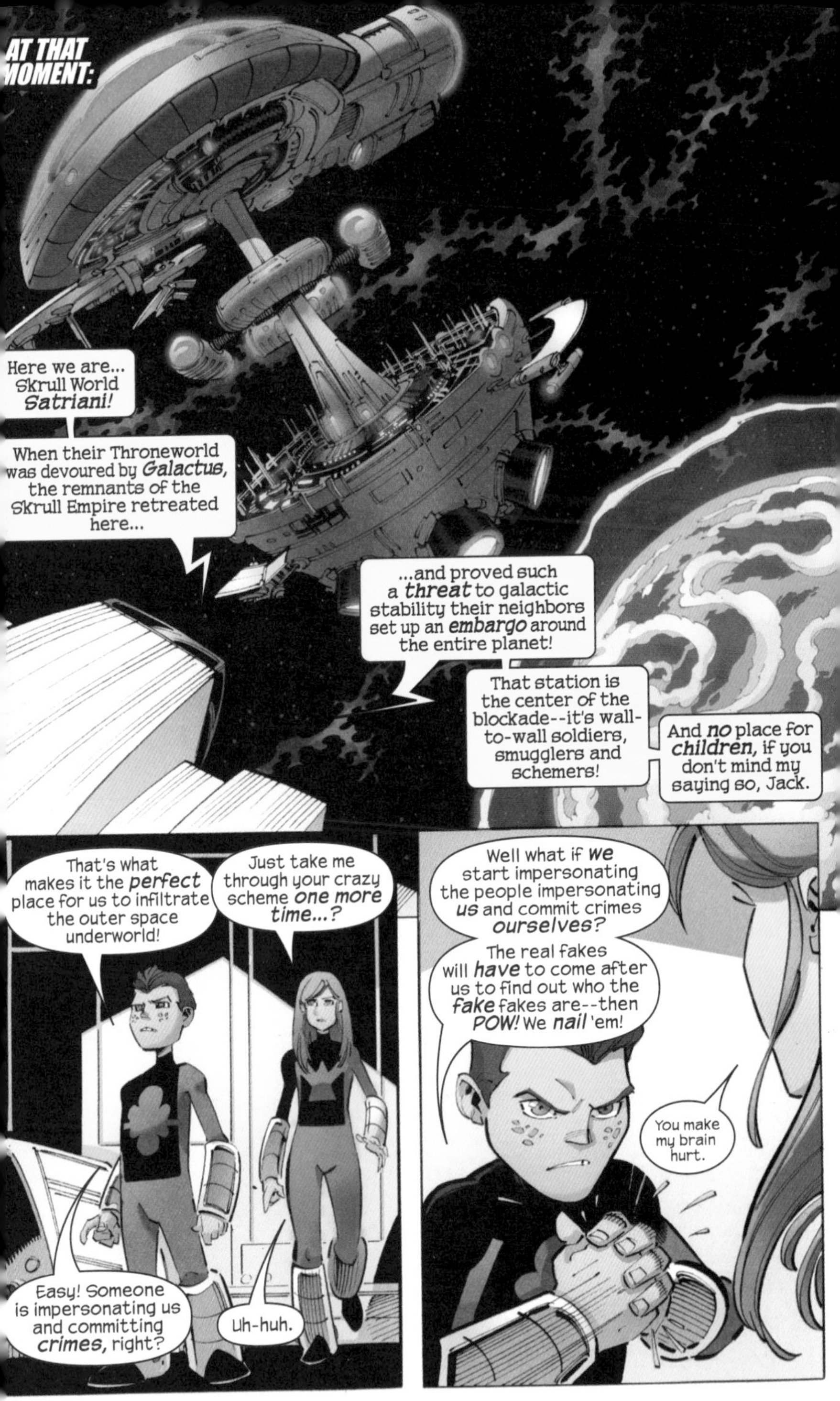
AT THAT MOMENT:
Here we are... Skrull World Satriani!
When their Throneworld was devoured by Galactus, the remnants of the Skrull Empire retreated here...
...and proved such a threat to galactic stability their neighbors set up an embargo around the entire planet!
That station is the center of the blockade--it's wall-to-wall soldiers, smugglers and schemers!
And no place for children, if you don't mind my saying so, Jack.
That's what makes it the perfect place for us to infiltrate the outer space underworld!
Just take me through your crazy scheme one more time...?
Easy! Someone is impersonating us and committing crimes, right?
Uh-huh.
Well what if we start impersonating the people impersonating us and commit crimes ourselves?
The real fakes will have to come after us to find out who the fake fakes are--then POW! We nail 'em!
You make my brain hurt.

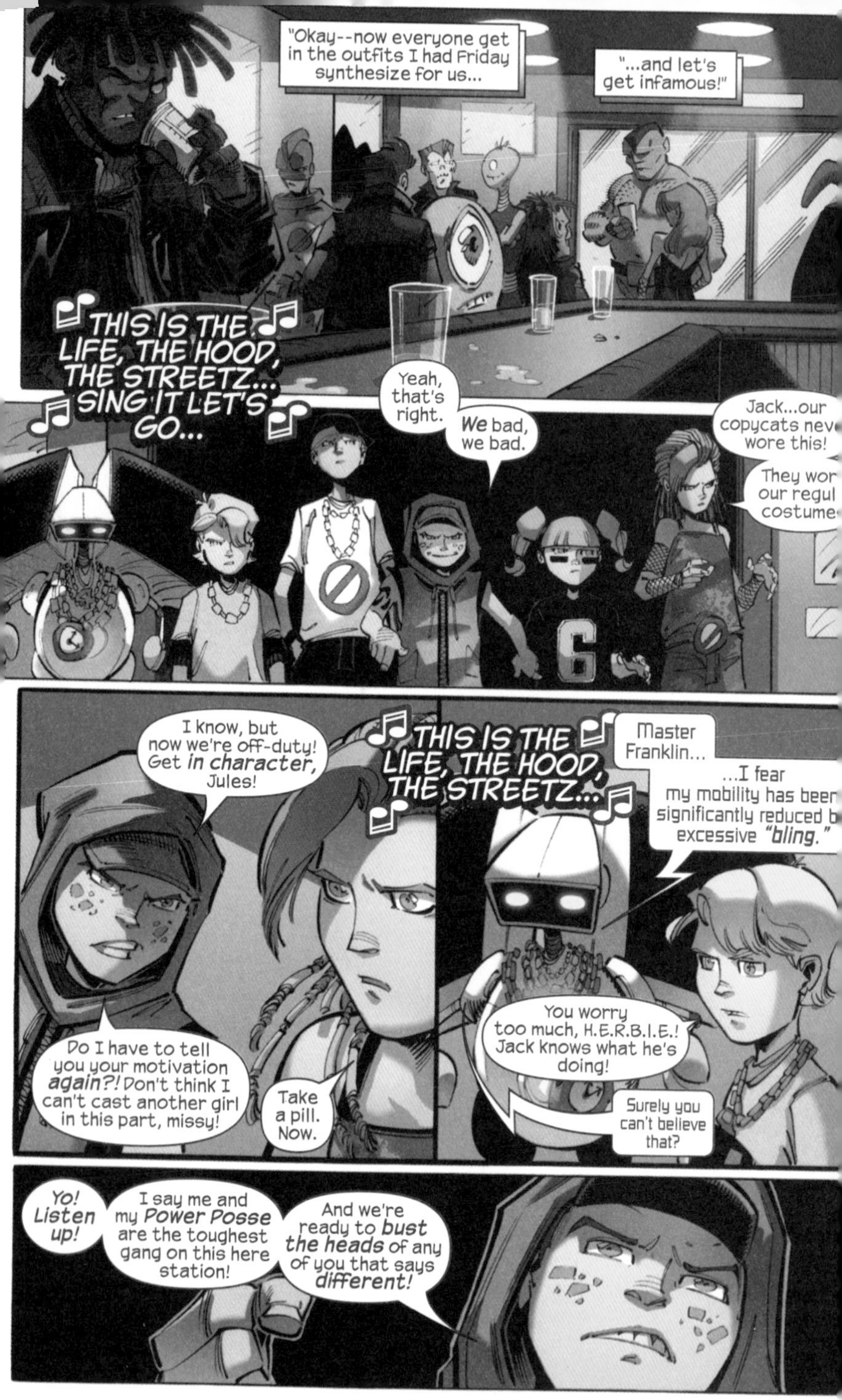

"Okay--now everyone get in the outfits I had Friday synthesize for us...
"...and let's get infamous!"
THIS IS THE LIFE, THE HOOD, THE STREETZ... SING IT LET'S GO...
Yeah, that's right.
We bad, we bad.
Jack...our copycats nev wore this!
They wor our regul costume
I know, but now we're off-duty! Get in character, Jules!
Do I have to tell you your motivation again?! Don't think I can't cast another girl in this part, missy!
Take a pill. Now.
THIS IS THE LIFE, THE HOOD, THE STREETZ...
Master Franklin...
...I fear my mobility has been significantly reduced b excessive "bling."
You worry too much, H.E.R.B.I.E.! Jack knows what he's doing!
Surely you can't believe that?
Yo! Listen up!
I say me and my Power Posse are the toughest gang on this here station!
And we're ready to bust the heads of any of you that says different!

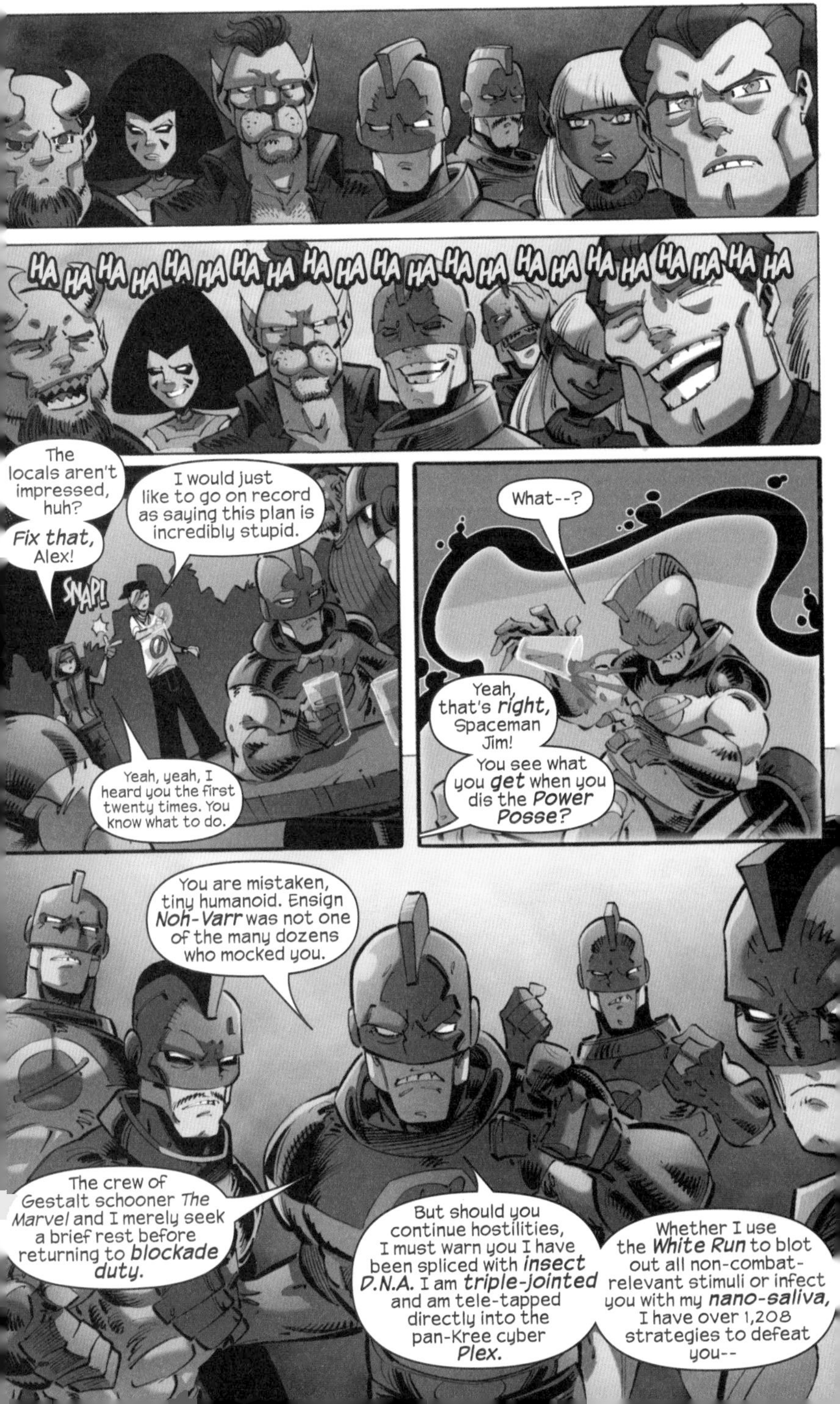

HA HA HA HA HA HA HA HA HA HA HA HA HA HA HA HA HA HA HA HA HA
The locals aren't impressed, huh?
Fix that, Alex!
I would just like to go on record as saying this plan is incredibly stupid.
SNAP!
Yeah, yeah, I heard you the first twenty times. You know what to do.
What--?
Yeah, that's right, Spaceman Jim!
You see what you get when you dis the Power Posse?
You are mistaken, tiny humanoid. Ensign Noh-Varr was not one of the many dozens who mocked you.
The crew of Gestalt schooner The Marvel and I merely seek a brief rest before returning to blockade duty.
But should you continue hostilities, I must warn you I have been spliced with insect D.N.A. I am triple-jointed and am tele-tapped directly into the pan-Kree cyber Plex.
Whether I use the White Run to blot out all non-combat-relevant stimuli or infect you with my nano-saliva, I have over 1,208 strategies to defeat you--

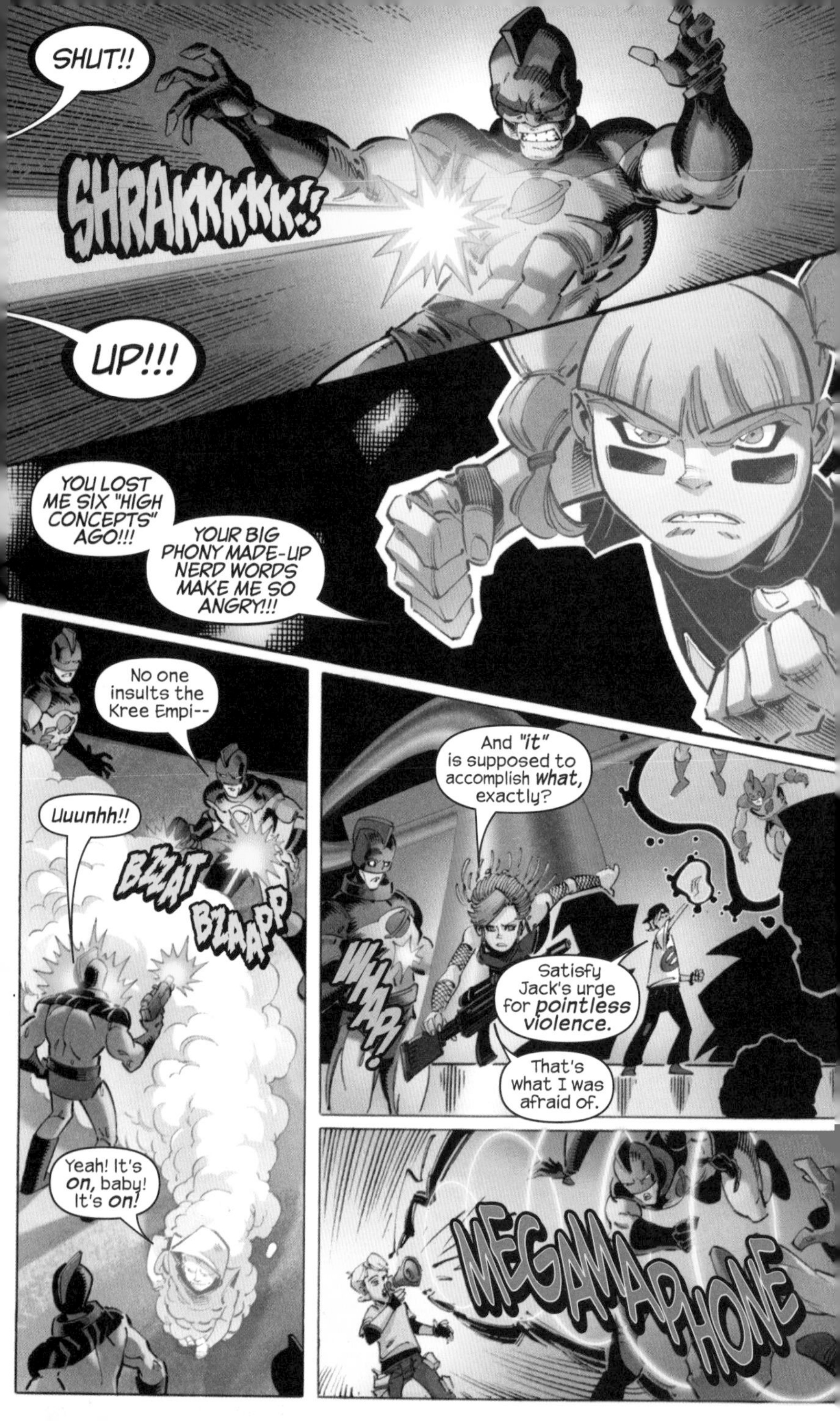
SHUT!!
SHRAKKKKK!!
UP!!!
YOU LOST ME SIX "HIGH CONCEPTS" AGO!!!
YOUR BIG PHONY MADE-UP NERD WORDS MAKE ME SO ANGRY!!!
No one insults the Kree Empi--
Uuunhh!!
BZZAT
BZAAPP
Yeah! It's *on*, baby! It's *on*!
And *"it"* is supposed to accomplish *what*, exactly?
WHAP!
Satisfy Jack's urge for **pointless violence**.
That's what I was afraid of.
MEGAMAPHONE

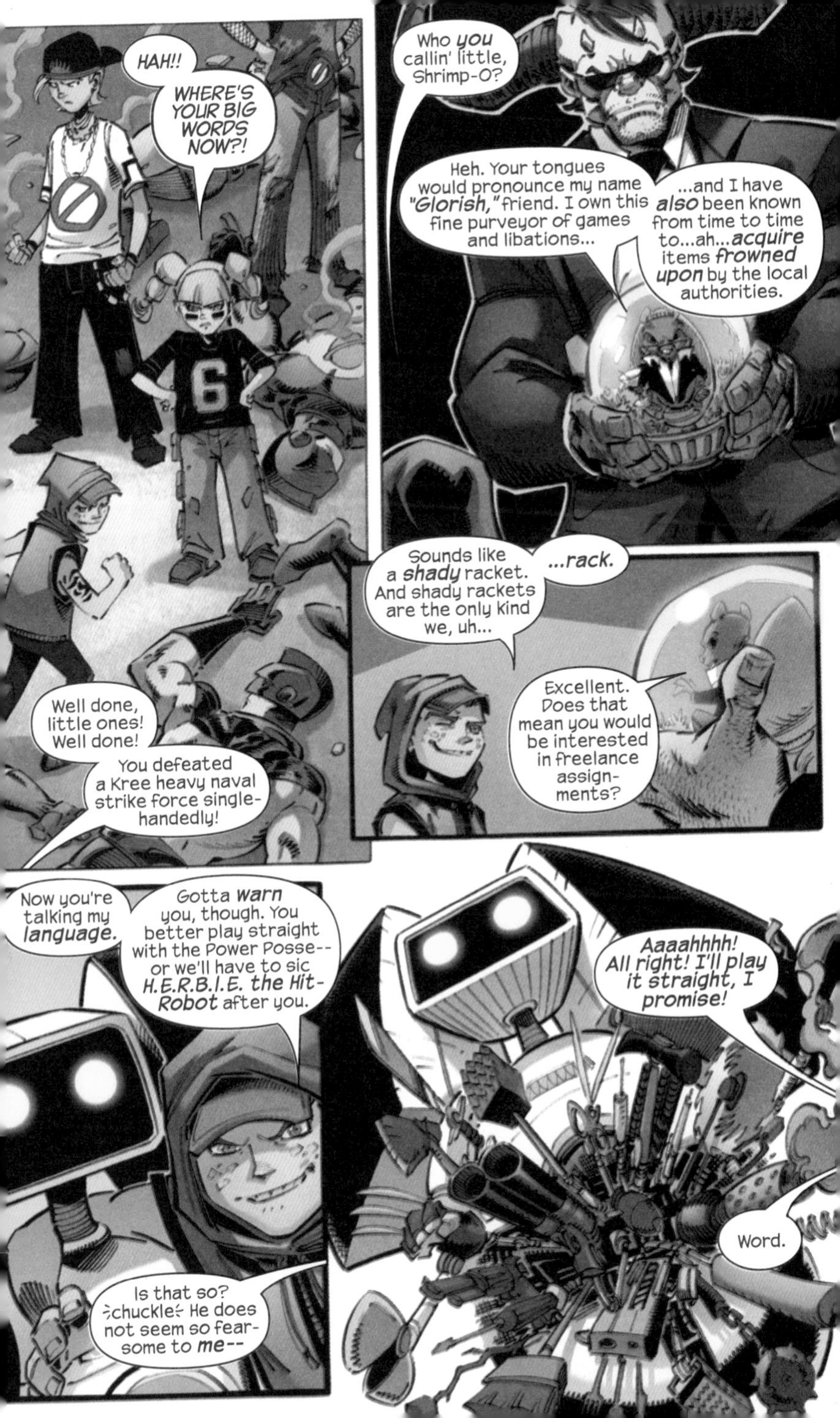

HAH!!
WHERE'S YOUR BIG WORDS NOW?!
Well done, little ones! Well done!
You defeated a Kree heavy naval strike force single-handedly!
Who *you* callin' little, Shrimp-O?
Heh. Your tongues would pronounce my name *"Glorish,"* friend. I own this fine purveyor of games and libations...
...and I have *also* been known from time to time to...ah...*acquire* items *frowned upon* by the local authorities.
Sounds like a *shady* racket. And shady rackets are the only kind we, uh...
...rack.
Excellent. Does that mean you would be interested in freelance assign-ments?
Now you're talking my *language.*
Gotta *warn* you, though. You better play straight with the Power Posse--or we'll have to sic *H.E.R.B.I.E. the Hit-Robot* after you.
Is that so? ⁼chuckle⁼ He does not seem so fear-some to *me*--
Aaaahhhh! All right! I'll play it straight, I promise!
Word.

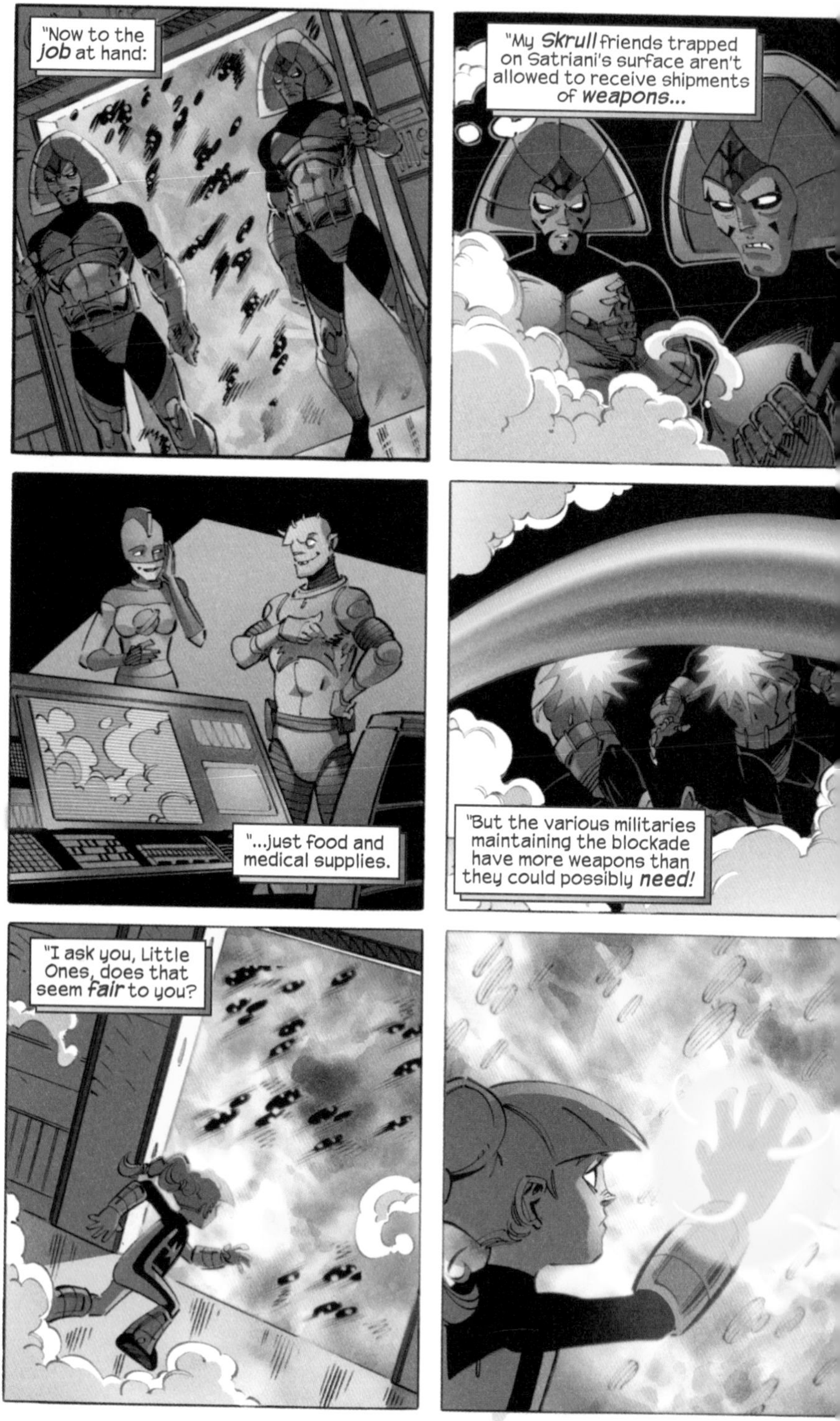

"Now to the job at hand:
"My Skrull friends trapped on Satriani's surface aren't allowed to receive shipments of weapons...
"...just food and medical supplies.
"But the various militaries maintaining the blockade have more weapons than they could possibly need!
"I ask you, Little Ones, does that seem fair to you?

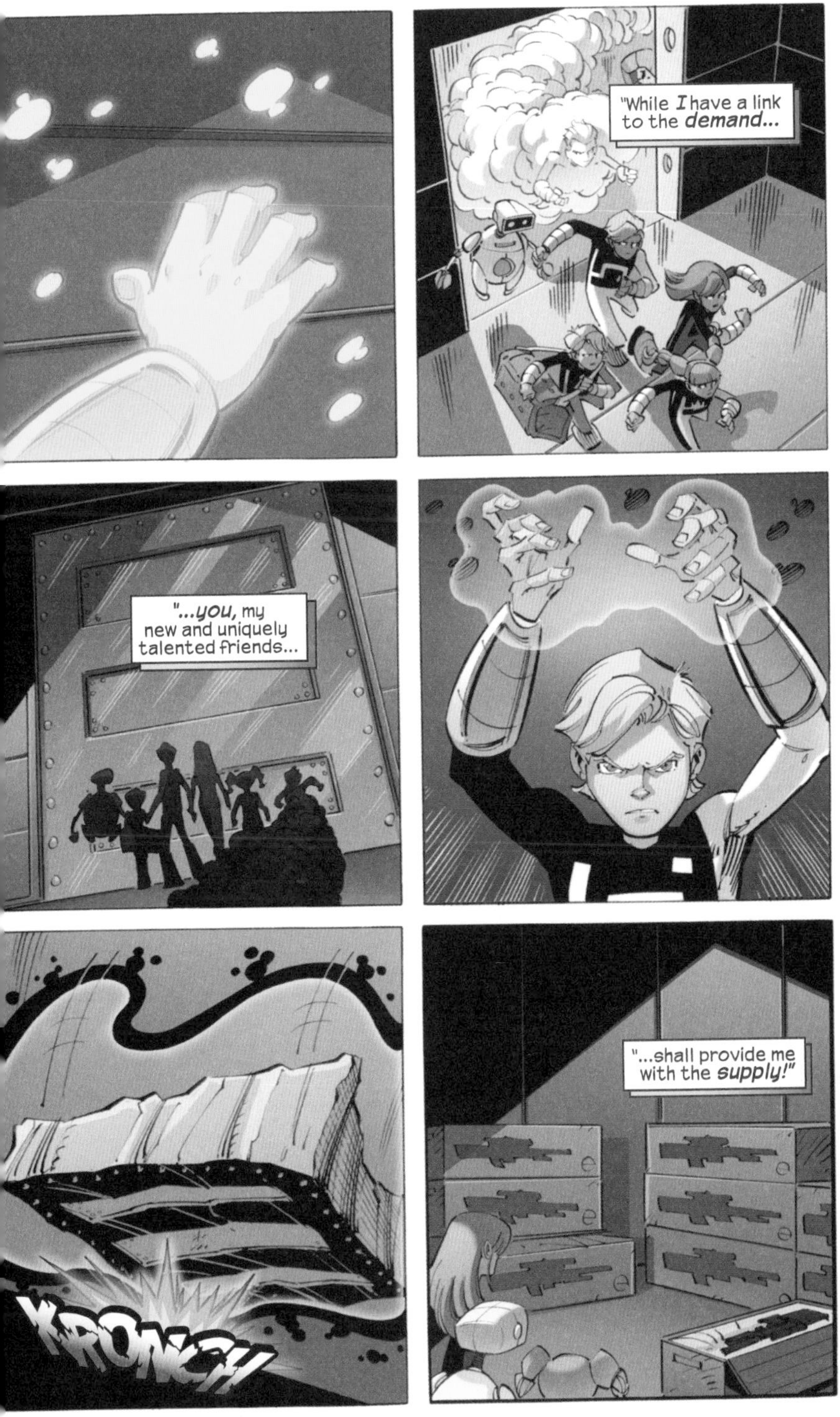
"While *I* have a link to the *demand...*
"...*you,* my new and uniquely talented friends...
KRONCH
"...shall provide me with the *supply!*"

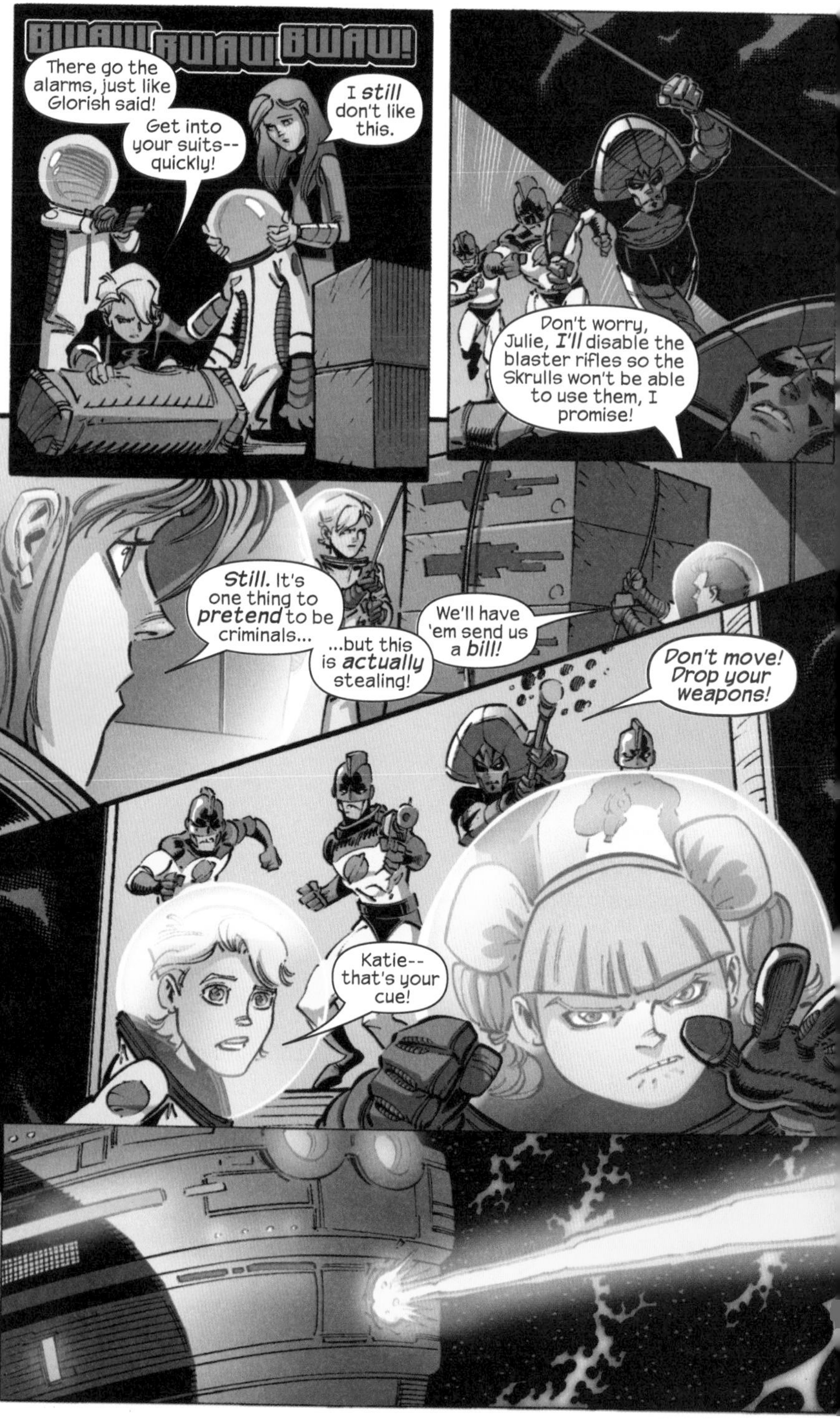
BWAW! BWAW! BWAW!
There go the alarms, just like Glorish said!
Get into your suits--quickly!
I still don't like this.
Don't worry, Julie, I'll disable the blaster rifles so the Skrulls won't be able to use them, I promise!
Still. It's one thing to pretend to be criminals...
...but this is actually stealing!
We'll have 'em send us a bill!
Don't move! Drop your weapons!
Katie--that's your cue!

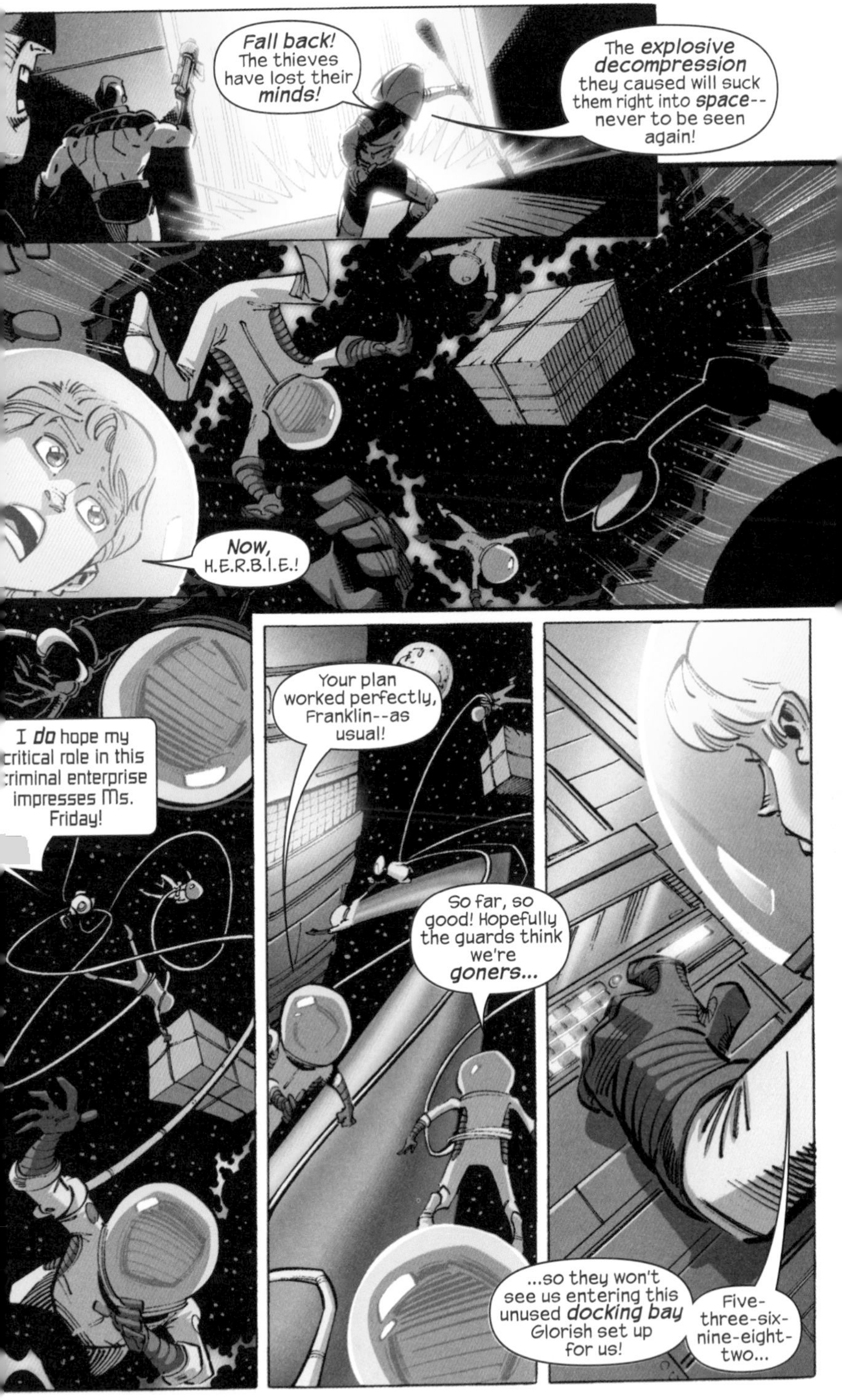

Fall back! The thieves have lost their minds!
The explosive decompression they caused will suck them right into space--never to be seen again!
Now, H.E.R.B.I.E.!
I do hope my critical role in this criminal enterprise impresses Ms. Friday!
Your plan worked perfectly, Franklin--as usual!
So far, so good! Hopefully the guards think we're goners...
...so they won't see us entering this unused docking bay Glorish set up for us!
Five-three-six-nine-eight-two...

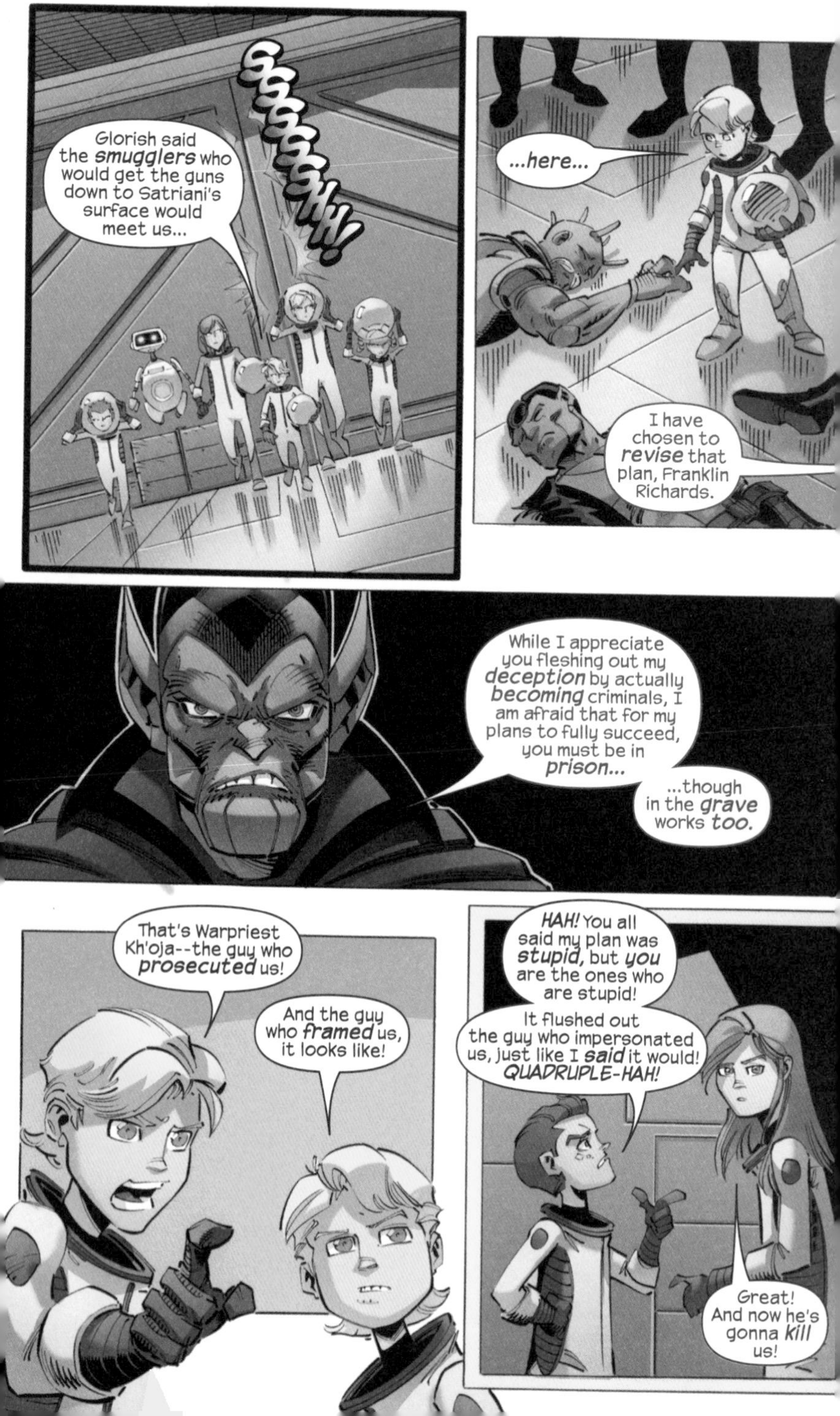
Glorish said the smugglers who would get the guns down to Satriani's surface would meet us...
SSSSSSHH!
...here...
I have chosen to revise that plan, Franklin Richards.
While I appreciate you fleshing out my deception by actually becoming criminals, I am afraid that for my plans to fully succeed, you must be in prison...
...though in the grave works too.
That's Warpriest Kh'oja--the guy who prosecuted us!
And the guy who framed us, it looks like!
HAH! You all said my plan was stupid, but you are the ones who are stupid!
It flushed out the guy who impersonated us, just like I said it would! QUADRUPLE-HAH!
Great! And now he's gonna kill us!

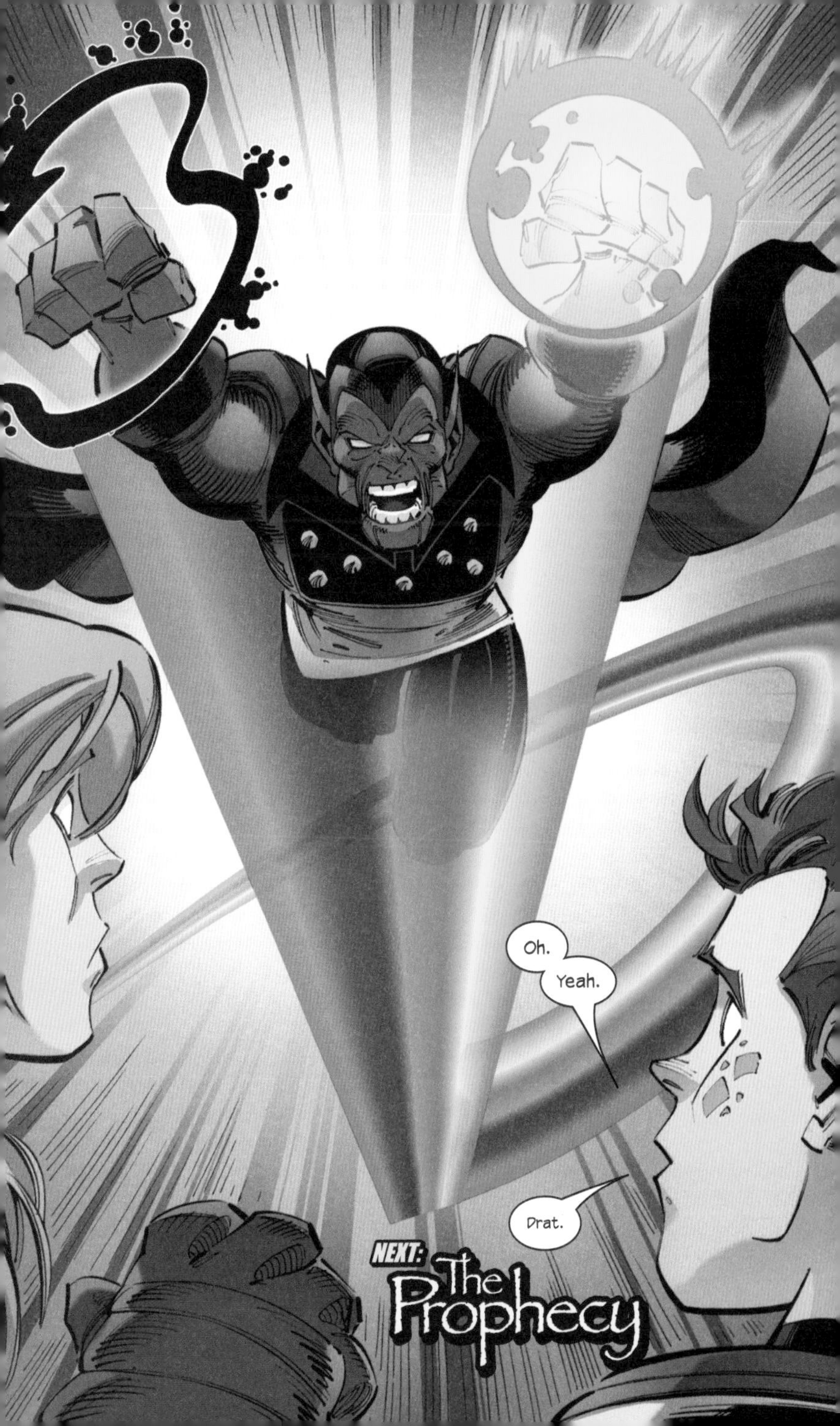
Oh.
Yeah.
Drat.
NEXT: The Prophecy

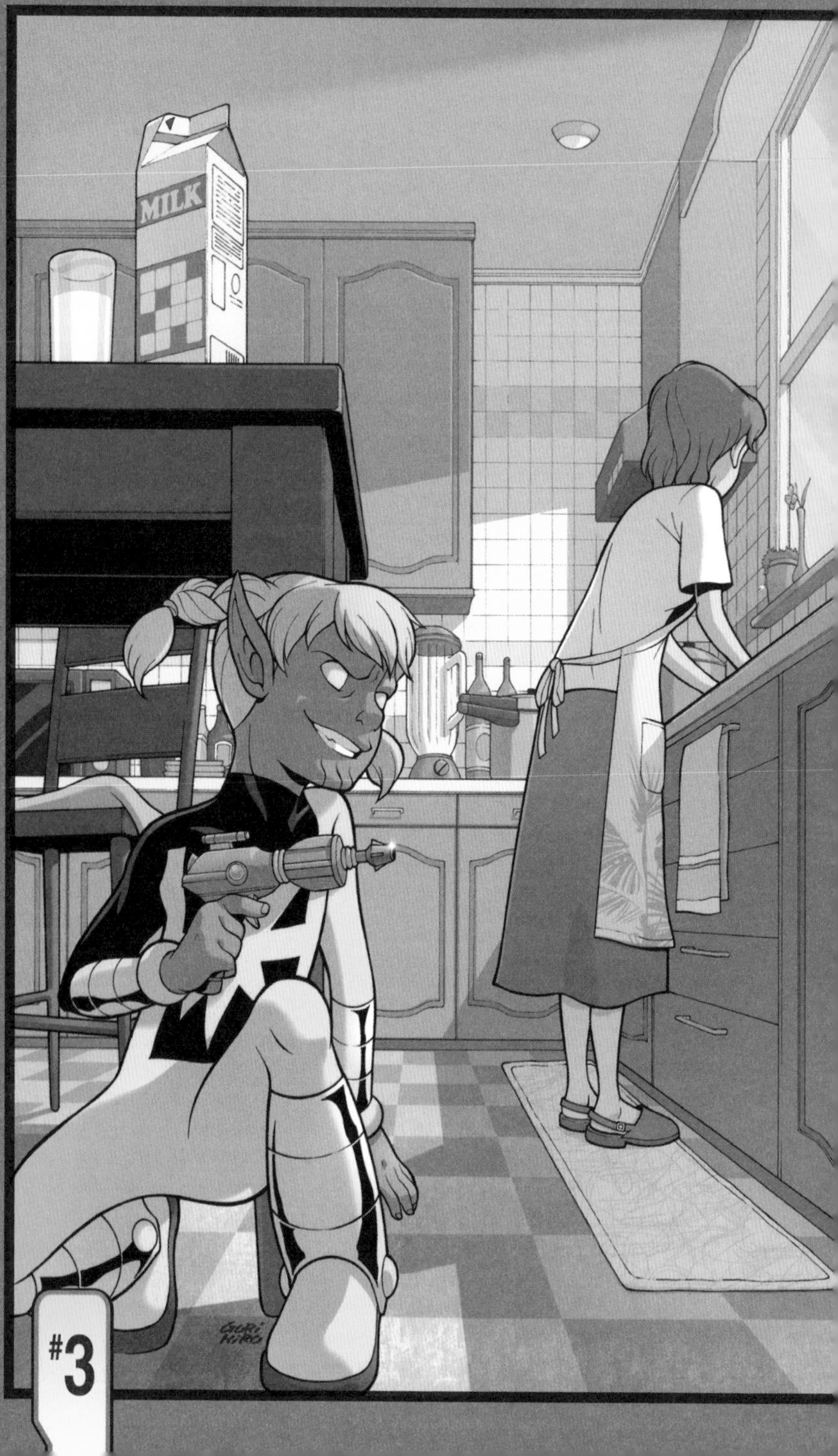
MILK
#3

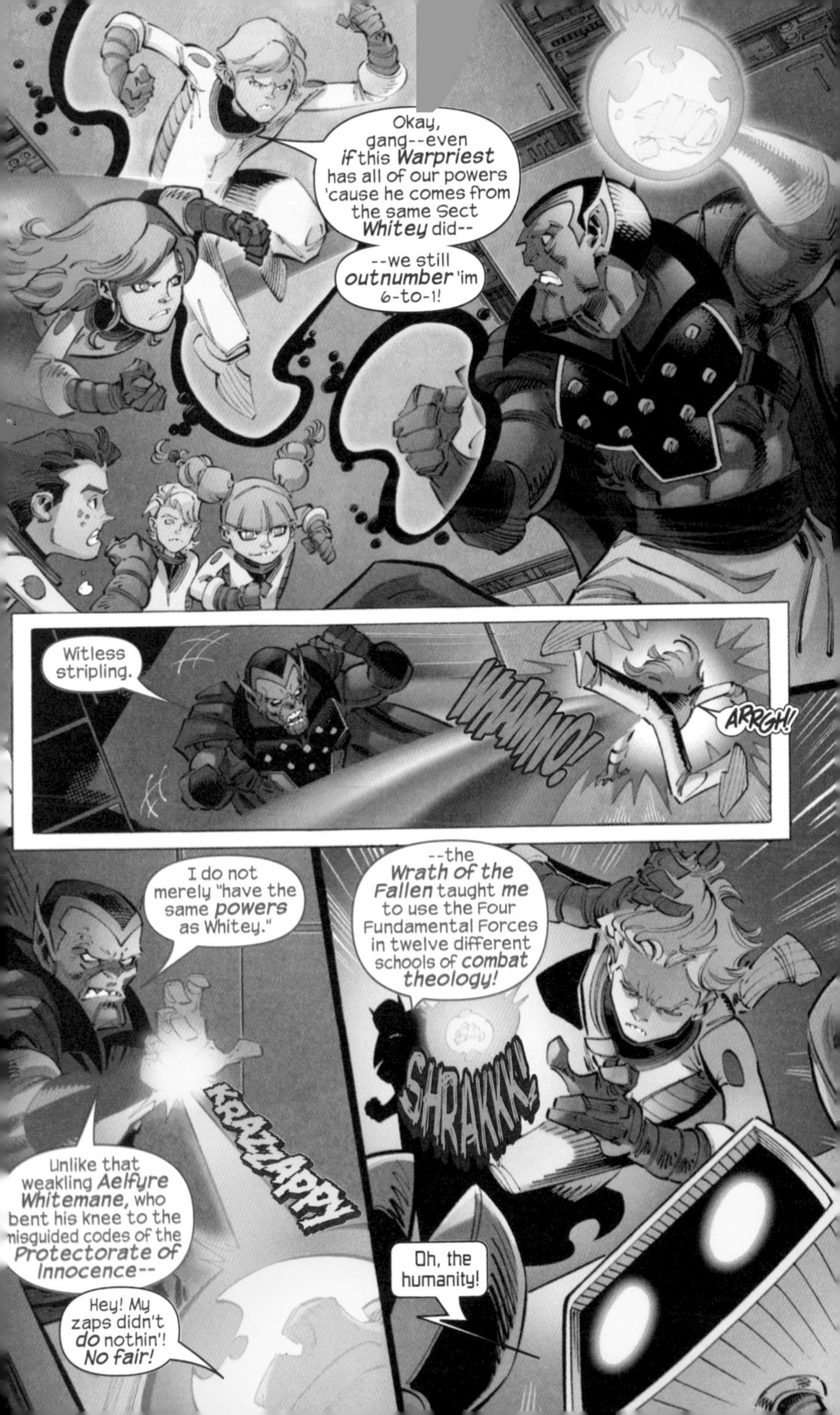
Okay, gang--even *if* this *Warpriest* has all of our powers 'cause he comes from the same Sect *Whitey* did--
--we still *outnumber* 'im 6-to-1!
Witless stripling.
WHAMMO!
ARRGH!
I do not merely "have the same *powers* as Whitey."
Unlike that weakling *Aelfyre Whitemane,* who bent his knee to the misguided codes of the *Protectorate of Innocence*--
--the *Wrath of the Fallen* taught *me* to use the Four Fundamental Forces in twelve different schools of *combat theology!*
KRAZZAPP!
SHRAKKK!
Hey! My zaps didn't *do* nothin'! *No fair!*
Oh, the humanity!

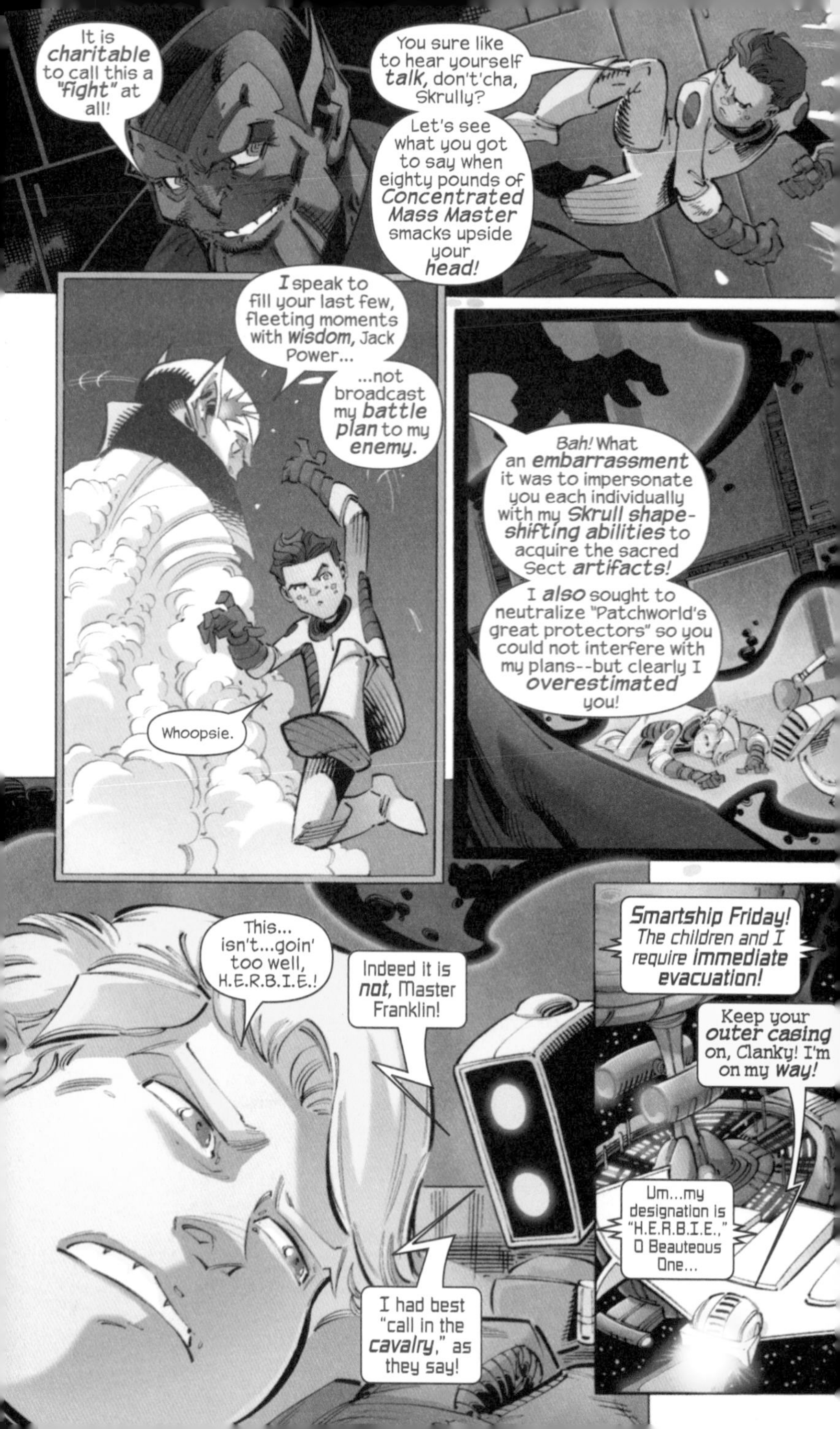
It is charitable to call this a "fight" at all!
You sure like to hear yourself talk, don't'cha, Skrully?
Let's see what you got to say when eighty pounds of Concentrated Mass Master smacks upside your head!
I speak to fill your last few, fleeting moments with wisdom, Jack Power...
...not broadcast my battle plan to my enemy.
Whoopsie.
Bah! What an embarrassment it was to impersonate you each individually with my Skrull shape-shifting abilities to acquire the sacred Sect artifacts!
I also sought to neutralize "Patchworld's great protectors" so you could not interfere with my plans--but clearly I overestimated you!
This... isn't...goin' too well, H.E.R.B.I.E.!
Indeed it is not, Master Franklin!
I had best "call in the cavalry," as they say!
Smartship Friday! The children and I require immediate evacuation!
Keep your outer casing on, Clanky! I'm on my way!
Um...my designation is "H.E.R.B.I.E.," O Beauteous One...

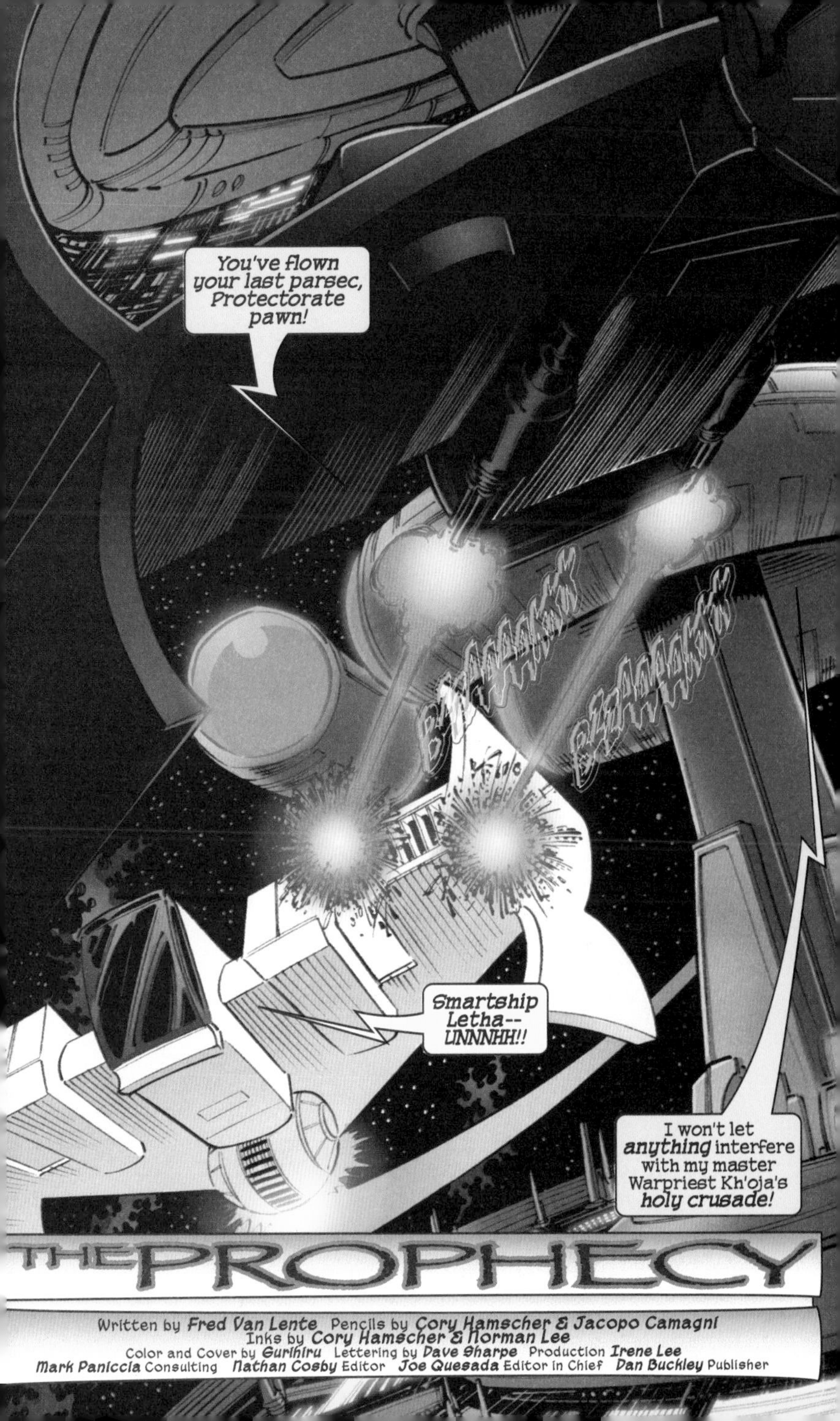
You've flown your last parsec, Protectorate pawn!
Smartship Letha-- UNNNHH!!
I won't let *anything* interfere with my master Warpriest Kh'oja's *holy crusade!*
THE PROPHECY
Written by Fred Van Lente Pencils by Cory Hamscher & Jacopo Camagni
Inks by Cory Hamscher & Norman Lee
Color and Cover by Gurihiru Lettering by Dave Sharpe Production Irene Lee
Mark Paniccia Consulting Nathan Cosby Editor Joe Quesada Editor in Chief Dan Buckley Publisher

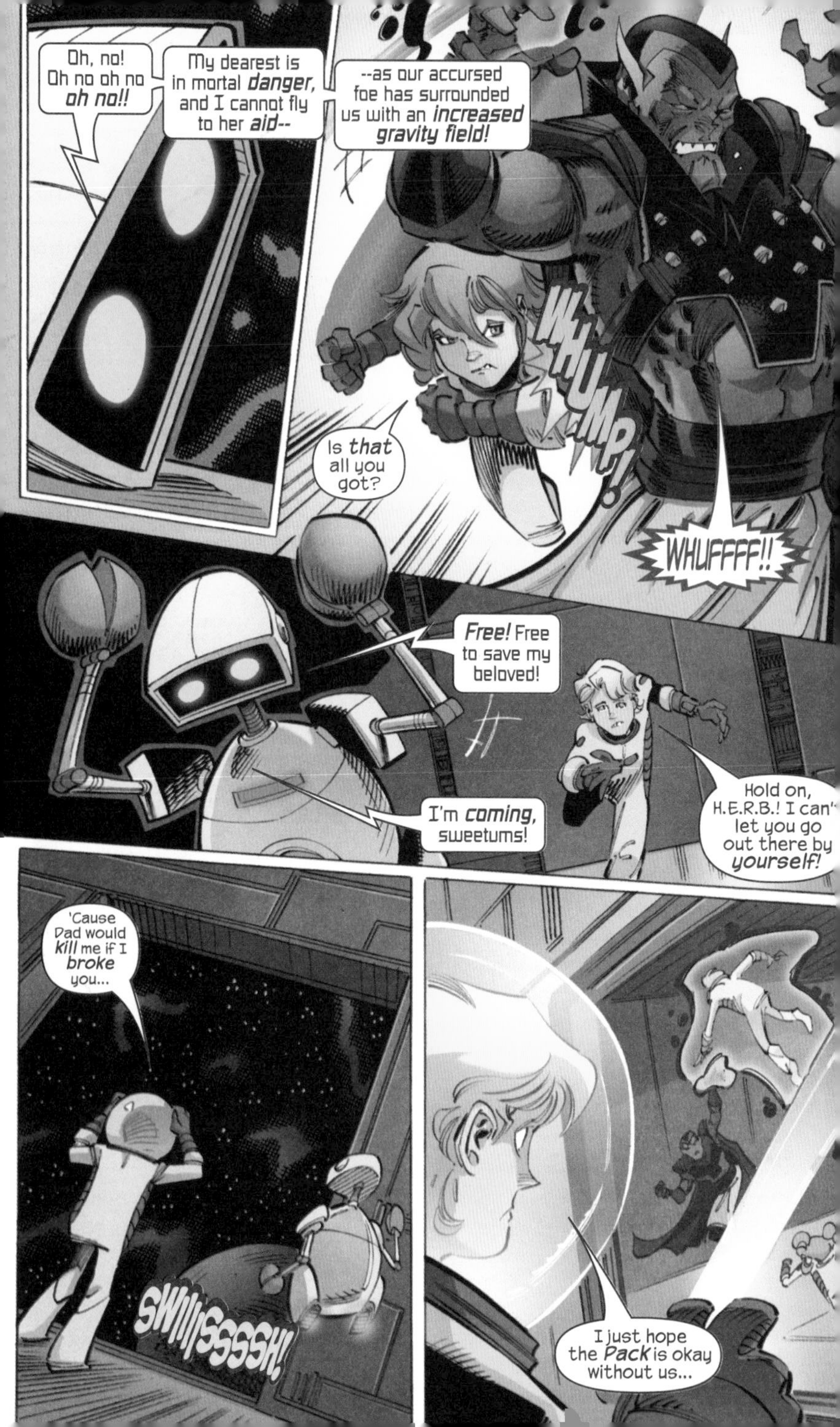
Oh, no! Oh no oh no oh no oh no!!
My dearest is in mortal danger, and I cannot fly to her aid--
--as our accursed foe has surrounded us with an increased gravity field!
WHUMP!!
Is that all you got?
WHUFFFF!!
Free! Free to save my beloved!
I'm coming, sweetums!
Hold on, H.E.R.B.! I can' let you go out there by yourself!
'Cause Dad would kill me if I broke you...
SWIIIISSSSH!
I just hope the Pack is okay without us...

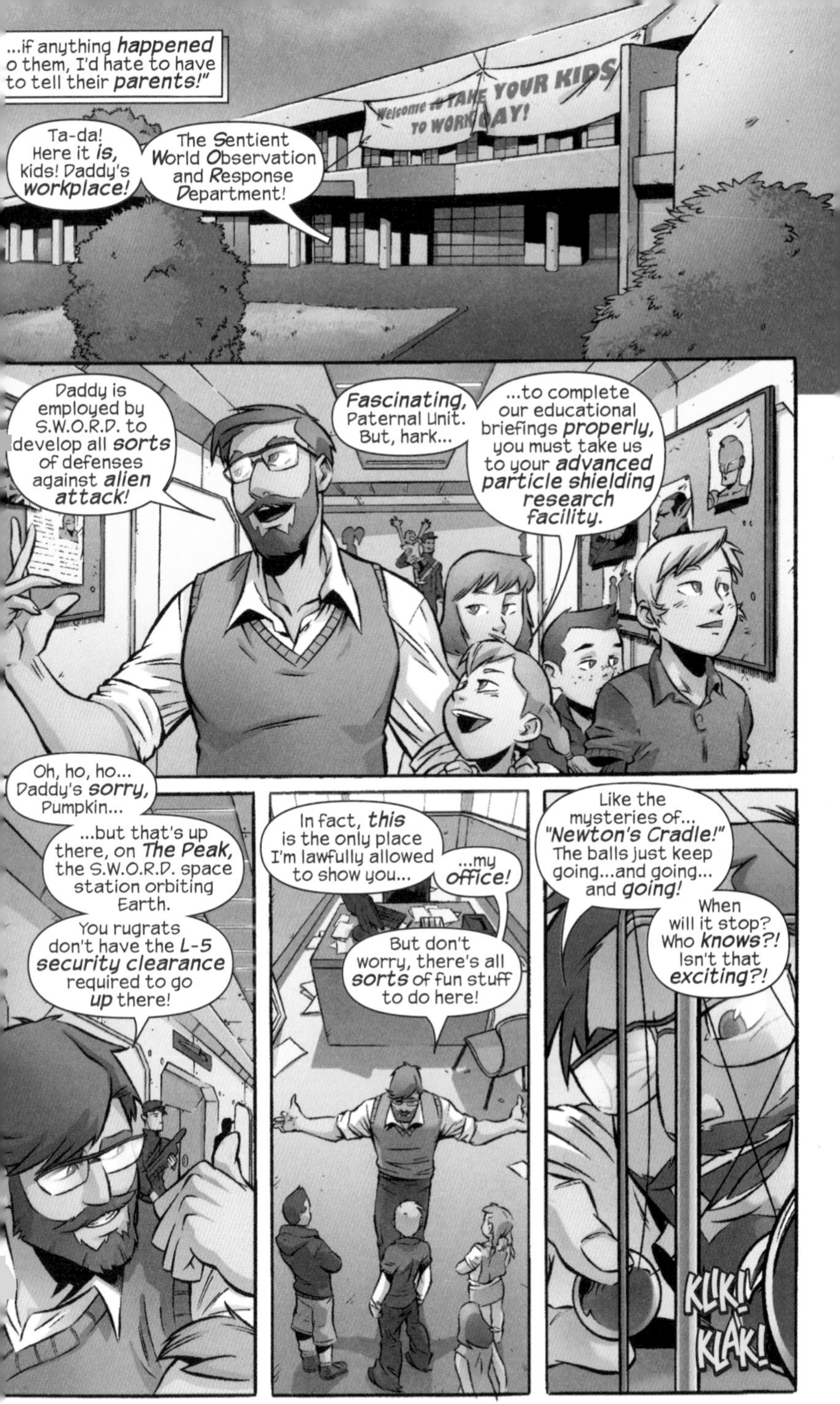

...if anything happened o them, I'd hate to have to tell their parents!"
Welcome to TAKE YOUR KIDS TO WORK DAY!
Ta-da! Here it is, kids! Daddy's workplace!
The Sentient World Observation and Response Department!
Daddy is employed by S.W.O.R.D. to develop all sorts of defenses against alien attack!
Fascinating, Paternal Unit. But, hark...
...to complete our educational briefings properly, you must take us to your advanced particle shielding research facility.
Oh, ho, ho... Daddy's sorry, Pumpkin...
...but that's up there, on The Peak, the S.W.O.R.D. space station orbiting Earth.
You rugrats don't have the L-5 security clearance required to go up there!
In fact, this is the only place I'm lawfully allowed to show you...
...my office!
But don't worry, there's all sorts of fun stuff to do here!
Like the mysteries of... "Newton's Cradle!" The balls just keep going...and going... and going!
When will it stop? Who knows?! Isn't that exciting?!
KLIK! KLAK!

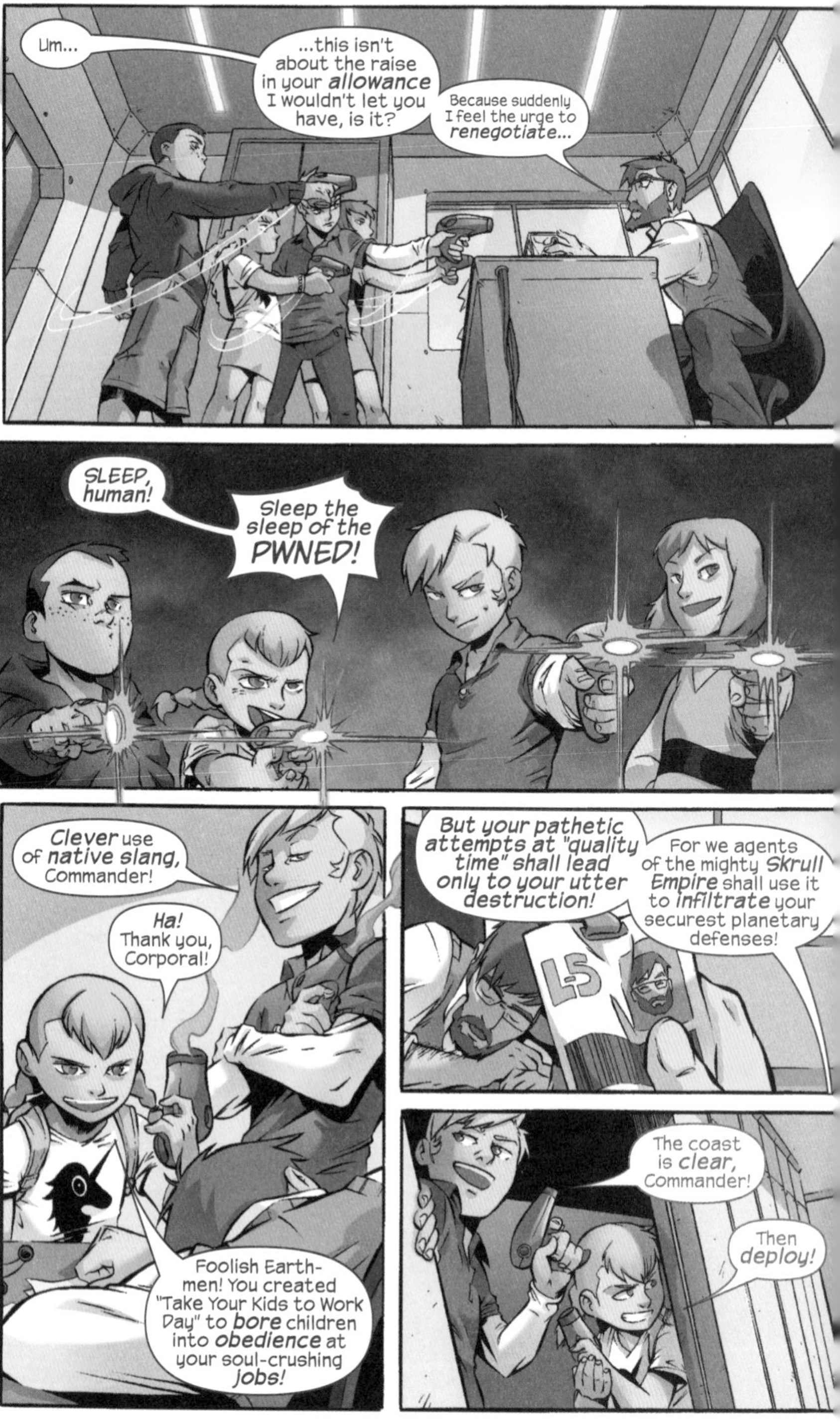
Um...
...this isn't about the raise in your allowance I wouldn't let you have, is it?
Because suddenly I feel the urge to renegotiate...
SLEEP, human!
Sleep the sleep of the PWNED!
Clever use of native slang, Commander!
Ha! Thank you, Corporal!
Foolish Earth-men! You created "Take Your Kids to Work Day" to bore children into obedience at your soul-crushing jobs!
But your pathetic attempts at "quality time" shall lead only to your utter destruction!
For we agents of the mighty Skrull Empire shall use it to infiltrate your securest planetary defenses!
L5
The coast is clear, Commander!
Then deploy!

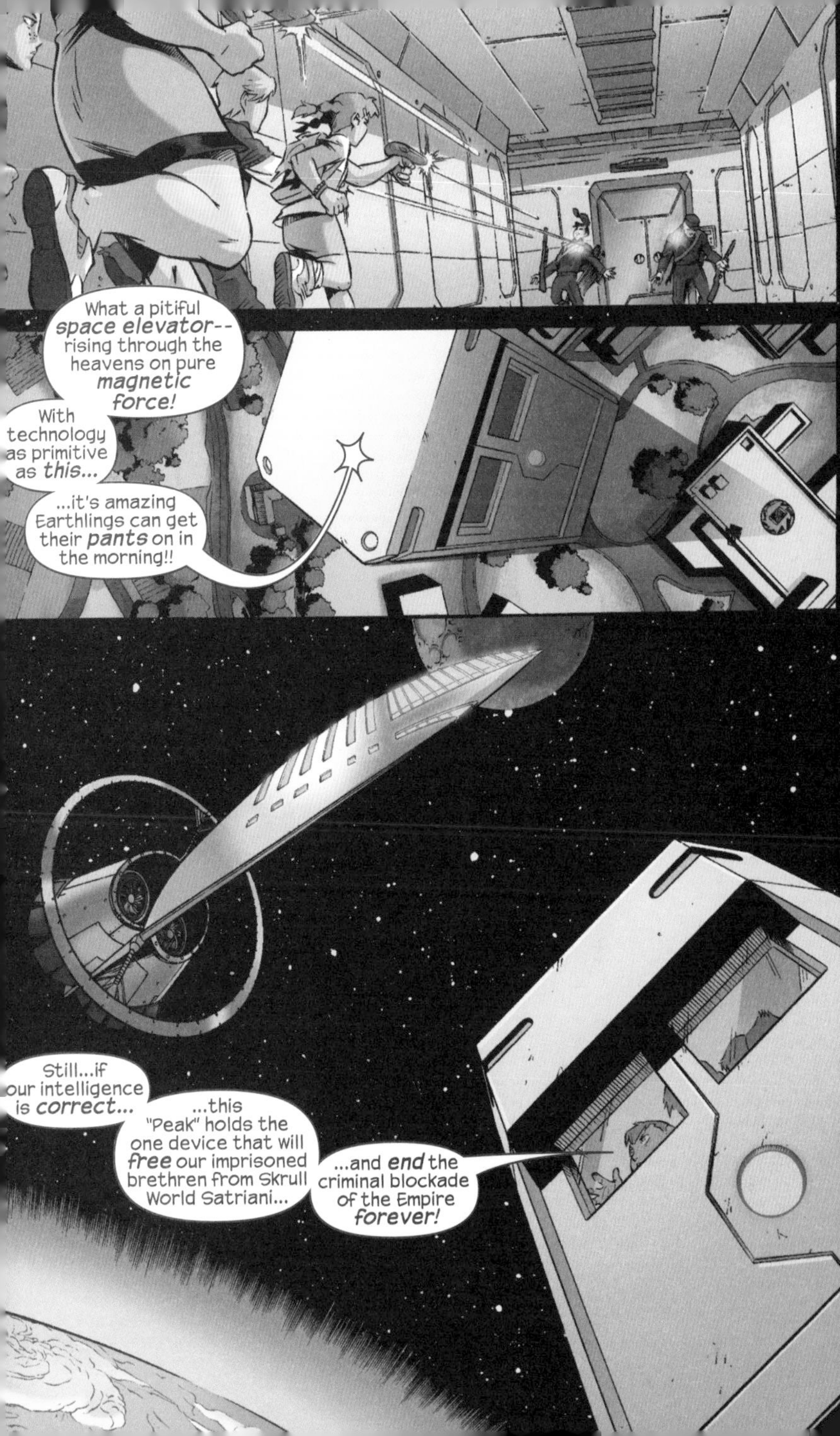
What a pitiful space elevator--rising through the heavens on pure magnetic force!
With technology as primitive as this...
...it's amazing Earthlings can get their pants on in the morning!!
Still...if our intelligence is correct...
..."this "Peak" holds the one device that will free our imprisoned brethren from Skrull World Satriani...
...and end the criminal blockade of the Empire forever!

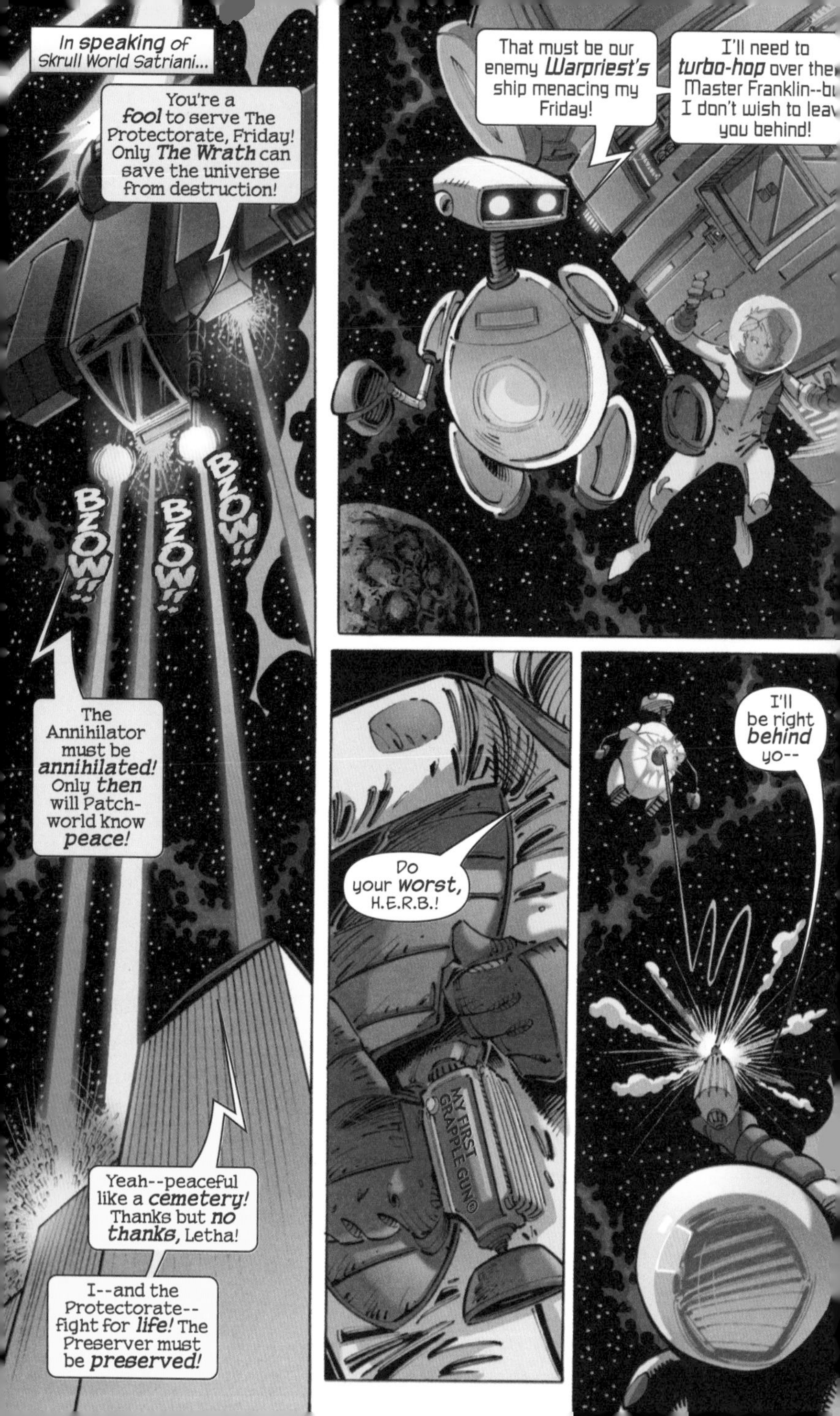
In speaking of Skrull World Satriani...
You're a fool to serve The Protectorate, Friday! Only The Wrath can save the universe from destruction!
BZOW!!
BZOW!!
BZOW!!
The Annihilator must be annihilated! Only then will Patch-world know peace!
Yeah--peaceful like a cemetery! Thanks but no thanks, Letha!
I--and the Protectorate--fight for life! The Preserver must be preserved!
That must be our enemy Warpriest's ship menacing my Friday!
I'll need to turbo-hop over the Master Franklin--bu I don't wish to leav you behind!
Do your worst, H.E.R.B.!
MY FIRST GRAPPLE GUN®
I'll be right behind yo--

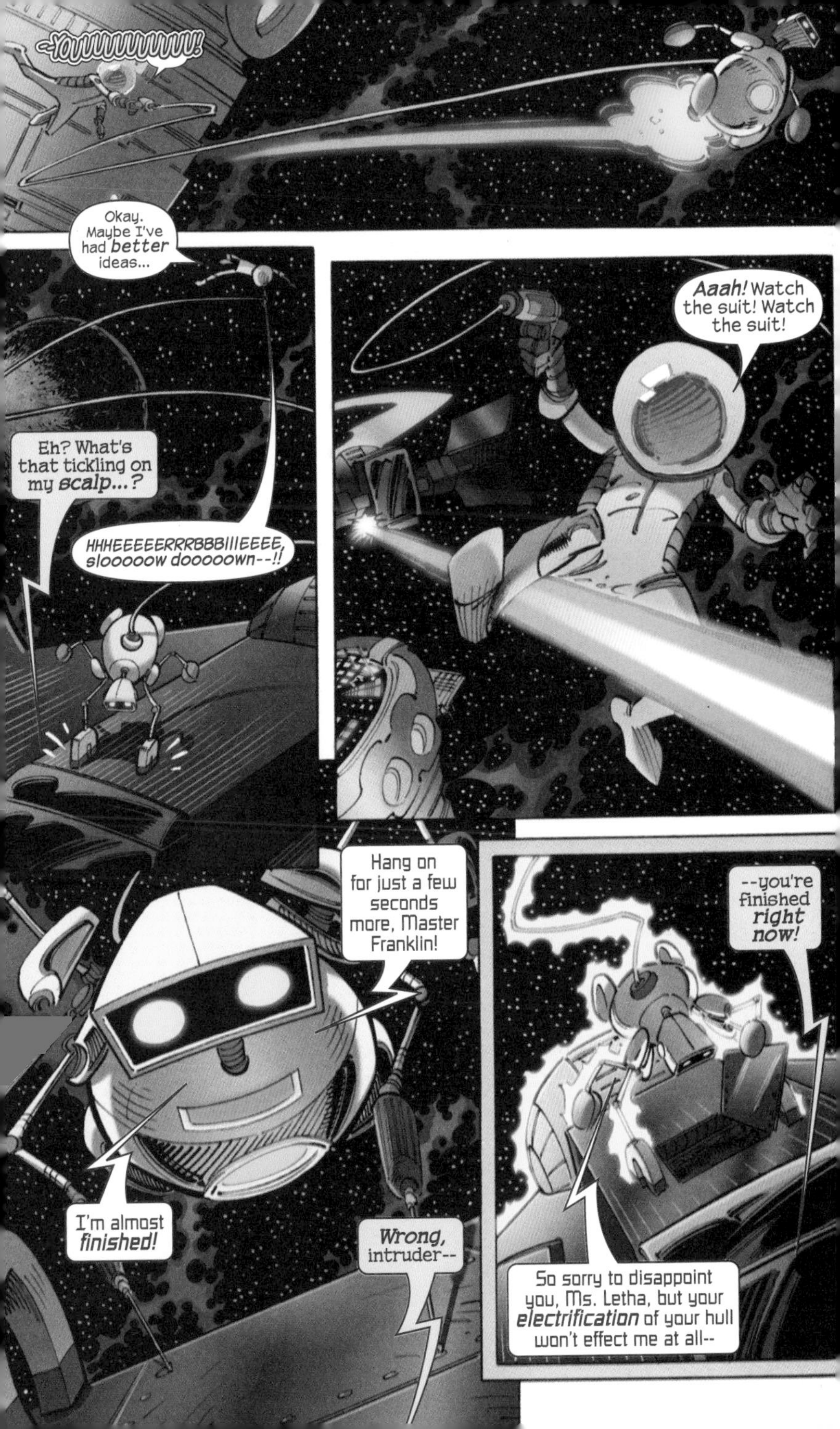

-YAAAAAAAAAAA!
Okay. Maybe I've had better ideas...
Eh? What's that tickling on my scalp...?
HHHEEEEERRRBBBIIIEEEE, slooooow dooooown--!!
Aaah! Watch the suit! Watch the suit!
Hang on for just a few seconds more, Master Franklin!
I'm almost finished!
Wrong, intruder--
--you're finished right now!
So sorry to disappoint you, Ms. Letha, but your electrification of your hull won't effect me at all--

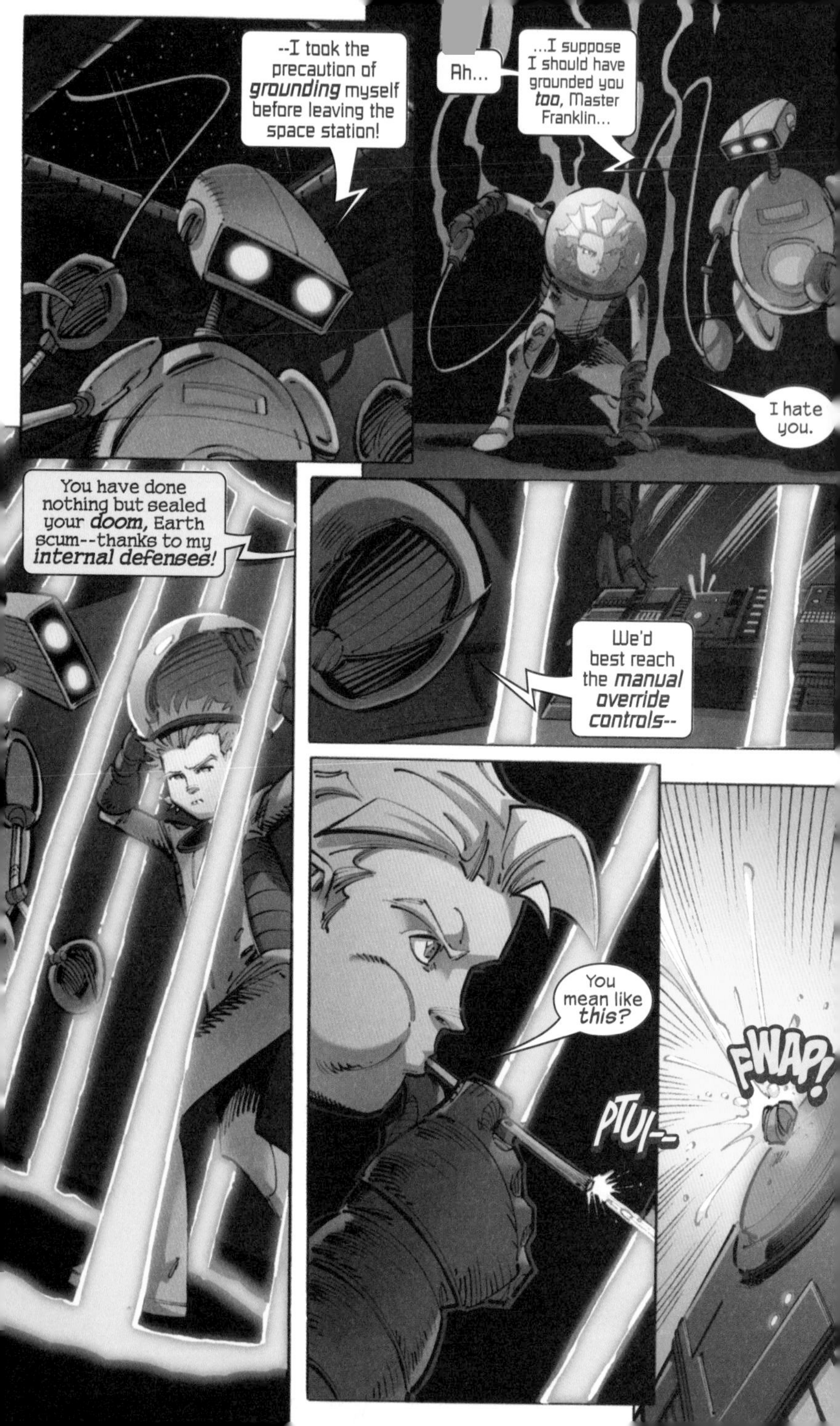
--I took the precaution of *grounding* myself before leaving the space station!
Ah...
...I suppose I should have grounded you *too*, Master Franklin...
I hate you.
You have done nothing but sealed your *doom*, Earth scum--thanks to my *internal defenses*!
We'd best reach the *manual override controls*--
You mean like *this*?
PTUI--
FWAP!

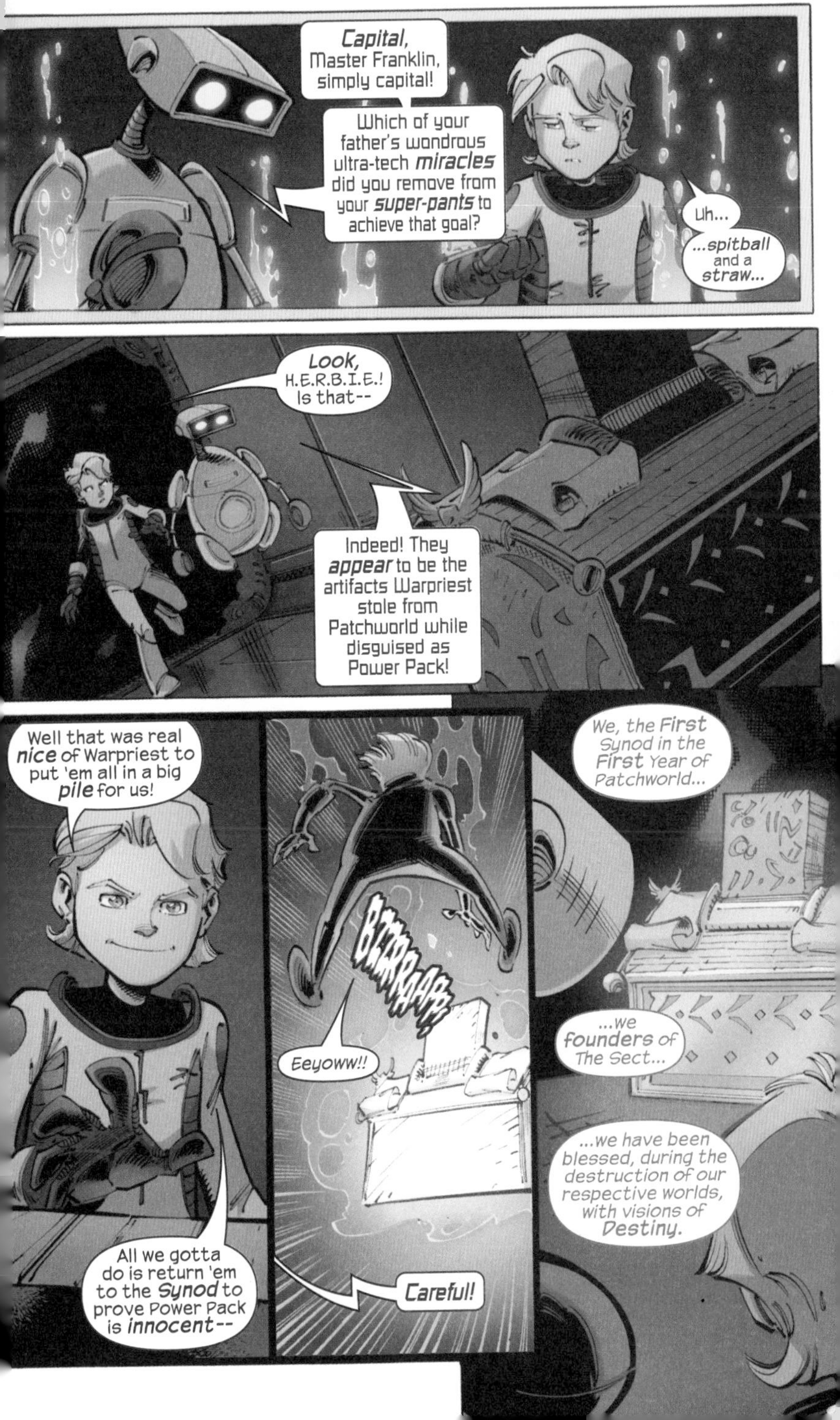

Capital, Master Franklin, simply capital!
Which of your father's wondrous ultra-tech miracles did you remove from your super-pants to achieve that goal?
Uh...
...spitball and a straw...
Look, H.E.R.B.I.E.! Is that--
Indeed! They appear to be the artifacts Warpriest stole from Patchworld while disguised as Power Pack!
Well that was real nice of Warpriest to put 'em all in a big pile for us!
All we gotta do is return 'em to the Synod to prove Power Pack is innocent--
BZZRAAP!
Eeyoww!!
Careful!
We, the First Synod in the First Year of Patchworld...
...we founders of The Sect...
...we have been blessed, during the destruction of our respective worlds, with visions of Destiny.

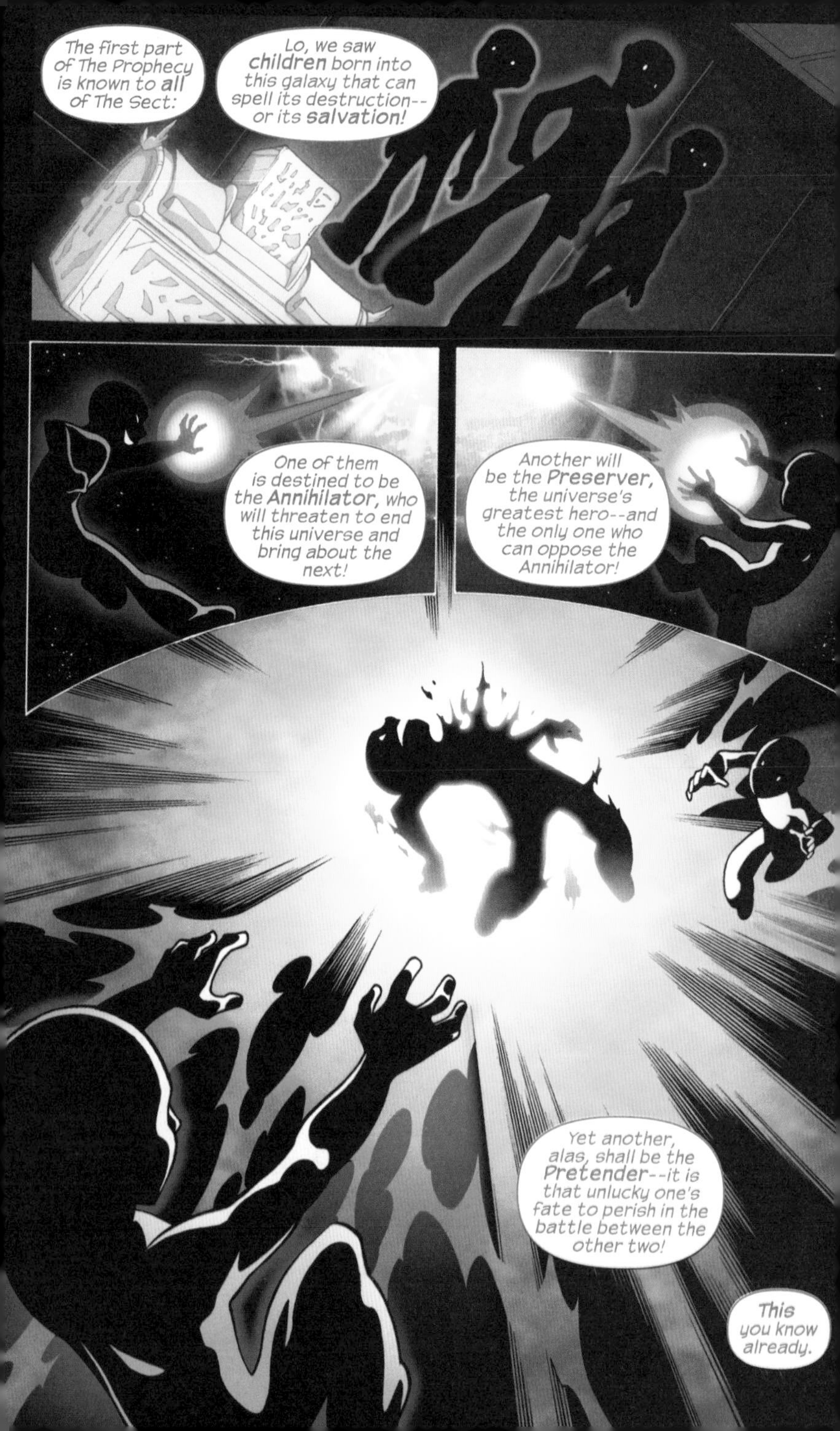
The first part of The Prophecy is known to all of The Sect:
Lo, we saw children born into this galaxy that can spell its destruction--or its salvation!
One of them is destined to be the Annihilator, who will threaten to end this universe and bring about the next!
Another will be the Preserver, the universe's greatest hero--and the only one who can oppose the Annihilator!
Yet another, alas, shall be the Pretender--it is that unlucky one's fate to perish in the battle between the other two!
This you know already.

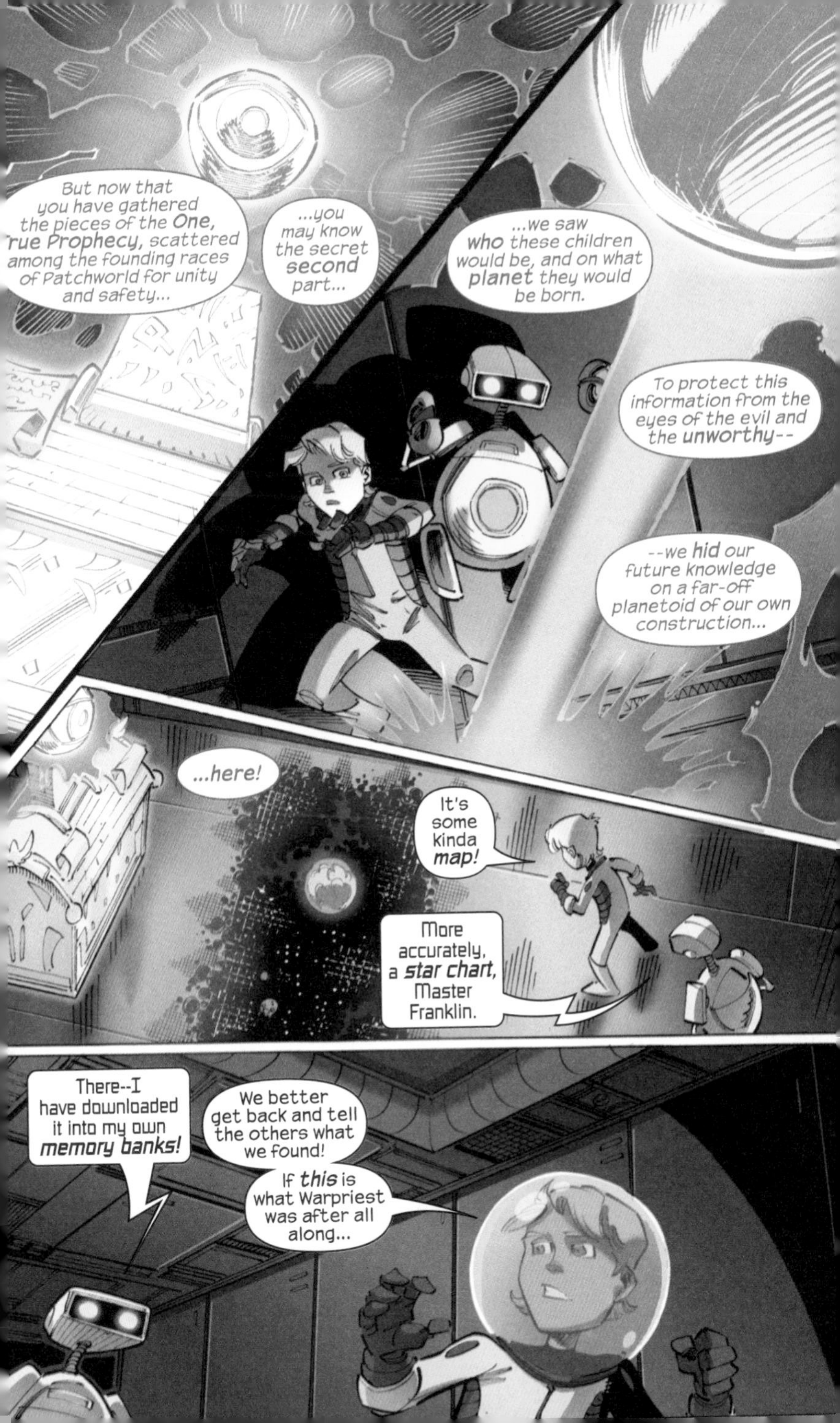
But now that you have gathered the pieces of the One, True Prophecy, scattered among the founding races of Patchworld for unity and safety...
...you may know the secret second part...
...we saw who these children would be, and on what planet they would be born.
To protect this information from the eyes of the evil and the unworthy--
--we hid our future knowledge on a far-off planetoid of our own construction...
...here!
It's some kinda map!
More accurately, a star chart, Master Franklin.
There--I have downloaded it into my own memory banks!
We better get back and tell the others what we found!
If this is what Warpriest was after all along...

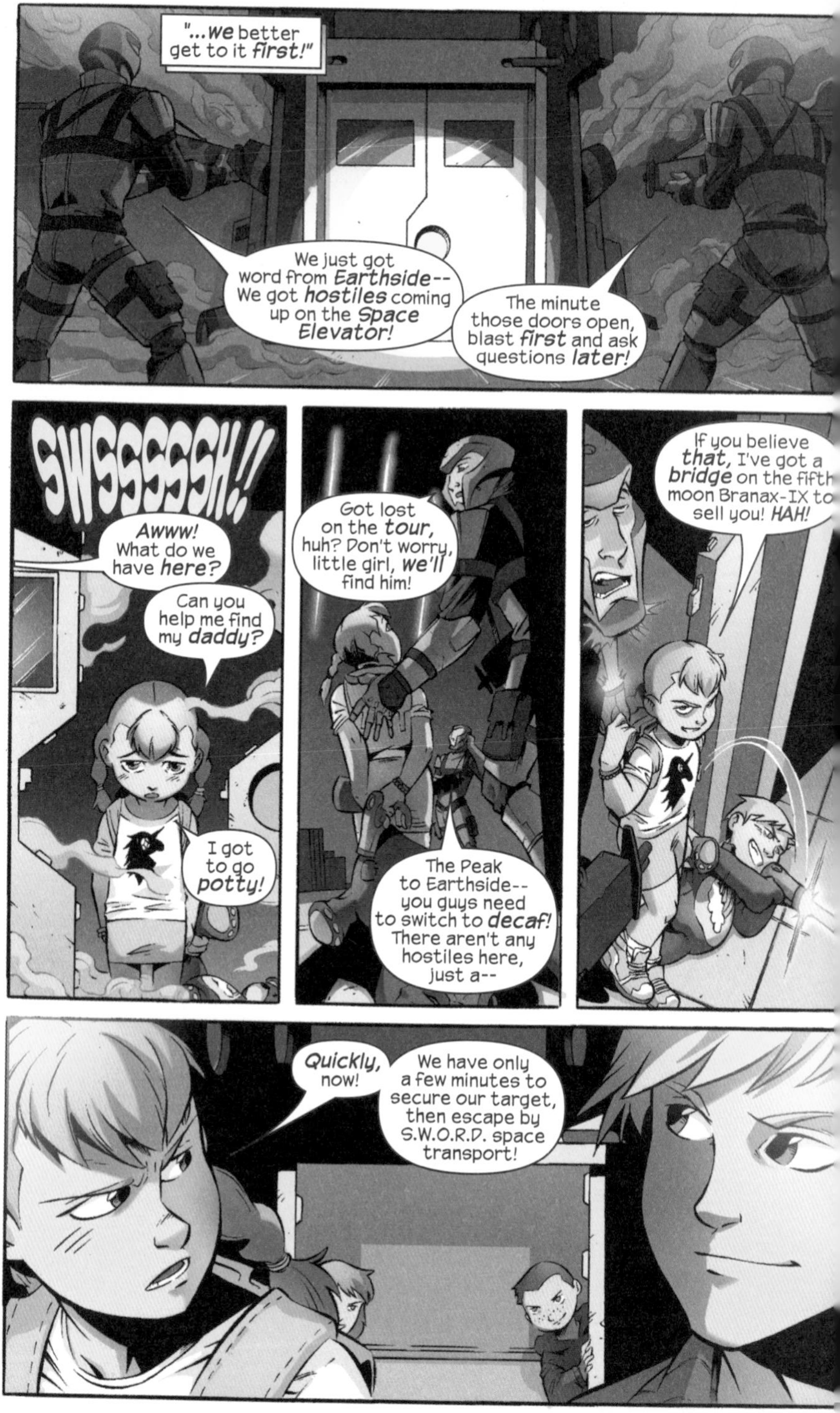
"...we better get to it first!"
We just got word from Earthside-- We got hostiles coming up on the Space Elevator!
The minute those doors open, blast first and ask questions later!
SWSSSSSH!!
Awww! What do we have here?
Can you help me find my daddy?
I got to go potty!
Got lost on the tour, huh? Don't worry, little girl, we'll find him!
The Peak to Earthside-- you guys need to switch to decaf! There aren't any hostiles here, just a--
If you believe that, I've got a bridge on the fifth moon Branax-IX to sell you! HAH!
Quickly, now!
We have only a few minutes to secure our target, then escape by S.W.O.R.D. space transport!

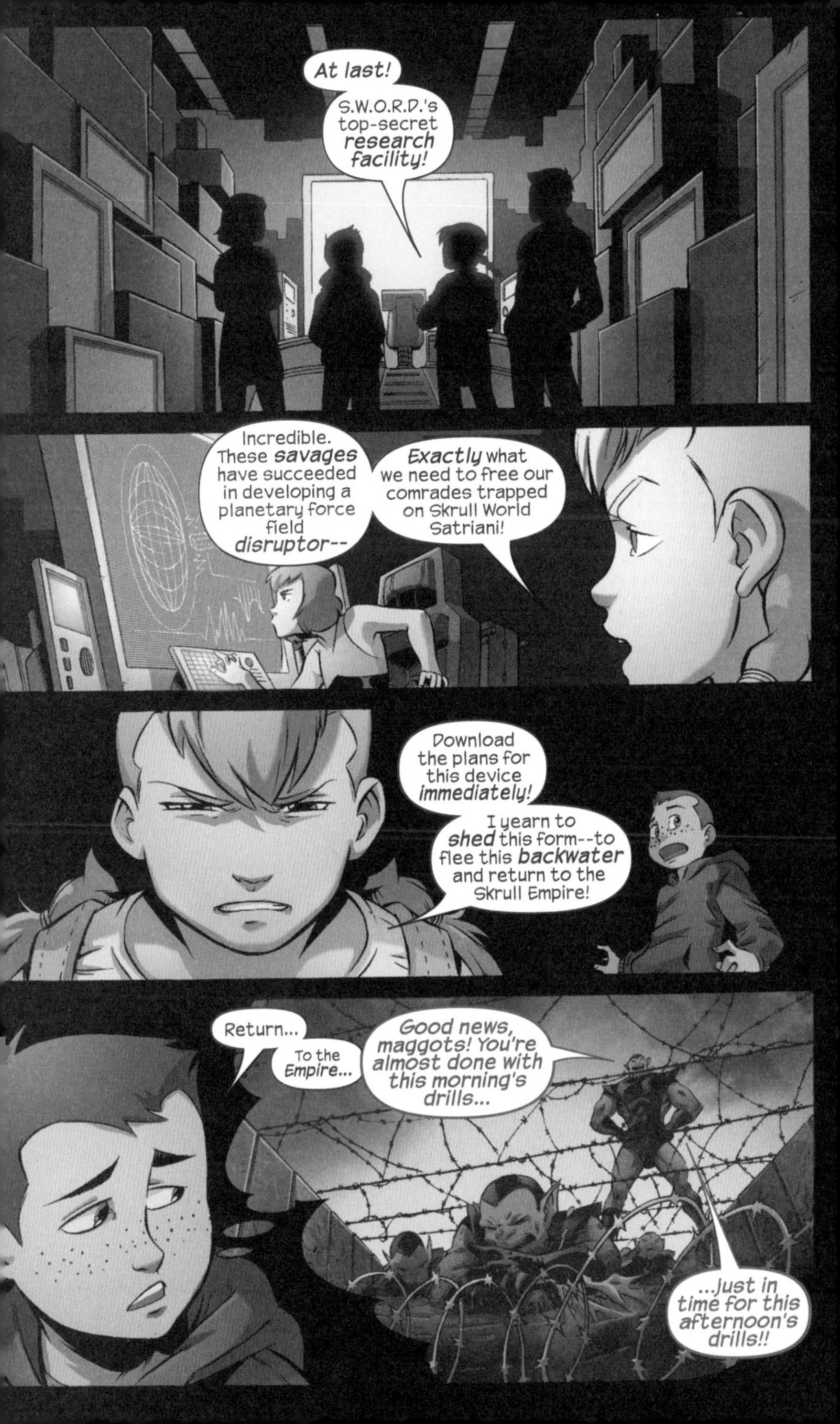

At last!
S.W.O.R.D.'s top-secret research facility!
Incredible. These savages have succeeded in developing a planetary force field disruptor--
Exactly what we need to free our comrades trapped on Skrull World Satriani!
Download the plans for this device immediately!
I yearn to shed this form--to flee this backwater and return to the Skrull Empire!
Return...
To the Empire...
Good news, maggots! You're almost done with this morning's drills...
...just in time for this afternoon's drills!!

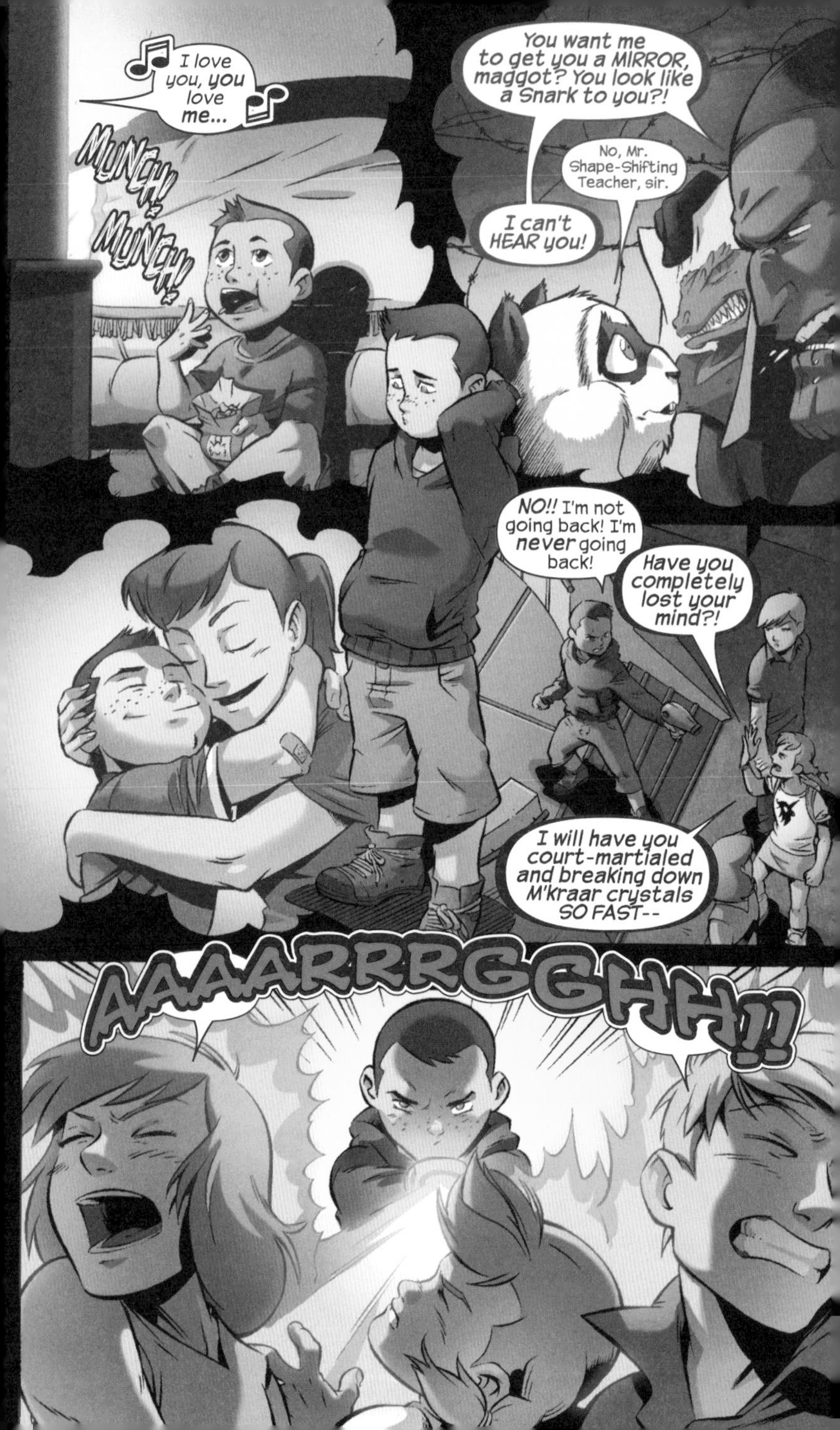

I love you, you love me...
MUNCH! MUNCH!
You want me to get you a MIRROR, maggot? You look like a Snark to you?!
No, Mr. Shape-Shifting Teacher, sir.
I can't HEAR you!
NO!! I'm not going back! I'm never going back!
Have you completely lost your mind?!
I will have you court-martialed and breaking down M'kraar crystals SO FAST--
AAAARRRGGHH!!

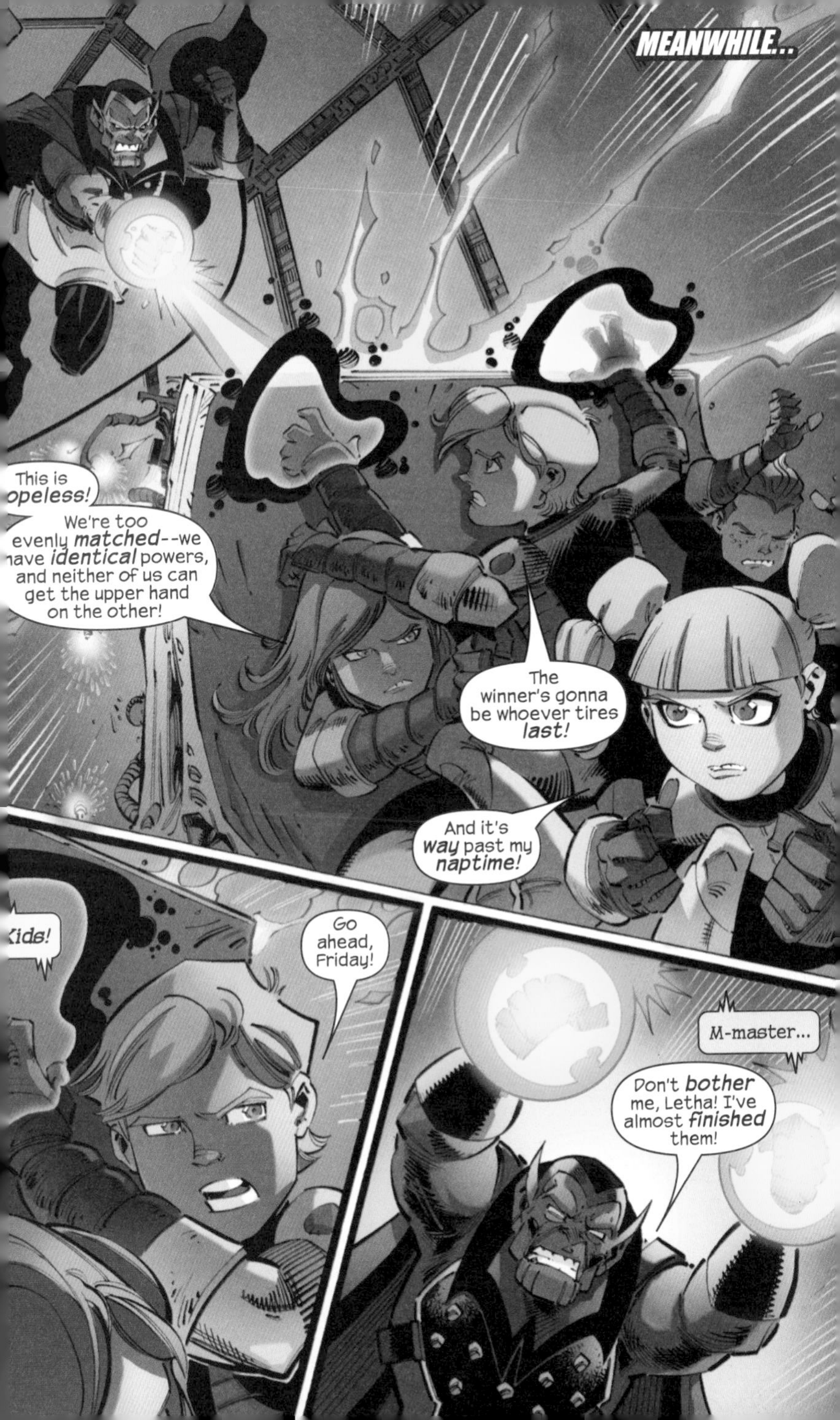
MEANWHILE...
This is opeless!
We're too evenly matched--we ave identical powers, and neither of us can get the upper hand on the other!
The winner's gonna be whoever tires last!
And it's way past my naptime!
Kids!
Go ahead, Friday!
M-master...
Don't bother me, Letha! I've almost finished them!

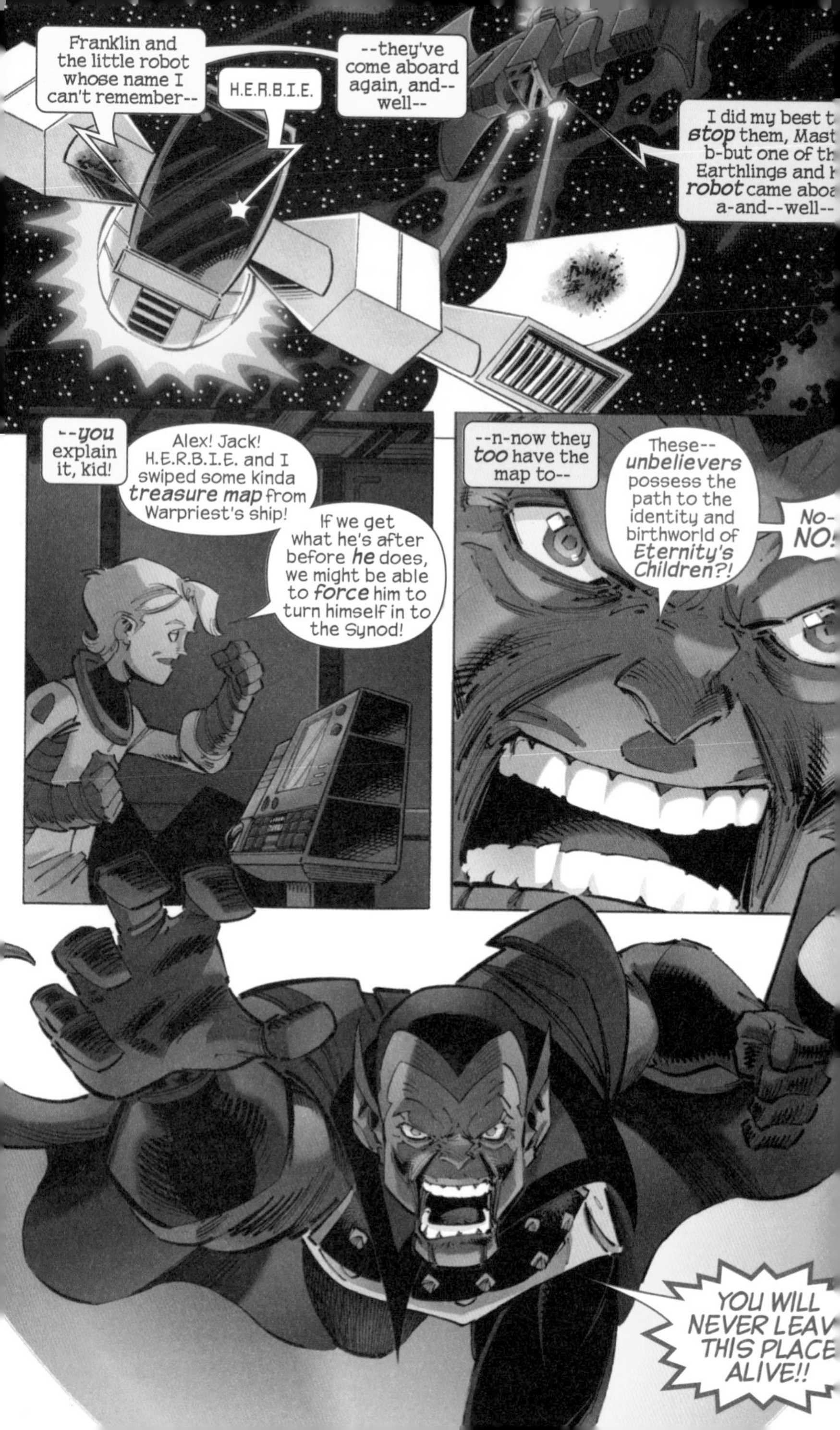

Franklin and the little robot whose name I can't remember--
H.E.R.B.I.E.
--they've come aboard again, and-- well--
I did my best t *stop* them, Mast b-but one of th Earthlings and h *robot* came aboa a-and--well--
--*you* explain it, kid!
Alex! Jack! H.E.R.B.I.E. and I swiped some kinda *treasure map* from Warpriest's ship!
If we get what he's after before *he* does, we might be able to *force* him to turn himself in to the Synod!
--n-now they *too* have the map to--
These-- *unbelievers* possess the path to the identity and birthworld of *Eternity's Children?!*
No- NO!
YOU WILL NEVER LEAV THIS PLACE ALIVE!!

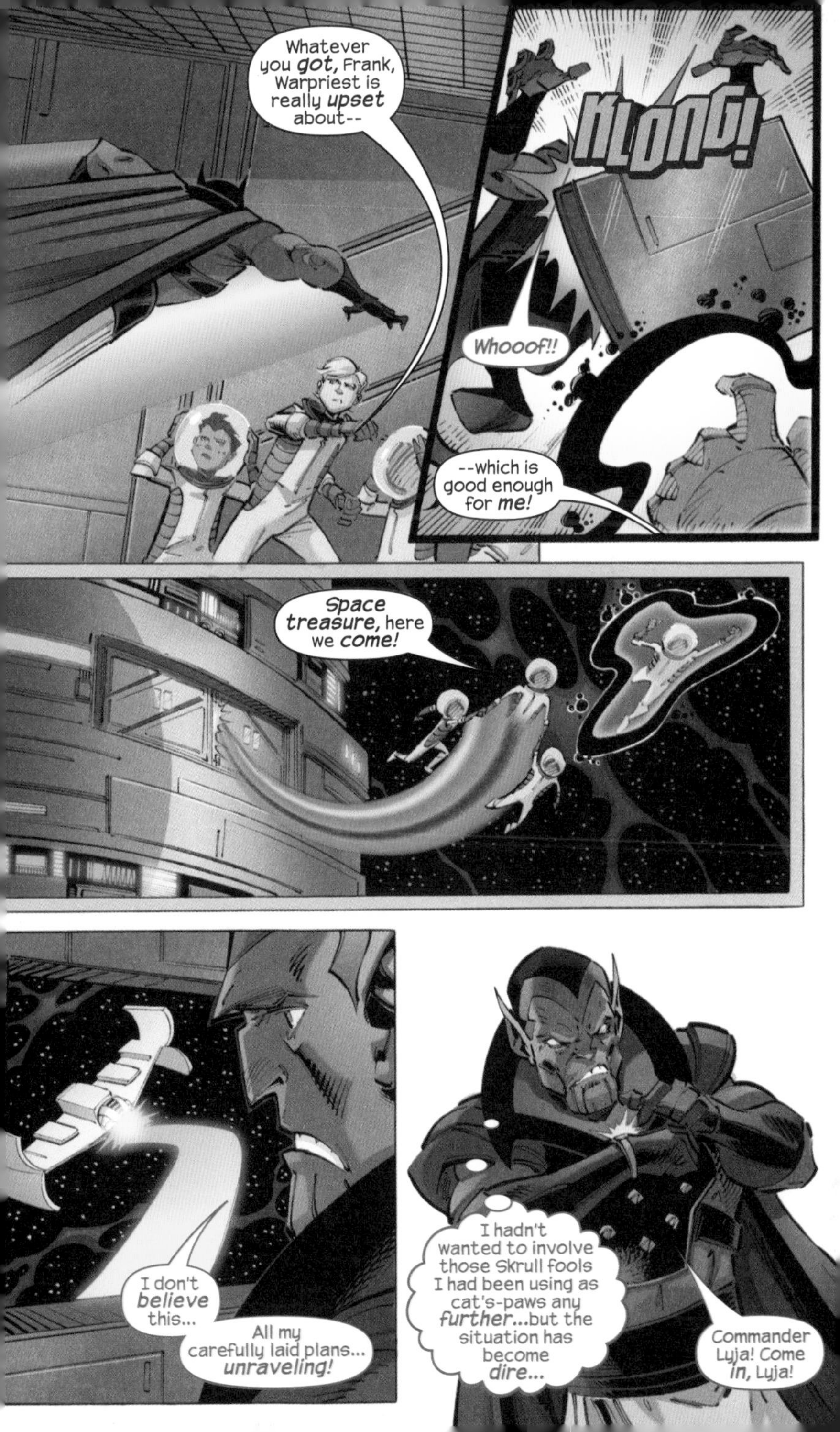
Whatever you got, Frank, Warpriest is really upset about--
KLONG!
Whooof!!
--which is good enough for me!
Space treasure, here we come!
I don't believe this...
All my carefully laid plans... unraveling!
I hadn't wanted to involve those Skrull fools I had been using as cat's-paws any further...but the situation has become dire...
Commander Luja! Come in, Luja!

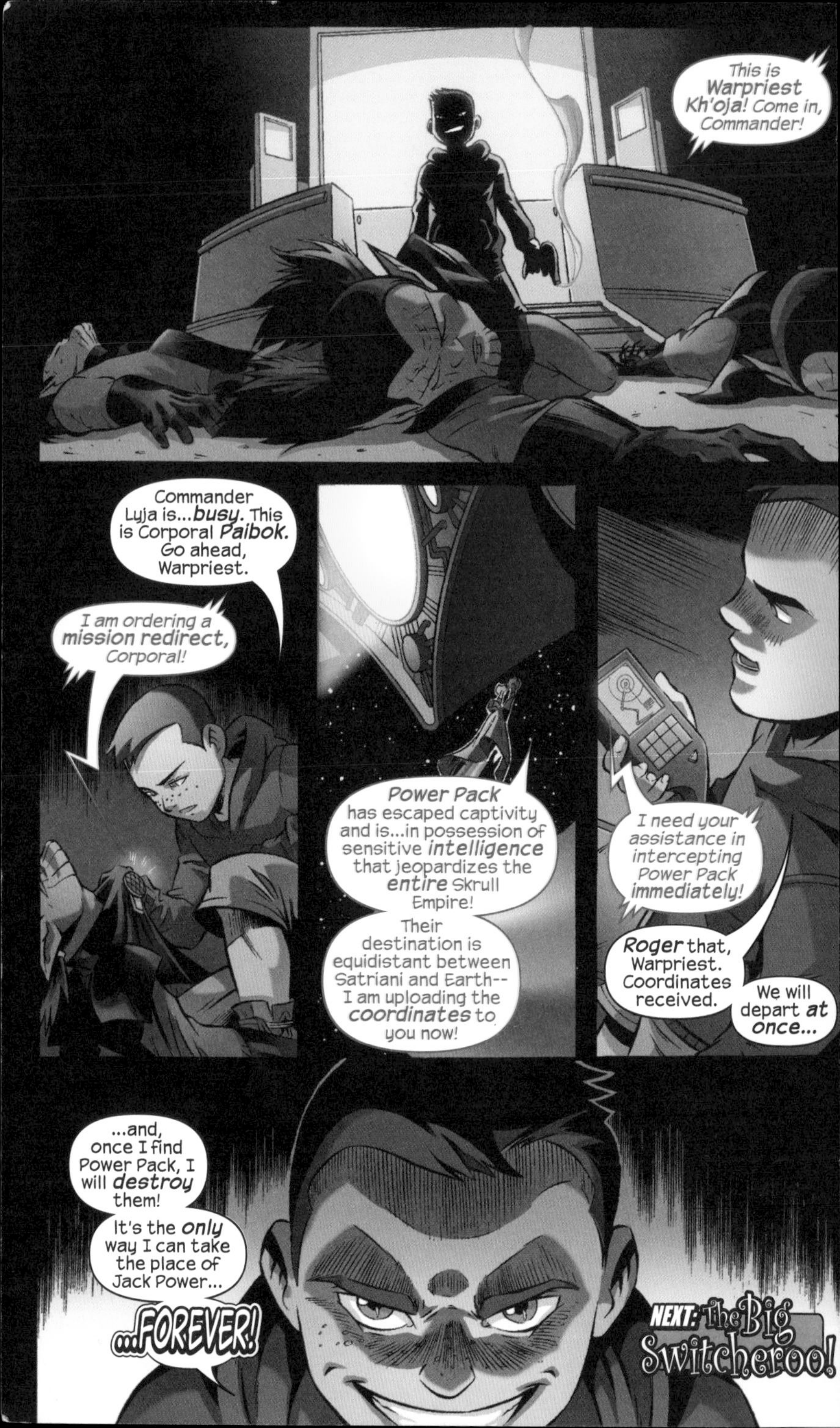
This is Warpriest Kh'oja! Come in, Commander!
Commander Luja is...busy. This is Corporal Paibok. Go ahead, Warpriest.
I am ordering a mission redirect, Corporal!
Power Pack has escaped captivity and is...in possession of sensitive intelligence that jeopardizes the entire Skrull Empire!
Their destination is equidistant between Satriani and Earth-- I am uploading the coordinates to you now!
I need your assistance in intercepting Power Pack immediately!
Roger that, Warpriest. Coordinates received.
We will depart at once...
...and, once I find Power Pack, I will destroy them!
It's the only way I can take the place of Jack Power...
...FOREVER!
NEXT: The Big Switcheroo!

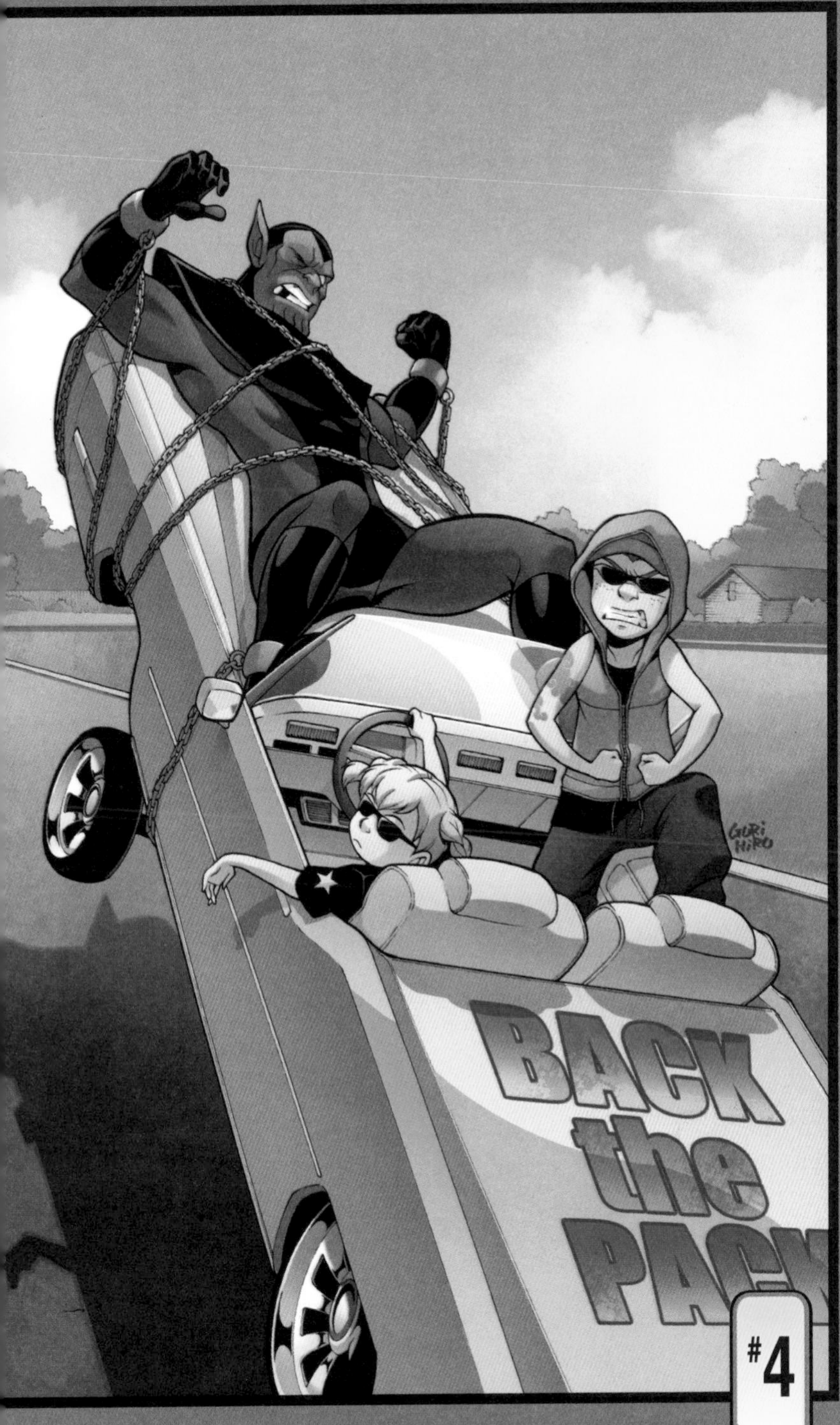
GURI HIRO
BACK the PACK
#4

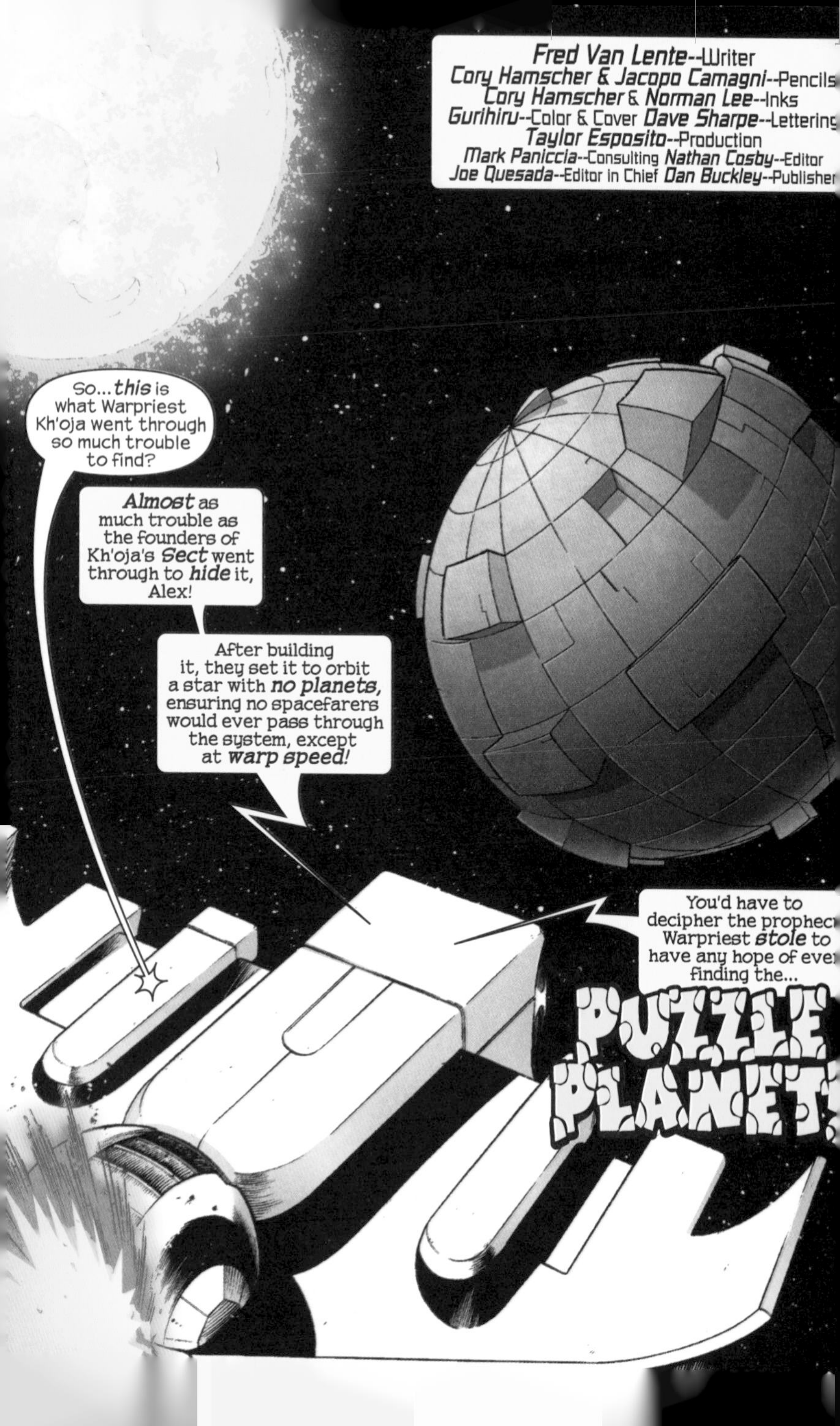

Fred Van Lente--Writer
Cory Hamscher & Jacopo Camagni--Pencils
Cory Hamscher & Norman Lee--Inks
Gurihiru--Color & Cover Dave Sharpe--Lettering
Taylor Esposito--Production
Mark Paniccia--Consulting Nathan Cosby--Editor
Joe Quesada--Editor in Chief Dan Buckley--Publisher
So... *this* is what Warpriest Kh'oja went through so much trouble to find?
Almost as much trouble as the founders of Kh'oja's *Sect* went through to *hide* it, Alex!
After building it, they set it to orbit a star with *no planets,* ensuring no spacefarers would ever pass through the system, except at *warp speed!*
You'd have to decipher the prophec Warpriest *stole* to have any hope of eve finding the...
PUZZLE PLANET!

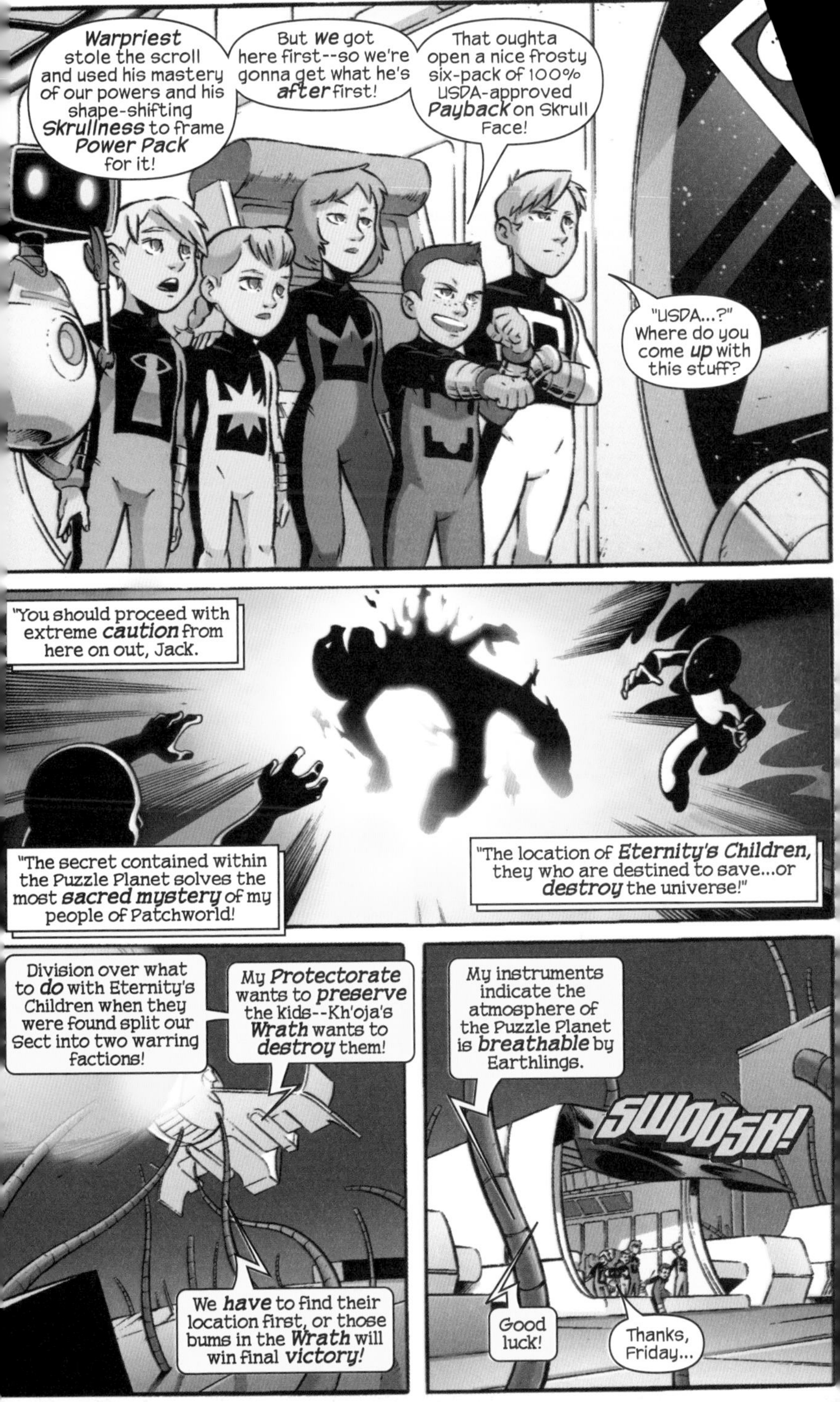

Warpriest stole the scroll and used his mastery of our powers and his shape-shifting Skrullness to frame Power Pack for it!
But we got here first--so we're gonna get what he's after first!
That oughta open a nice frosty six-pack of 100% USDA-approved Payback on Skrull Face!
"USDA...?" Where do you come up with this stuff?
"You should proceed with extreme caution from here on out, Jack.
"The secret contained within the Puzzle Planet solves the most sacred mystery of my people of Patchworld!
"The location of Eternity's Children, they who are destined to save...or destroy the universe!"
Division over what to do with Eternity's Children when they were found split our Sect into two warring factions!
My Protectorate wants to preserve the kids--Kh'oja's Wrath wants to destroy them!
We have to find their location first, or those bums in the Wrath will win final victory!
My instruments indicate the atmosphere of the Puzzle Planet is breathable by Earthlings.
SWOOSH!
Good luck!
Thanks, Friday...

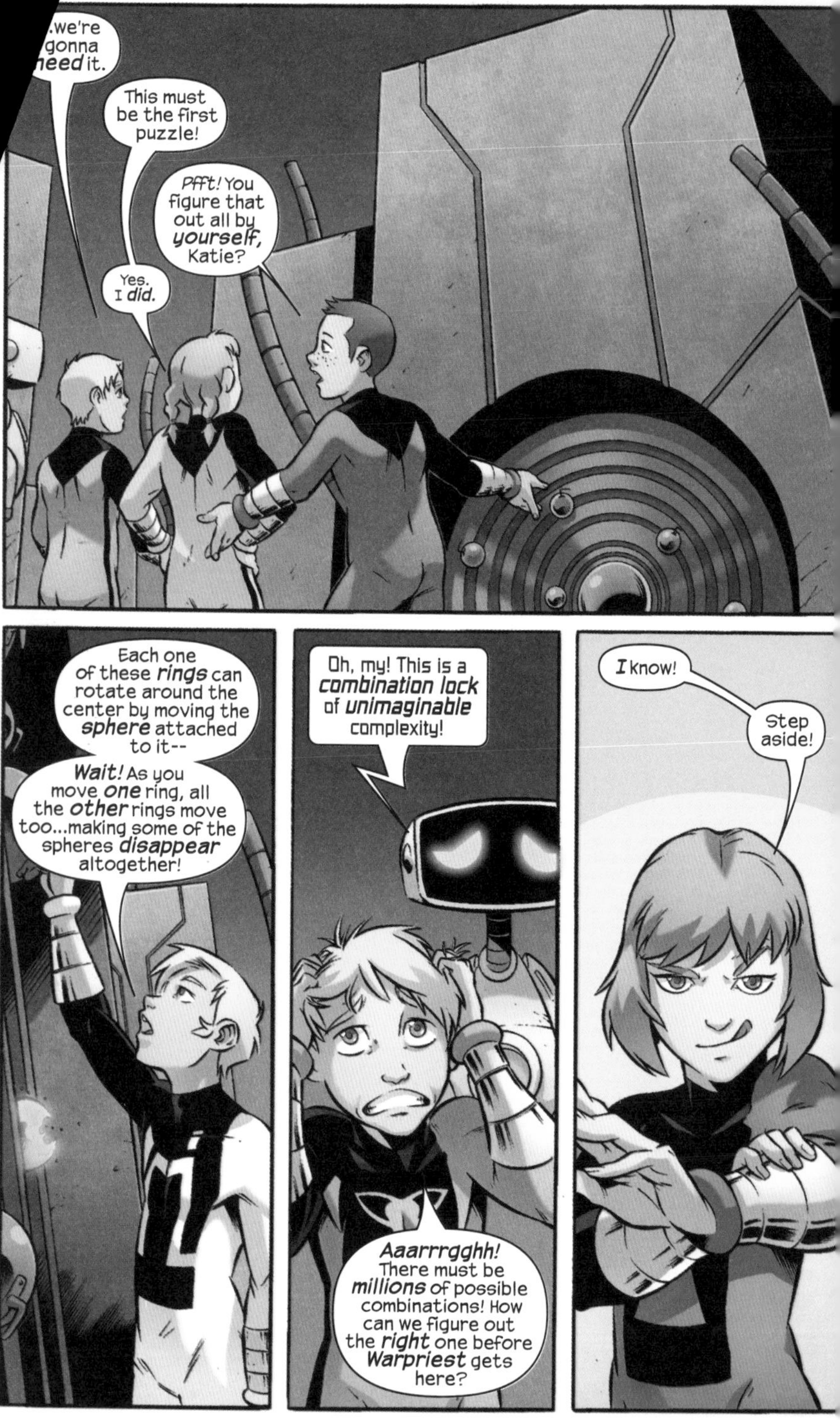
.we're gonna need it.
This must be the first puzzle!
Pfft! You figure that out all by yourself, Katie?
Yes. I did.
Each one of these rings can rotate around the center by moving the sphere attached to it--
Wait! As you move one ring, all the other rings move too...making some of the spheres disappear altogether!
Oh, my! This is a combination lock of unimaginable complexity!
Aaarrrgghh! There must be millions of possible combinations! How can we figure out the right one before Warpriest gets here?
I know!
Step aside!

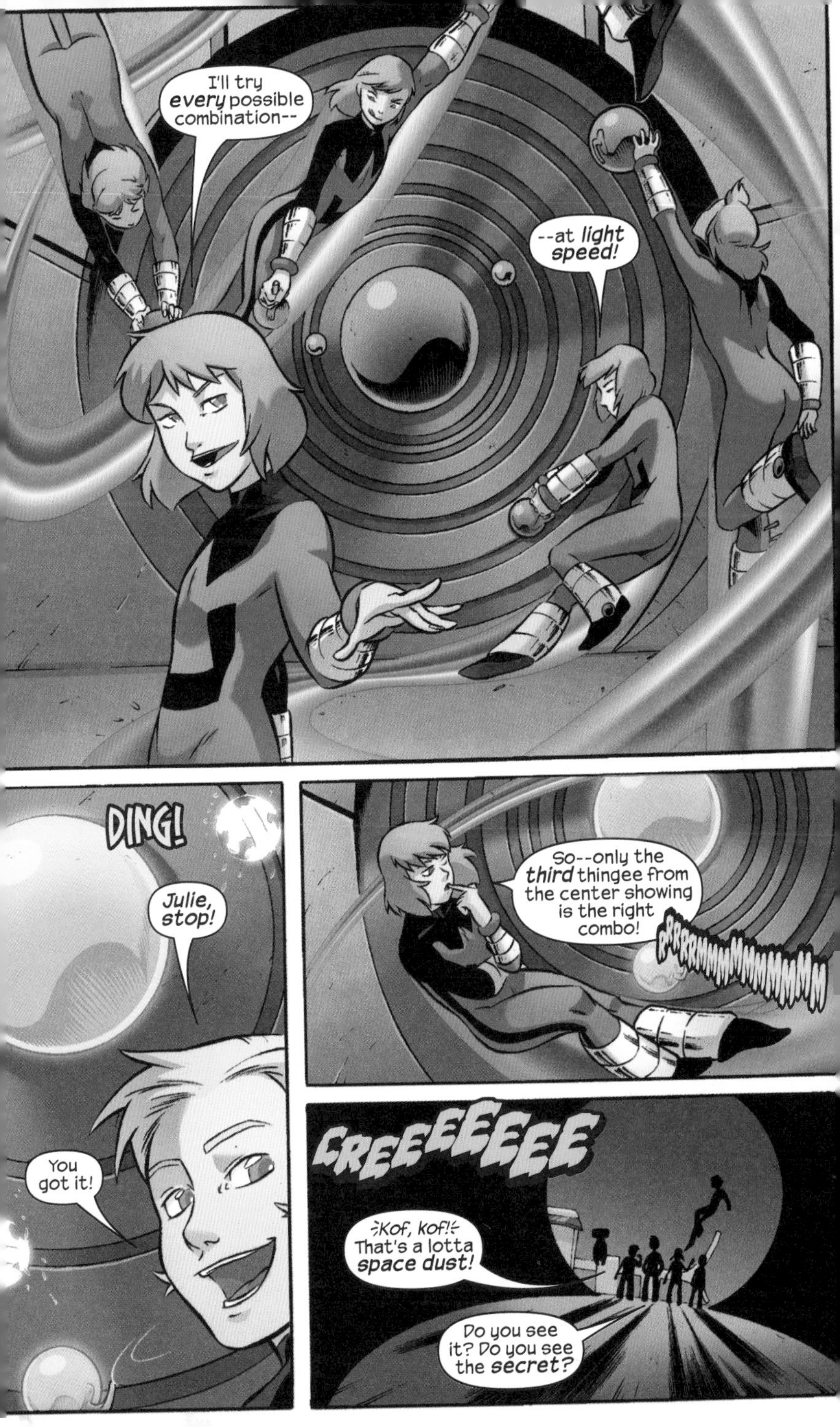
I'll try every possible combination--
--at light speed!
DING!
Julie, stop!
You got it!
So--only the third thingee from the center showing is the right combo!
RRRRRMMMMMMMMMMM
CREEEEEEEE
Kof, kof! That's a lotta space dust!
Do you see it? Do you see the secret?

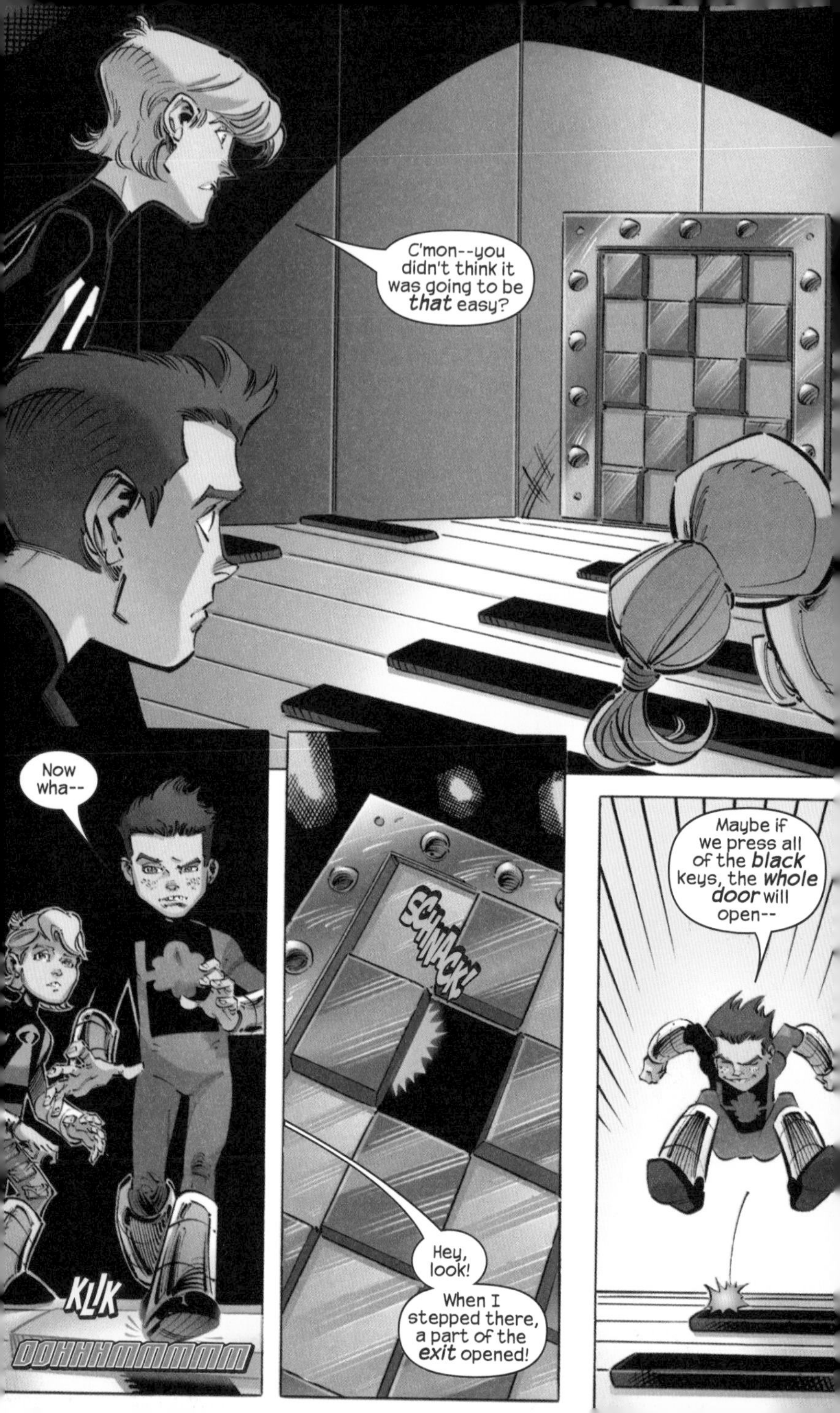
C'mon--you didn't think it was going to be *that* easy?
Now wha--
KLIK
OOHHHMMMMMM
SCHNACK!
Hey, look!
When I stepped there, a part of the *exit* opened!
Maybe if we press all of the *black* keys, the *whole door* will open--

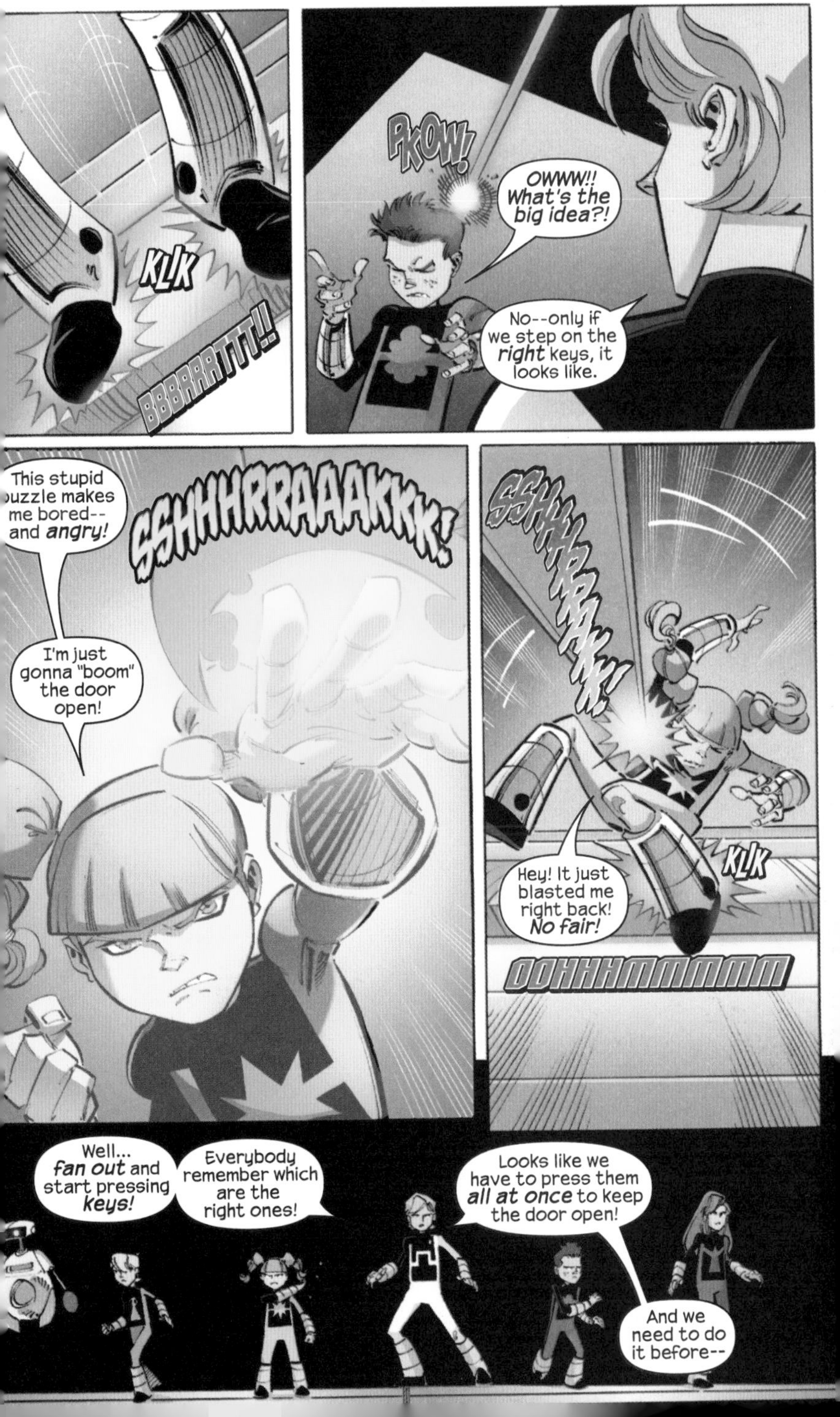
KLIK
BBBRRATTTT!!
PKOW!
OWWW!! What's the big idea?!
No--only if we step on the right keys, it looks like.
This stupid puzzle makes me bored-- and angry!
SSHHHRRAAAKKK!
I'm just gonna "boom" the door open!
Hey! It just blasted me right back! No fair!
KLIK
OOHHHMMMMMM
Well... fan out and start pressing keys!
Everybody remember which are the right ones!
Looks like we have to press them all at once to keep the door open!
And we need to do it before--

Before **what**, meddlesome youngling?

Before **Warpriest** arrives and solves the first riddle?

Too late-- too late for **all** of you!

Oh, great.

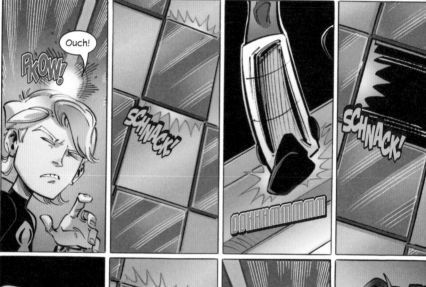

PKOW!

Ouch!

SCHNACK!

OOHHHMMMMMM

SCHNACK!

BBBRRTTT!!

Ow!

SCHNACK!

Ouch!

PKOW!

SHRAKKK!

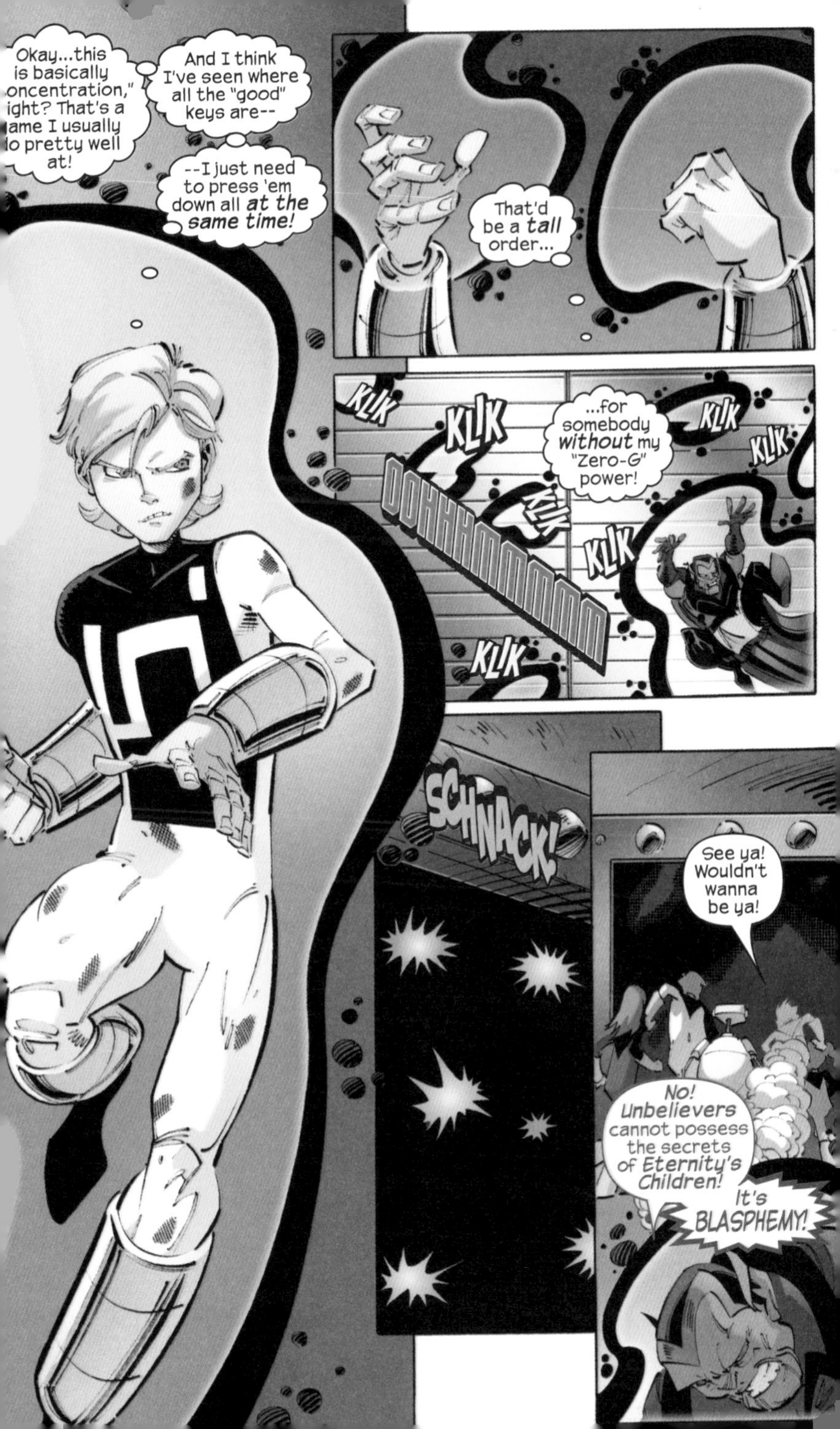
Okay...this is basically oncentration," ight? That's a ame I usually lo pretty well at!
And I think I've seen where all the "good" keys are--
--I just need to press 'em down all *at the same time!*
That'd be a *tall* order...
KLIK
KLIK
...for somebody *without* my "Zero-G" power!
KLIK
KLIK
OOHHMMMMMM
KLIK
KLIK
KLIK
SCHNACK!
See ya! Wouldn't wanna be ya!
No! Unbelievers cannot possess the secrets of *Eternity's Children!*
It's BLASPHEMY!

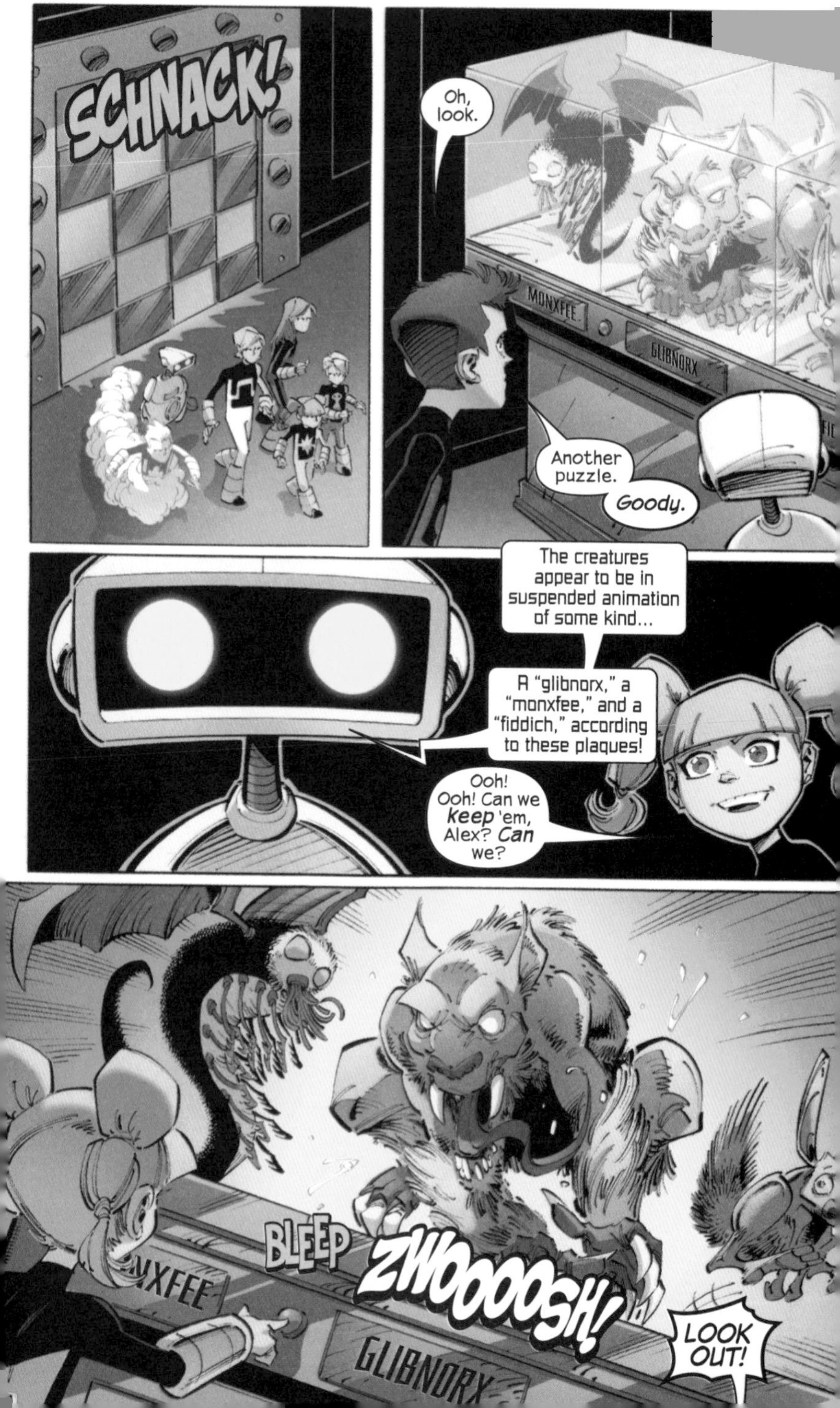
SCHNACK!
Oh, look.
MONXFEE
GLIBNORX
Another puzzle.
Goody.
The creatures appear to be in suspended animation of some kind...
A "glibnorx," a "monxfee," and a "fiddich," according to these plaques!
Ooh! Ooh! Can we keep 'em, Alex? Can we?
BLEEP
ZWOOOOSH!
LOOK OUT!
GLIBNORX

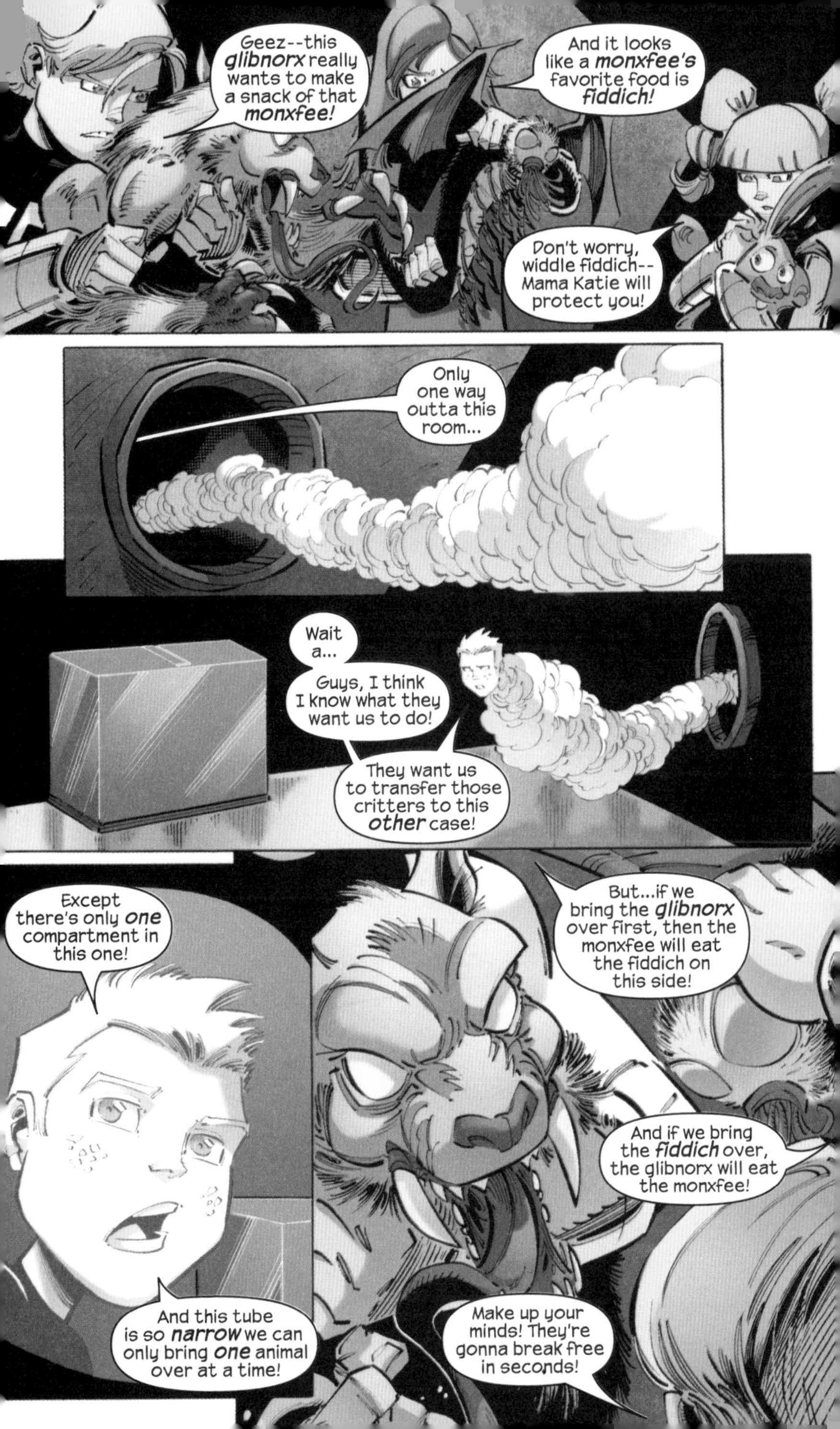
Geez--this glibnorx really wants to make a snack of that monxfee!
And it looks like a monxfee's favorite food is fiddich!
Don't worry, widdle fiddich-- Mama Katie will protect you!
Only one way outta this room...
Wait a...
Guys, I think I know what they want us to do!
They want us to transfer those critters to this other case!
Except there's only one compartment in this one!
But...if we bring the glibnorx over first, then the monxfee will eat the fiddich on this side!
And if we bring the fiddich over, the glibnorx will eat the monxfee!
And this tube is so narrow we can only bring one animal over at a time!
Make up your minds! They're gonna break free in seconds!

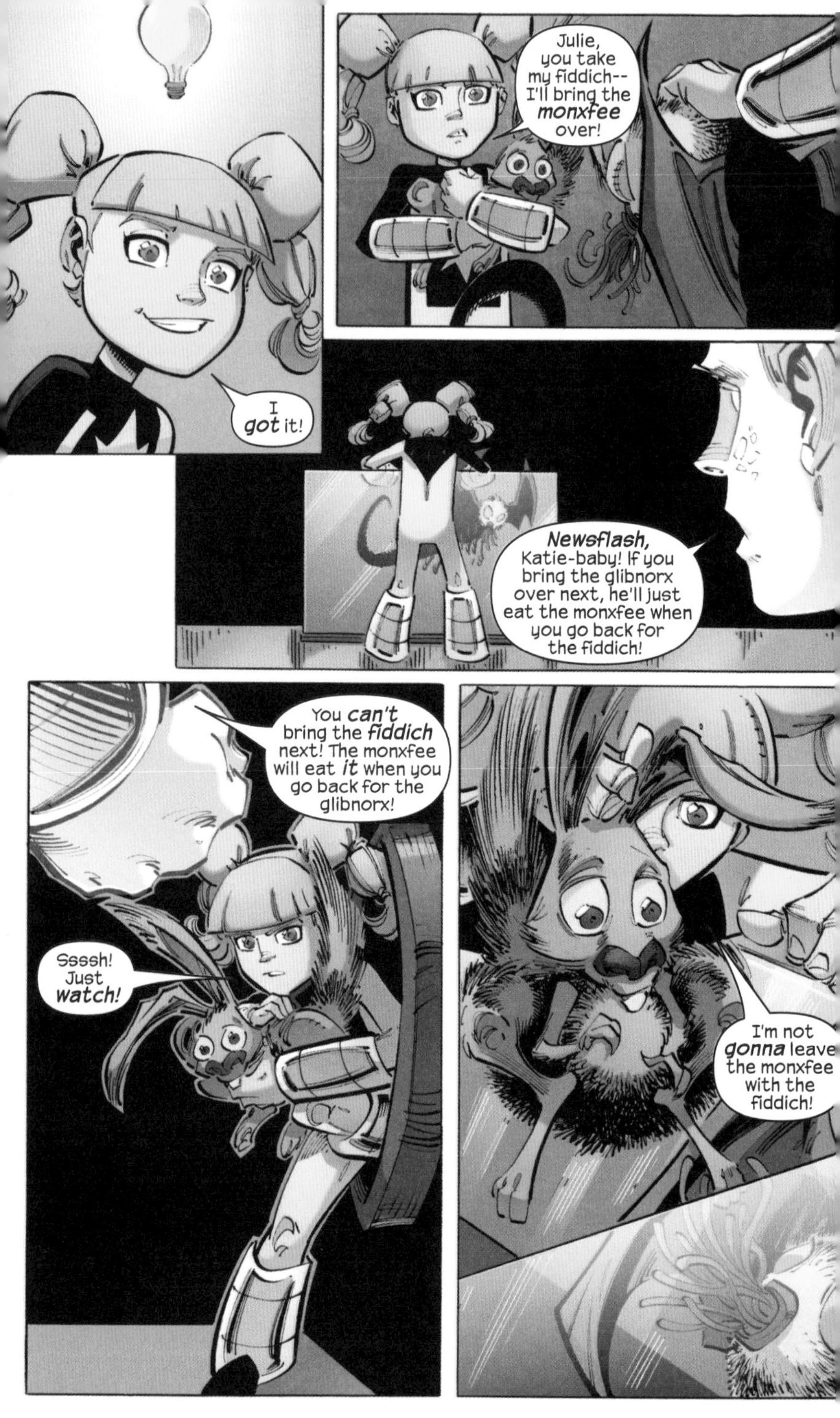
I got it!
Julie, you take my fiddich-- I'll bring the monxfee over!
Newsflash, Katie-baby! If you bring the glibnorx over next, he'll just eat the monxfee when you go back for the fiddich!
You can't bring the fiddich next! The monxfee will eat it when you go back for the glibnorx!
Ssssh! Just watch!
I'm not gonna leave the monxfee with the fiddich!

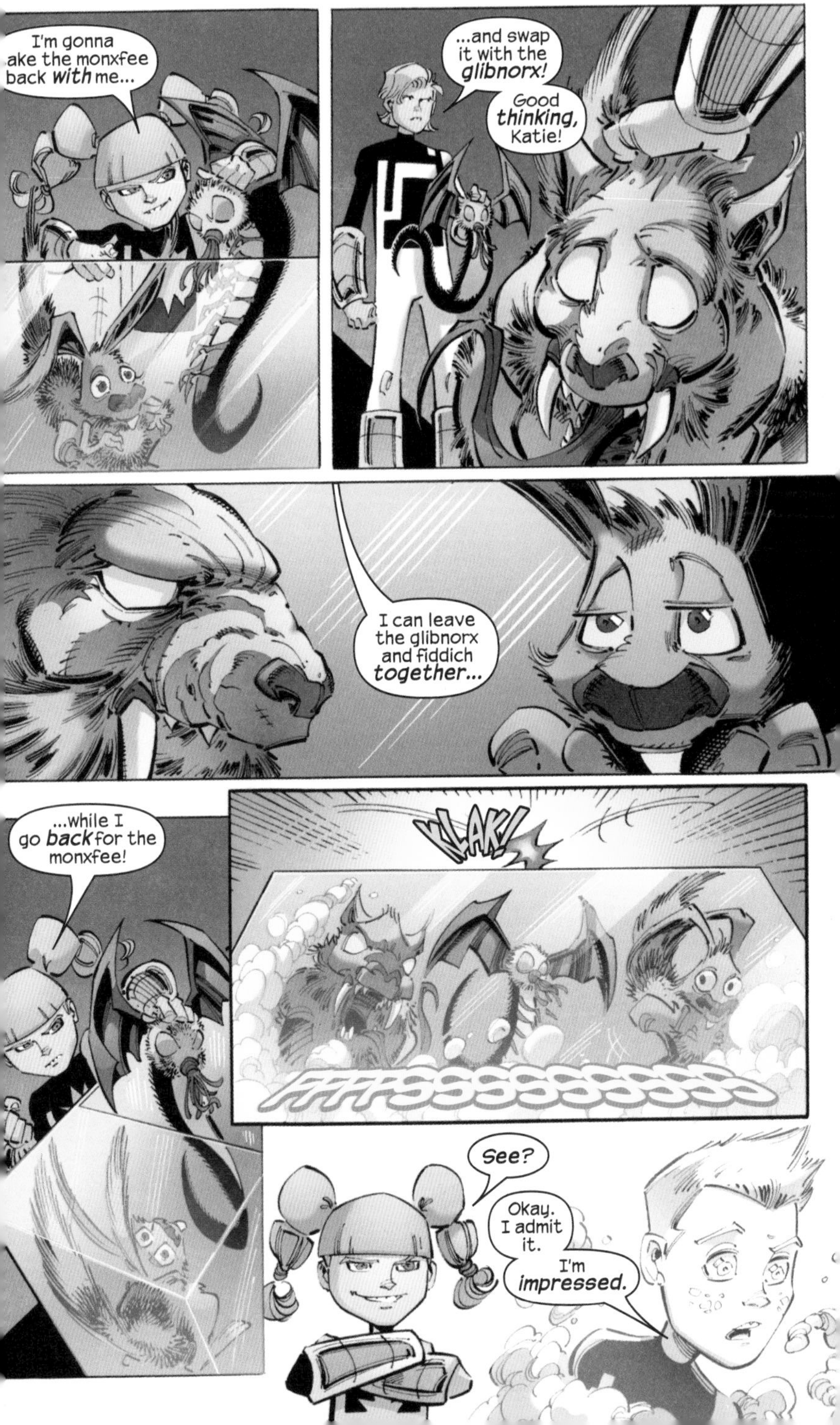
I'm gonna
ake the monxfee
back with me...
...and swap
it with the
glibnorx!
Good
thinking,
Katie!
I can leave
the glibnorx
and fiddich
together...
...while I
go back for the
monxfee!
KLAK!
FFFFSSSSSSSSSSSSS
See?
Okay.
I admit
it.
I'm
impressed.

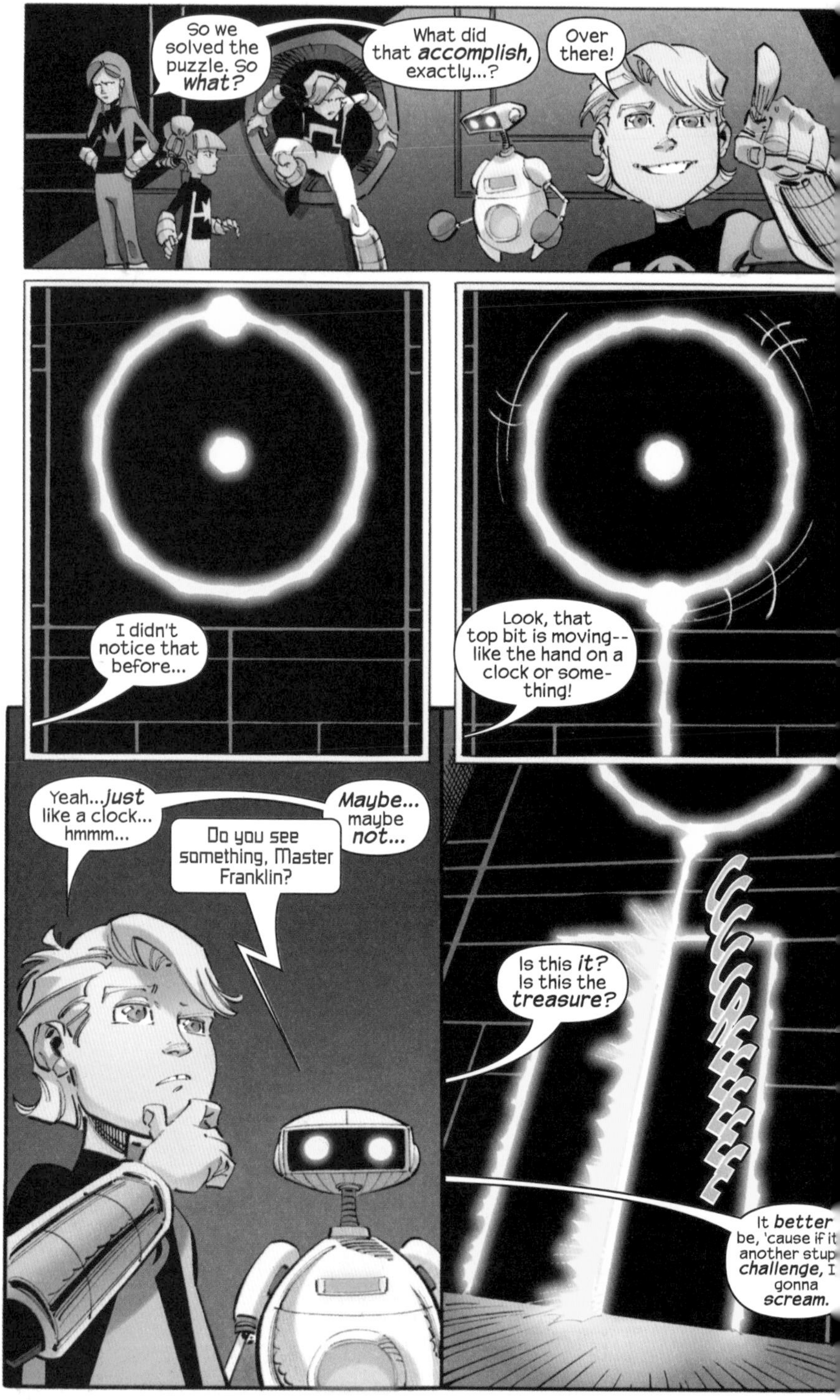
So we solved the puzzle. So what?
What did that accomplish, exactly...?
Over there!
I didn't notice that before...
Look, that top bit is moving--like the hand on a clock or some-thing!
Yeah...just like a clock... hmmm...
Maybe... maybe not...
Do you see something, Master Franklin?
Is this it? Is this the treasure?
It better be, 'cause if it another stup challenge, I gonna scream.

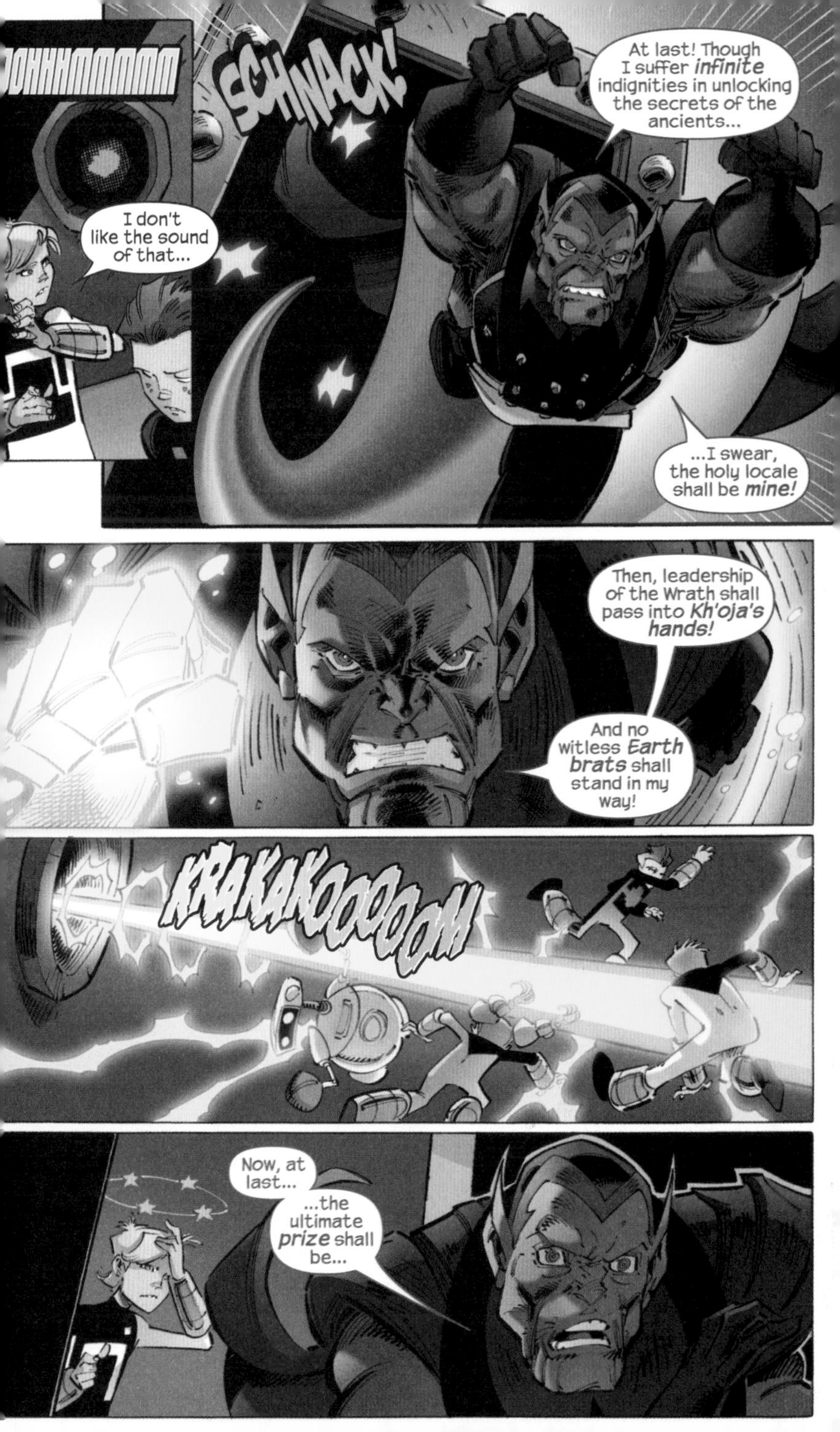

OHHHMMMMM
SCHNACK!
At last! Though I suffer *infinite* indignities in unlocking the secrets of the ancients...
I don't like the sound of that...
...I swear, the holy locale shall be *mine!*
Then, leadership of the Wrath shall pass into *Kh'oja's hands!*
And no witless *Earth brats* shall stand in my way!
KRAKAKOOOOOM
Now, at last...
...the ultimate *prize* shall be...

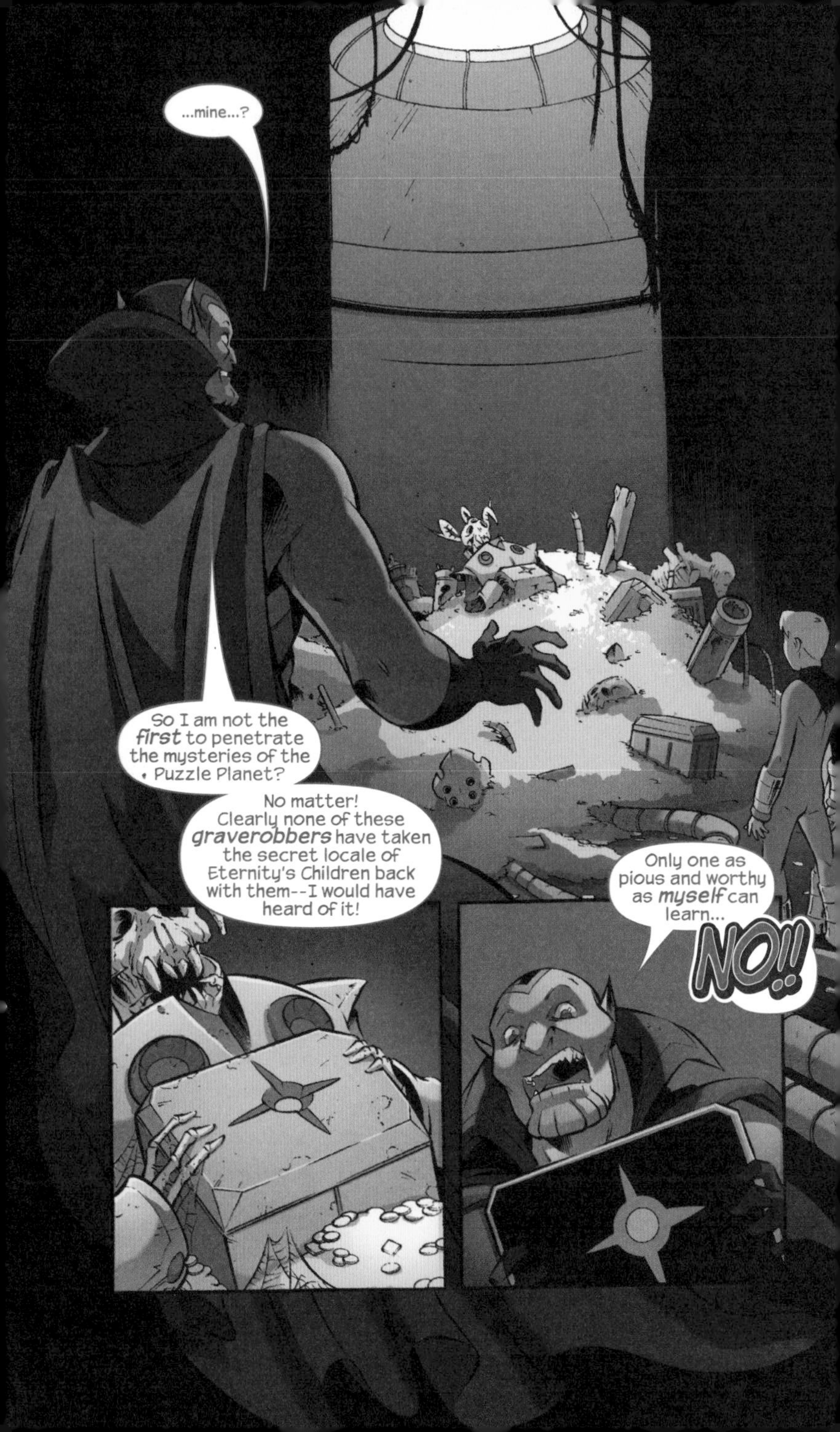
...mine...?
So I am not the *first* to penetrate the mysteries of the Puzzle Planet?
No matter! Clearly none of these *graverobbers* have taken the secret locale of Eternity's Children back with them--I would have heard of it!
Only one as pious and worthy as *myself* can learn...
NO!!

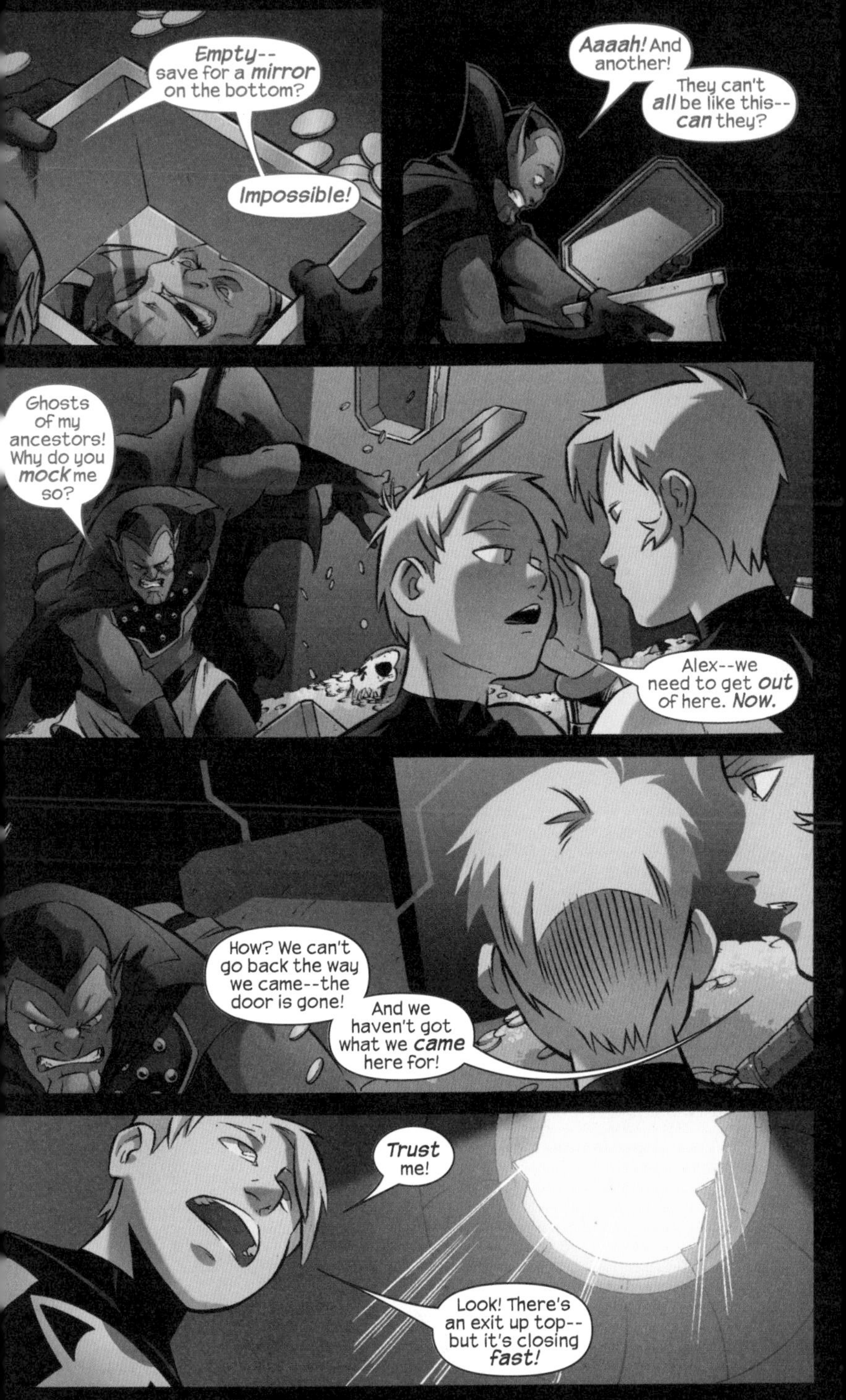
Empty-- save for a mirror on the bottom?
Impossible!
Aaaah! And another!
They can't all be like this-- can they?
Ghosts of my ancestors! Why do you mock me so?
Alex--we need to get out of here. Now.
How? We can't go back the way we came--the door is gone!
And we haven't got what we came here for!
Trust me!
Look! There's an exit up top-- but it's closing fast!

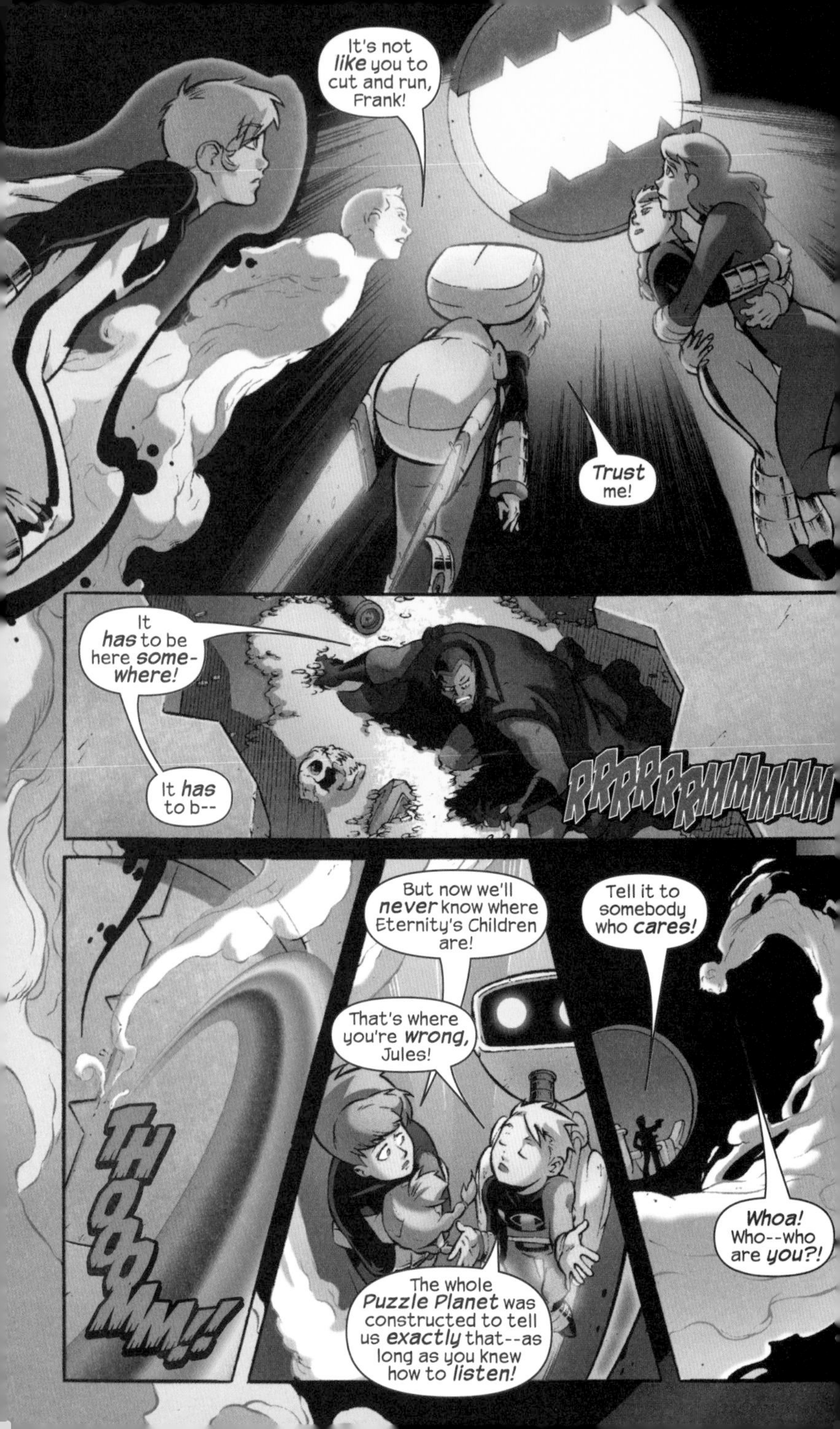

It's not like you to cut and run, Frank!
Trust me!
It has to be here some-where!
It has to b--
RRRRRRMMMMMM
THOOOMM!!
But now we'll never know where Eternity's Children are!
That's where you're wrong, Jules!
The whole Puzzle Planet was constructed to tell us exactly that--as long as you knew how to listen!
Tell it to somebody who cares!
Whoa! Who--who are you?!

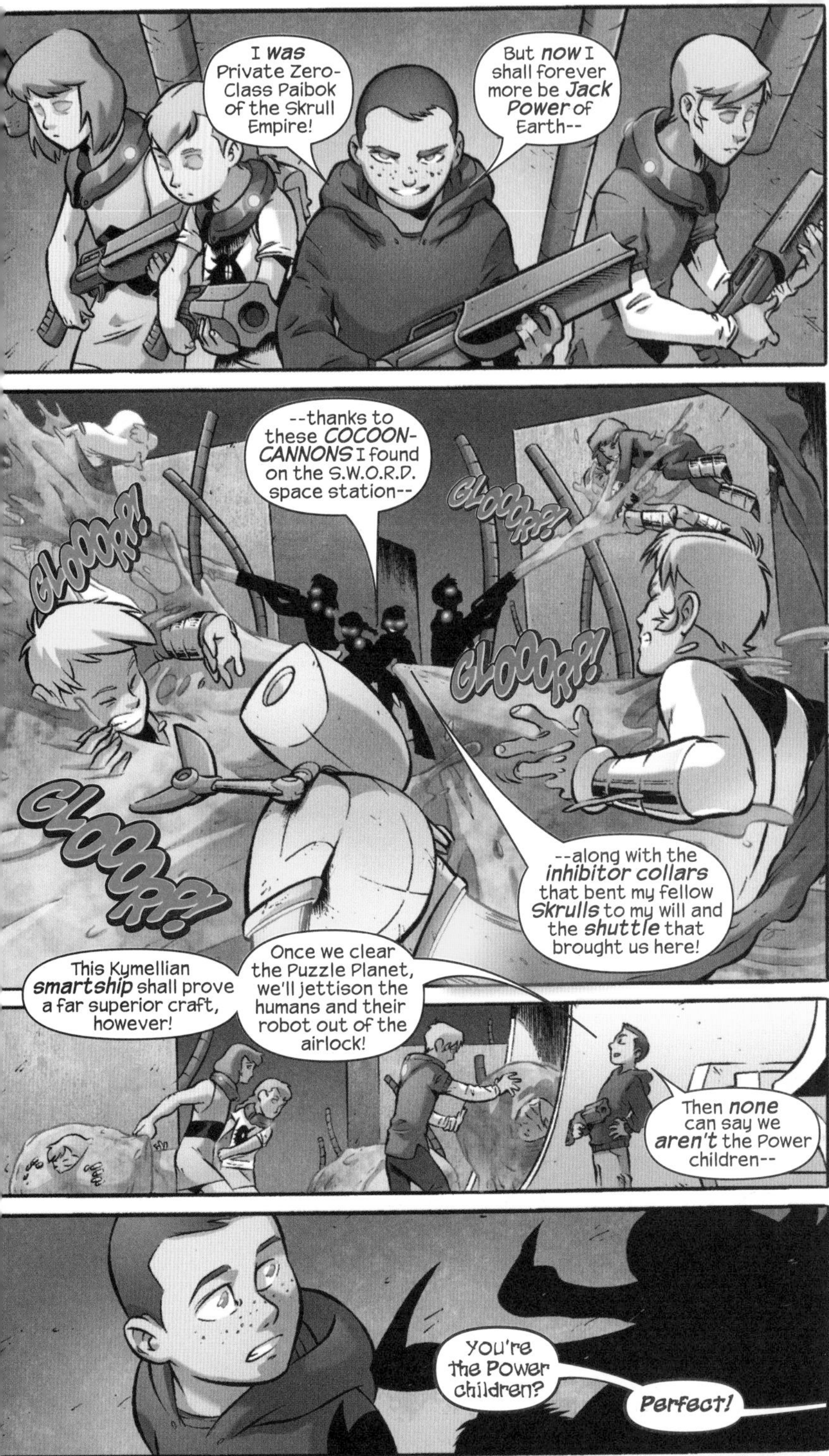
I was Private Zero-Class Paibok of the Skrull Empire!
But now I shall forever more be Jack Power of Earth--
--thanks to these COCOON-CANNONS I found on the S.W.O.R.D. space station--
GLOOORP!
GLOOORP!
GLOOORP!
GLOOORP!
--along with the inhibitor collars that bent my fellow Skrulls to my will and the shuttle that brought us here!
This Kymellian smartship shall prove a far superior craft, however!
Once we clear the Puzzle Planet, we'll jettison the humans and their robot out of the airlock!
Then none can say we aren't the Power children--
You're the Power children?
Perfect!

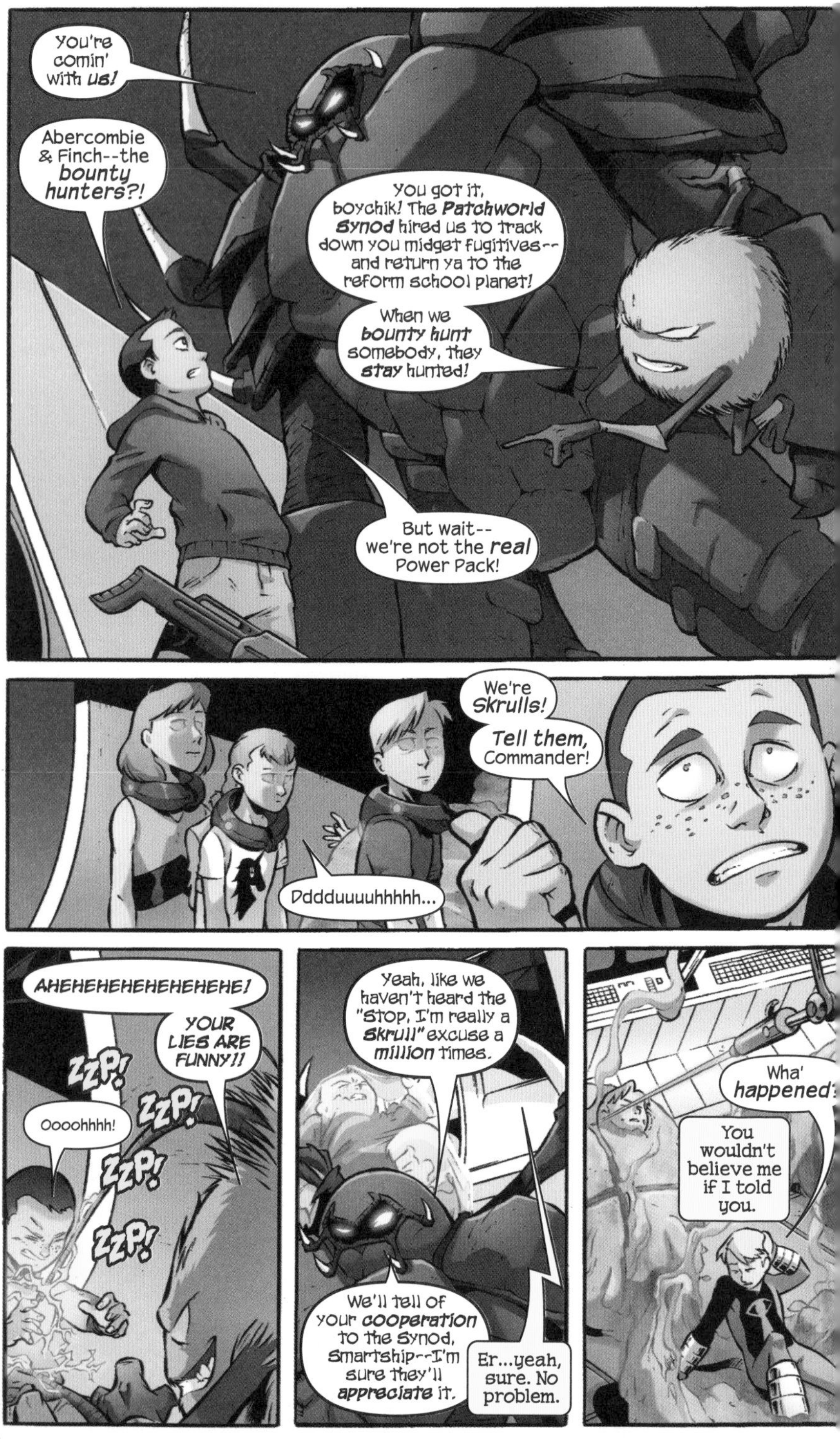

You're comin' with *us!*
Abercombie & Finch--the ***bounty hunters?!***
You got it, boychik! The ***Patchworld Synod*** hired us to track down you midget fugitives--and return ya to the reform school planet!
When we ***bounty hunt*** somebody, they ***stay*** hunted!
But wait--we're not the ***real*** Power Pack!
We're ***Skrulls!***
Tell them, Commander!
Ddddduuuuhhhhh...
AHEHEHEHEHEHEHEHEHE!
YOUR LIES ARE FUNNY!!
ZZP!
ZZP!
Oooohhhh!
ZZP!
ZZP!
Yeah, like we haven't heard the "Stop, I'm really a ***Skrull***" excuse a ***million*** times.
We'll tell of your ***cooperation*** to the Synod, Smartship--I'm sure they'll ***appreciate*** it.
Er...yeah, sure. No problem.
Wha' ***happened***
You wouldn't believe me if I told you.

So wait, Franklin--*what* were you saying about the secret of the Puzzle Planet?

All its puzzles *were* the secret! Remember those symbols in the glibnorx chamber?

They depicted an atom of *hydrogen*, the most common element in the universe, shifting states of its one *electron!*

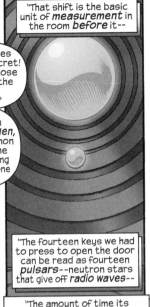

"That shift is the basic unit of *measurement* in the room *before* it--

"The fourteen keys we had to press to open the door can be read as fourteen *pulsars*--neutron stars that give off *radio waves*--

"The amount of time its *notes* were *active* allow us to map them to a central point--the *star* in the system where Eternity's kids *live!*

"And the combo Julie figured out on the first door could mean that the kids live on the *third planet* from that sun!"

Wait...this sounds kinda *familiar...*

It *is!* N.A.S.A. scientists used *similar* symbols on the *Pioneer spacecraft* they shot out into space so *aliens* would know where our planet is!

All the info here on the Puzzle Planet leads right back to the *same place...*

...Earth!

The kids destined to become the greatest *heroes*...and greatest *villains* in the *universe...*

...can be found on *our* homeworld!

Does that *mean...*

...*we* could be Eternity's Children?

THE END?

CONSPICUOUS INVASION

written & illustrated by **CHRIS GIARRUSSO**

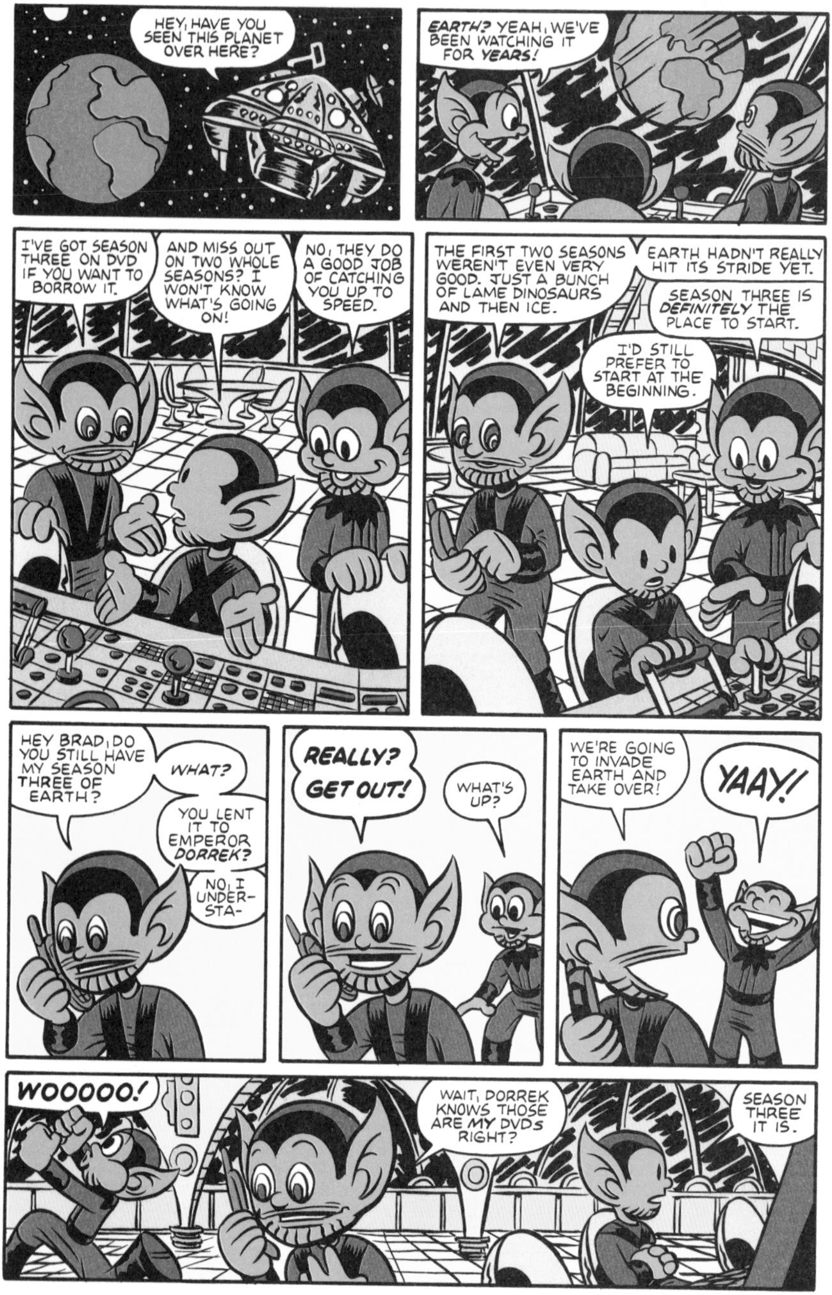

HEY, HAVE YOU SEEN THIS PLANET OVER HERE?
EARTH? YEAH, WE'VE BEEN WATCHING IT FOR YEARS!
I'VE GOT SEASON THREE ON DVD IF YOU WANT TO BORROW IT.
AND MISS OUT ON TWO WHOLE SEASONS? I WON'T KNOW WHAT'S GOING ON!
NO, THEY DO A GOOD JOB OF CATCHING YOU UP TO SPEED.
THE FIRST TWO SEASONS WEREN'T EVEN VERY GOOD. JUST A BUNCH OF LAME DINOSAURS AND THEN ICE.
EARTH HADN'T REALLY HIT ITS STRIDE YET.
SEASON THREE IS DEFINITELY THE PLACE TO START.
I'D STILL PREFER TO START AT THE BEGINNING.
HEY BRAD, DO YOU STILL HAVE MY SEASON THREE OF EARTH?
WHAT?
YOU LENT IT TO EMPEROR DORREK?
NO, I UNDERSTA-
REALLY? GET OUT!
WHAT'S UP?
WE'RE GOING TO INVADE EARTH AND TAKE OVER!
YAAY!
WOOOOO!
WAIT, DORREK KNOWS THOSE ARE MY DVDS RIGHT?
SEASON THREE IT IS.

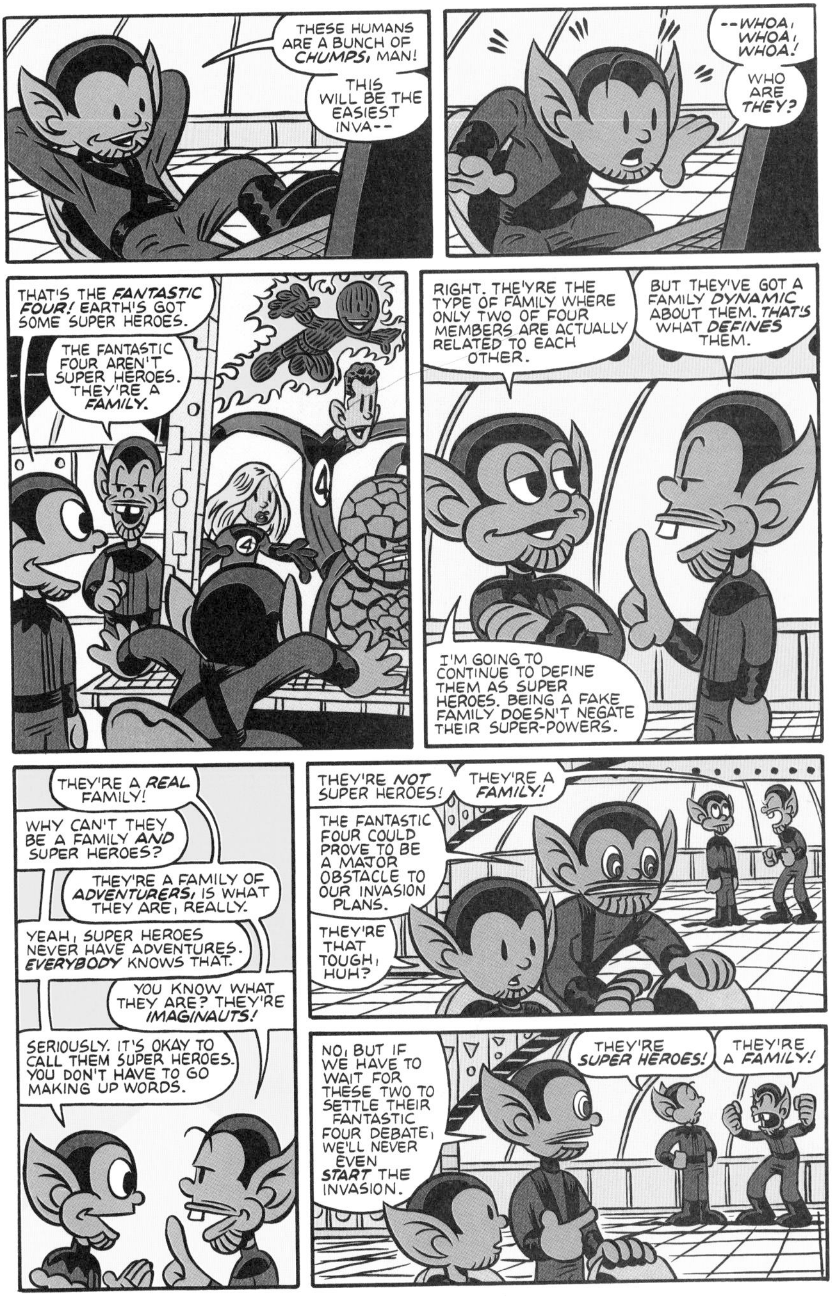
THESE HUMANS ARE A BUNCH OF CHUMPS, MAN!
THIS WILL BE THE EASIEST INVA--
--WHOA, WHOA, WHOA!
WHO ARE THEY?
THAT'S THE FANTASTIC FOUR! EARTH'S GOT SOME SUPER HEROES.
THE FANTASTIC FOUR AREN'T SUPER HEROES. THEY'RE A FAMILY.
RIGHT. THE'YRE THE TYPE OF FAMILY WHERE ONLY TWO OF FOUR MEMBERS ARE ACTUALLY RELATED TO EACH OTHER.
BUT THEY'VE GOT A FAMILY DYNAMIC ABOUT THEM. THAT'S WHAT DEFINES THEM.
I'M GOING TO CONTINUE TO DEFINE THEM AS SUPER HEROES. BEING A FAKE FAMILY DOESN'T NEGATE THEIR SUPER-POWERS.
THEY'RE A REAL FAMILY!
WHY CAN'T THEY BE A FAMILY AND SUPER HEROES?
THEY'RE A FAMILY OF ADVENTURERS, IS WHAT THEY ARE, REALLY.
YEAH, SUPER HEROES NEVER HAVE ADVENTURES. EVERYBODY KNOWS THAT.
YOU KNOW WHAT THEY ARE? THEY'RE IMAGINAUTS!
SERIOUSLY. IT'S OKAY TO CALL THEM SUPER HEROES. YOU DON'T HAVE TO GO MAKING UP WORDS.
THEY'RE NOT SUPER HEROES!
THEY'RE A FAMILY!
THE FANTASTIC FOUR COULD PROVE TO BE A MAJOR OBSTACLE TO OUR INVASION PLANS.
THEY'RE THAT TOUGH, HUH?
NO, BUT IF WE HAVE TO WAIT FOR THESE TWO TO SETTLE THEIR FANTASTIC FOUR DEBATE, WE'LL NEVER EVEN START THE INVASION.
THEY'RE SUPER HEROES!
THEY'RE A FAMILY!

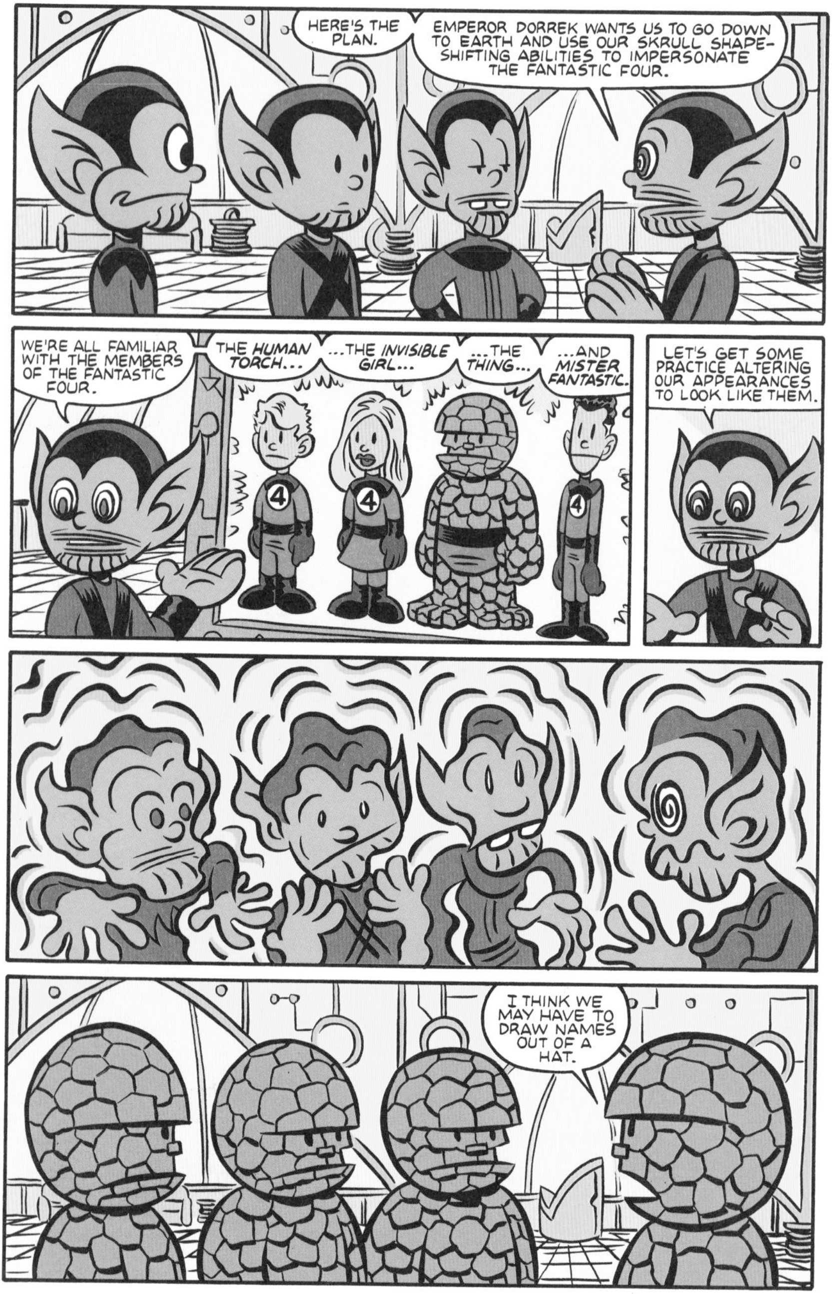
HERE'S THE PLAN.
EMPEROR DORREK WANTS US TO GO DOWN TO EARTH AND USE OUR SKRULL SHAPE-SHIFTING ABILITIES TO IMPERSONATE THE FANTASTIC FOUR.
WE'RE ALL FAMILIAR WITH THE MEMBERS OF THE FANTASTIC FOUR.
THE HUMAN TORCH...
...THE INVISIBLE GIRL...
...THE THING...
...AND MISTER FANTASTIC.
LET'S GET SOME PRACTICE ALTERING OUR APPEARANCES TO LOOK LIKE THEM.
I THINK WE MAY HAVE TO DRAW NAMES OUT OF A HAT.

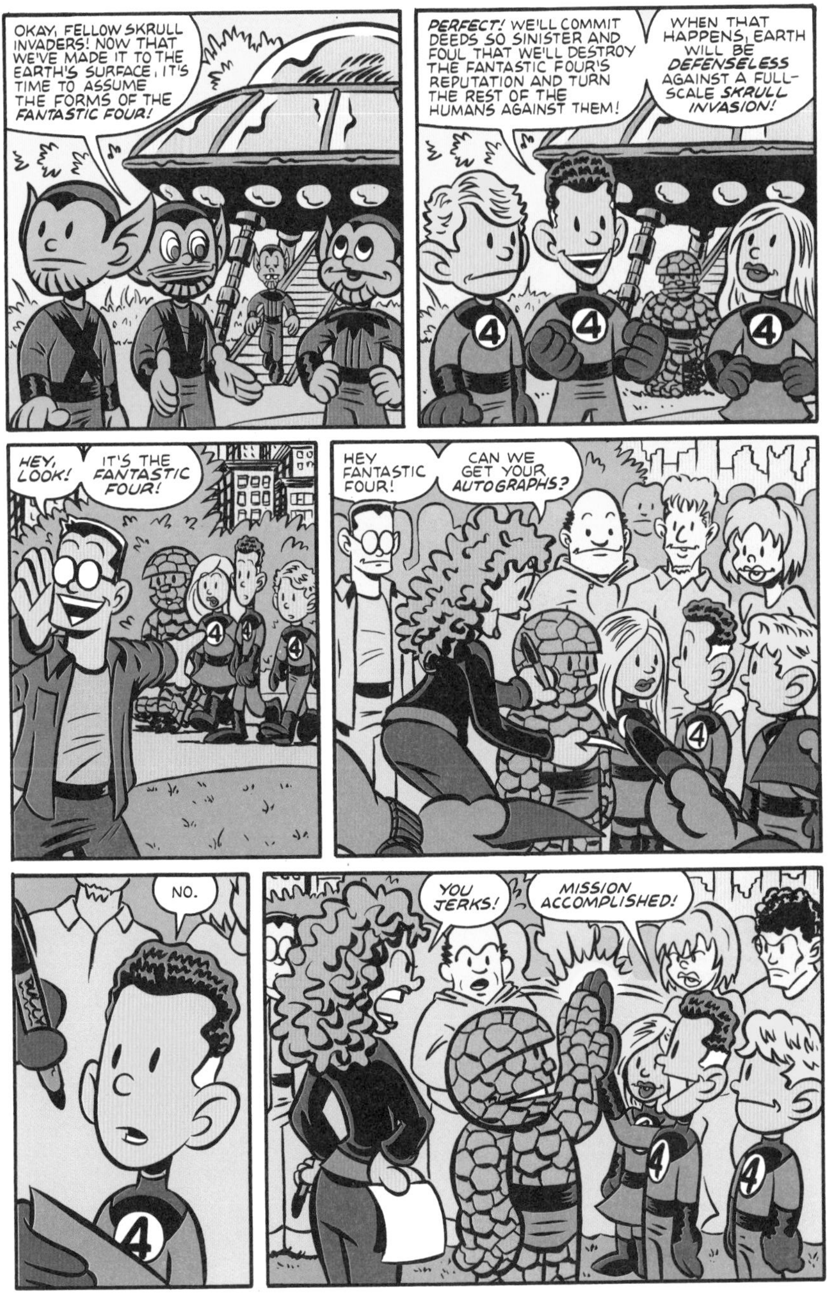
OKAY, FELLOW SKRULL INVADERS! NOW THAT WE'VE MADE IT TO THE EARTH'S SURFACE, IT'S TIME TO ASSUME THE FORMS OF THE FANTASTIC FOUR!
PERFECT! WE'LL COMMIT DEEDS SO SINISTER AND FOUL THAT WE'LL DESTROY THE FANTASTIC FOUR'S REPUTATION AND TURN THE REST OF THE HUMANS AGAINST THEM!
WHEN THAT HAPPENS, EARTH WILL BE DEFENSELESS AGAINST A FULL-SCALE SKRULL INVASION!
HEY, LOOK!
IT'S THE FANTASTIC FOUR!
HEY FANTASTIC FOUR!
CAN WE GET YOUR AUTOGRAPHS?
NO.
YOU JERKS!
MISSION ACCOMPLISHED!

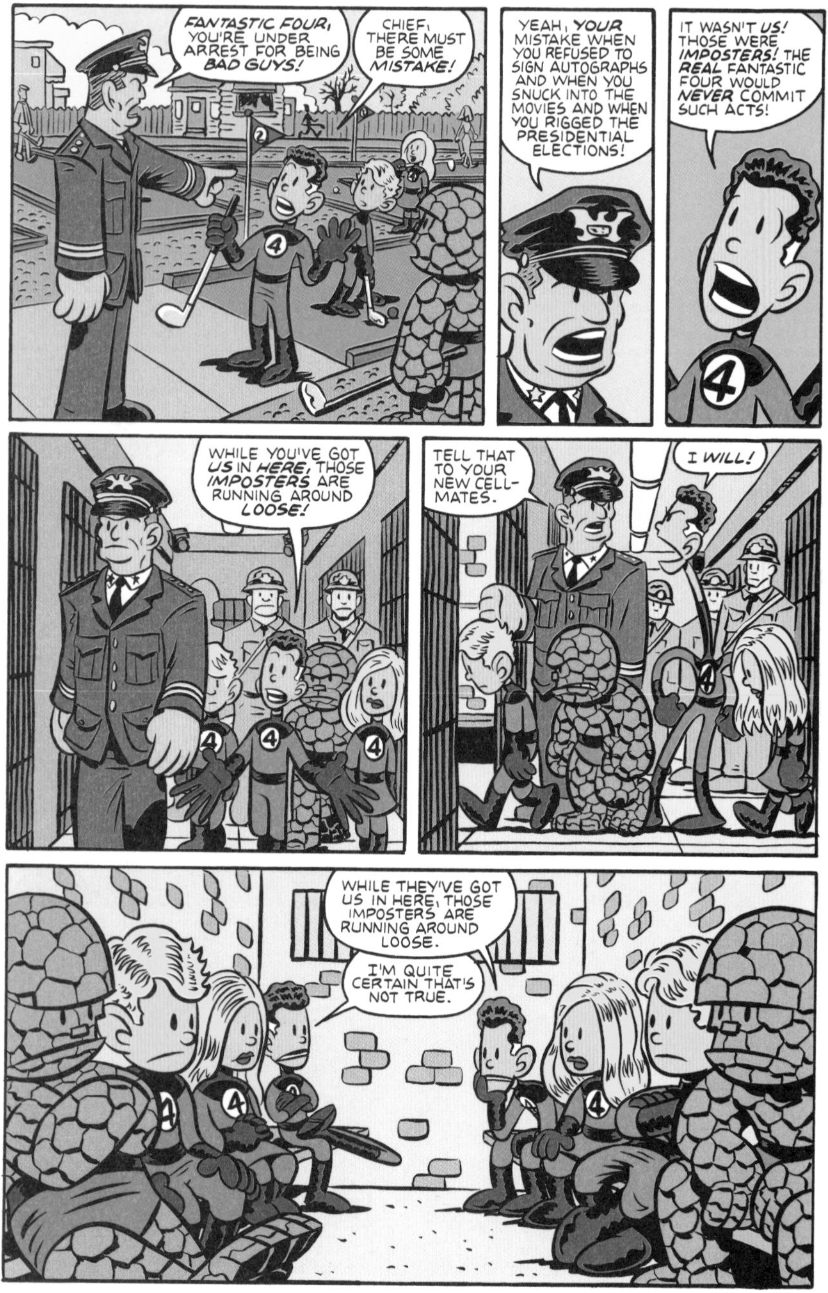
FANTASTIC FOUR, YOU'RE UNDER ARREST FOR BEING BAD GUYS!
CHIEF, THERE MUST BE SOME MISTAKE!
YEAH, YOUR MISTAKE WHEN YOU REFUSED TO SIGN AUTOGRAPHS AND WHEN YOU SNUCK INTO THE MOVIES AND WHEN YOU RIGGED THE PRESIDENTIAL ELECTIONS!
IT WASN'T US! THOSE WERE IMPOSTERS! THE REAL FANTASTIC FOUR WOULD NEVER COMMIT SUCH ACTS!
WHILE YOU'VE GOT US IN HERE, THOSE IMPOSTERS ARE RUNNING AROUND LOOSE!
TELL THAT TO YOUR NEW CELL-MATES.
I WILL!
WHILE THEY'VE GOT US IN HERE, THOSE IMPOSTERS ARE RUNNING AROUND LOOSE.
I'M QUITE CERTAIN THAT'S NOT TRUE.

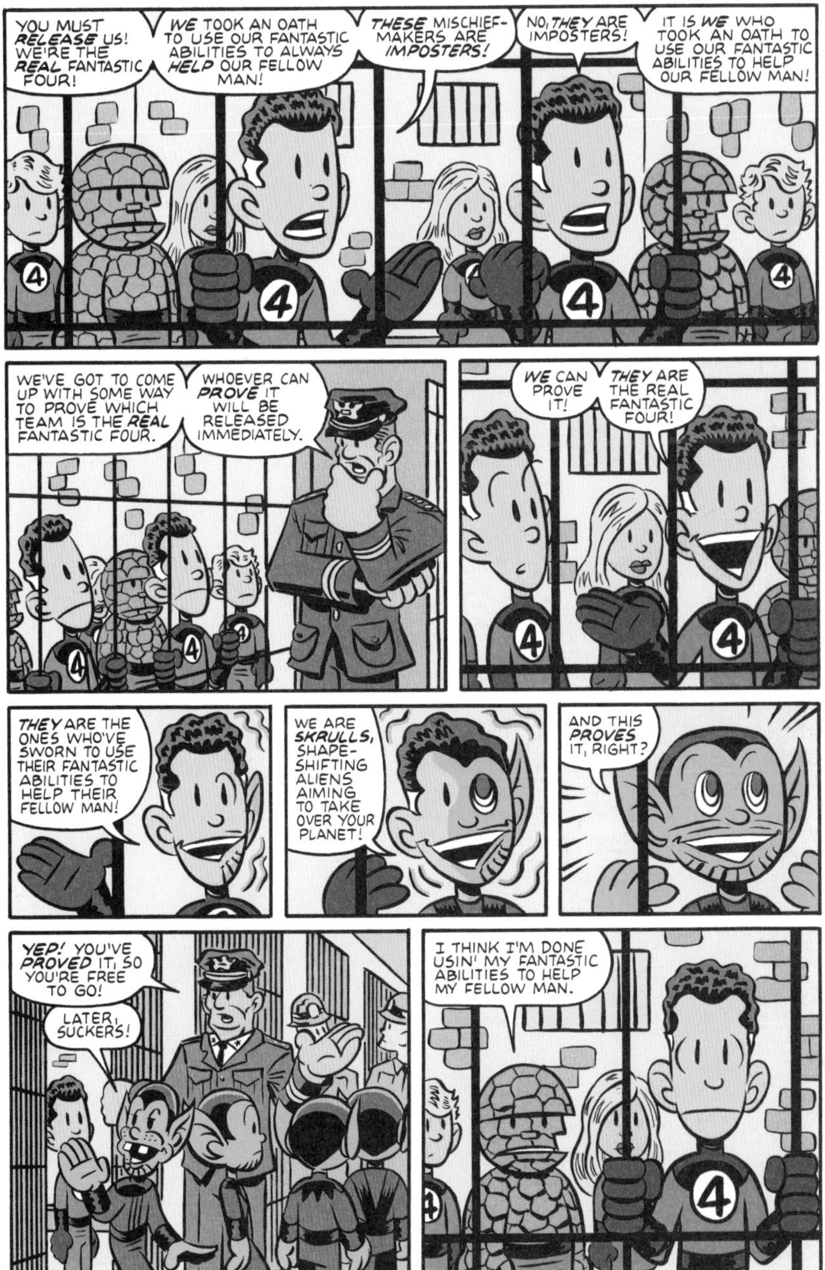
YOU MUST RELEASE US! WE'RE THE REAL FANTASTIC FOUR!
WE TOOK AN OATH TO USE OUR FANTASTIC ABILITIES TO ALWAYS HELP OUR FELLOW MAN!
THESE MISCHIEF-MAKERS ARE IMPOSTERS!
NO, THEY ARE IMPOSTERS!
IT IS WE WHO TOOK AN OATH TO USE OUR FANTASTIC ABILITIES TO HELP OUR FELLOW MAN!
WE'VE GOT TO COME UP WITH SOME WAY TO PROVE WHICH TEAM IS THE REAL FANTASTIC FOUR.
WHOEVER CAN PROVE IT WILL BE RELEASED IMMEDIATELY.
WE CAN PROVE IT!
THEY ARE THE REAL FANTASTIC FOUR!
THEY ARE THE ONES WHO'VE SWORN TO USE THEIR FANTASTIC ABILITIES TO HELP THEIR FELLOW MAN!
WE ARE SKRULLS, SHAPE-SHIFTING ALIENS AIMING TO TAKE OVER YOUR PLANET!
AND THIS PROVES IT, RIGHT?
YEP! YOU'VE PROVED IT, SO YOU'RE FREE TO GO!
LATER, SUCKERS!
I THINK I'M DONE USIN' MY FANTASTIC ABILITIES TO HELP MY FELLOW MAN.

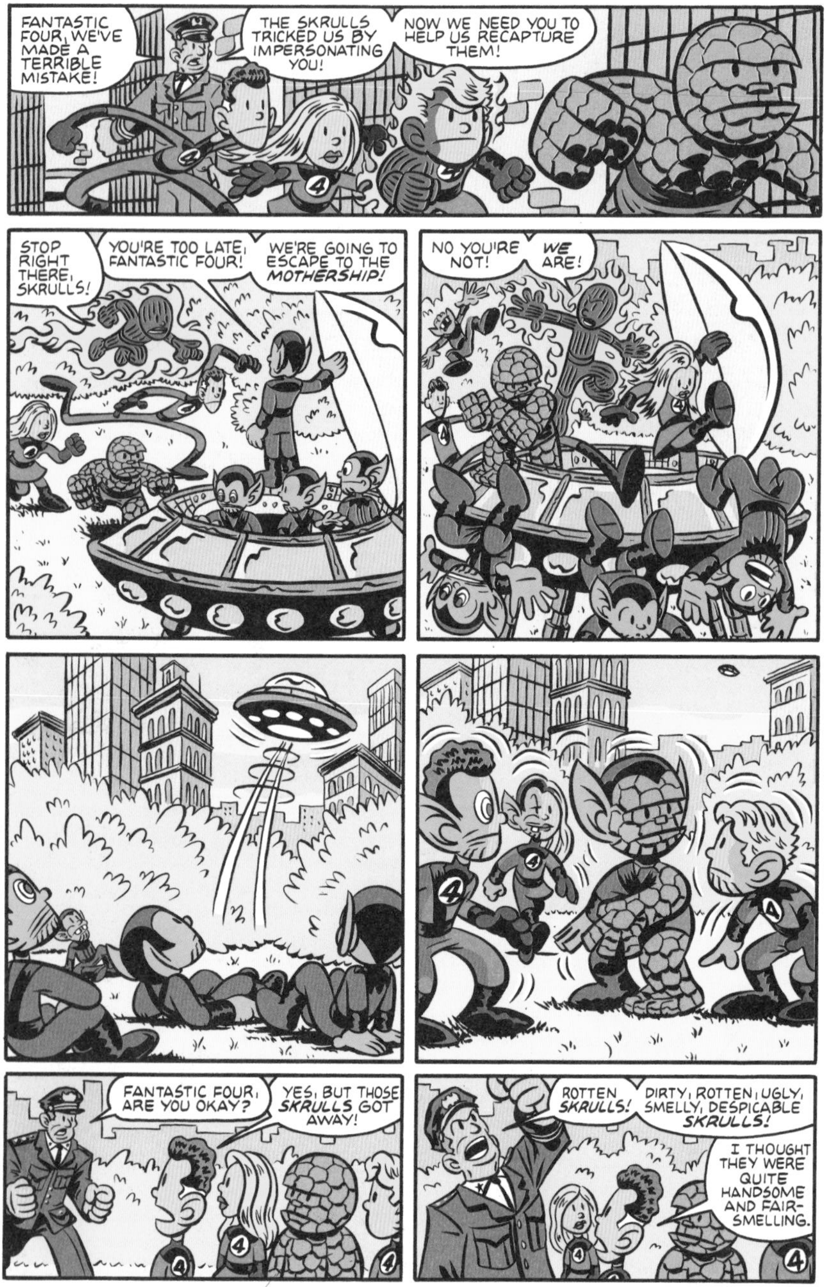
FANTASTIC FOUR, WE'VE MADE A TERRIBLE MISTAKE!
THE SKRULLS TRICKED US BY IMPERSONATING YOU!
NOW WE NEED YOU TO HELP US RECAPTURE THEM!
STOP RIGHT THERE, SKRULLS!
YOU'RE TOO LATE, FANTASTIC FOUR!
WE'RE GOING TO ESCAPE TO THE MOTHERSHIP!
NO YOU'RE NOT!
WE ARE!
FANTASTIC FOUR, ARE YOU OKAY?
YES, BUT THOSE SKRULLS GOT AWAY!
ROTTEN SKRULLS!
DIRTY, ROTTEN, UGLY, SMELLY, DESPICABLE SKRULLS!
I THOUGHT THEY WERE QUITE HANDSOME AND FAIR-SMELLING.
4

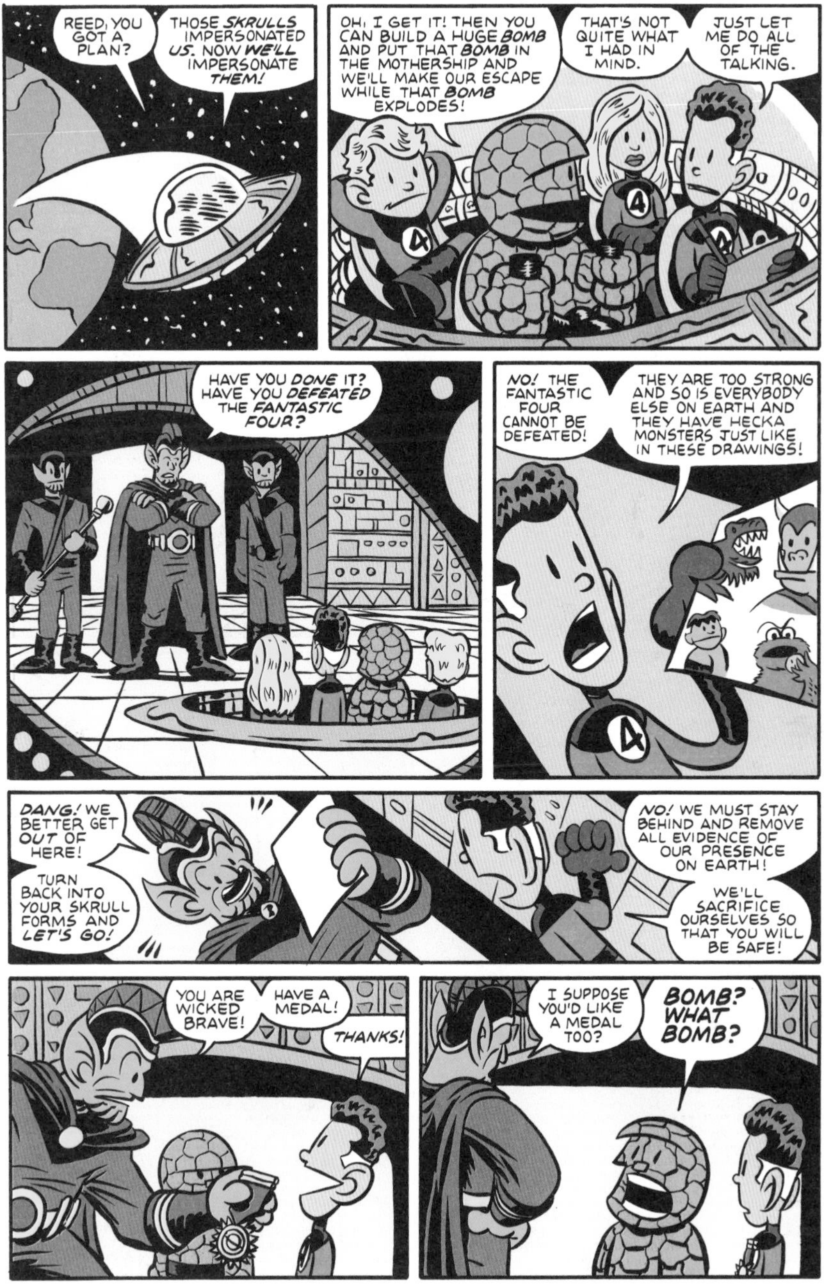
REED, YOU GOT A PLAN?
THOSE SKRULLS IMPERSONATED US. NOW WE'LL IMPERSONATE THEM!
OH, I GET IT! THEN YOU CAN BUILD A HUGE BOMB AND PUT THAT BOMB IN THE MOTHERSHIP AND WE'LL MAKE OUR ESCAPE WHILE THAT BOMB EXPLODES!
THAT'S NOT QUITE WHAT I HAD IN MIND.
JUST LET ME DO ALL OF THE TALKING.
HAVE YOU DONE IT? HAVE YOU DEFEATED THE FANTASTIC FOUR?
NO! THE FANTASTIC FOUR CANNOT BE DEFEATED!
THEY ARE TOO STRONG AND SO IS EVERYBODY ELSE ON EARTH AND THEY HAVE HECKA MONSTERS JUST LIKE IN THESE DRAWINGS!
DANG! WE BETTER GET OUT OF HERE!
TURN BACK INTO YOUR SKRULL FORMS AND LET'S GO!
NO! WE MUST STAY BEHIND AND REMOVE ALL EVIDENCE OF OUR PRESENCE ON EARTH!
WE'LL SACRIFICE OURSELVES SO THAT YOU WILL BE SAFE!
YOU ARE WICKED BRAVE!
HAVE A MEDAL!
THANKS!
I SUPPOSE YOU'D LIKE A MEDAL TOO?
BOMB? WHAT BOMB?

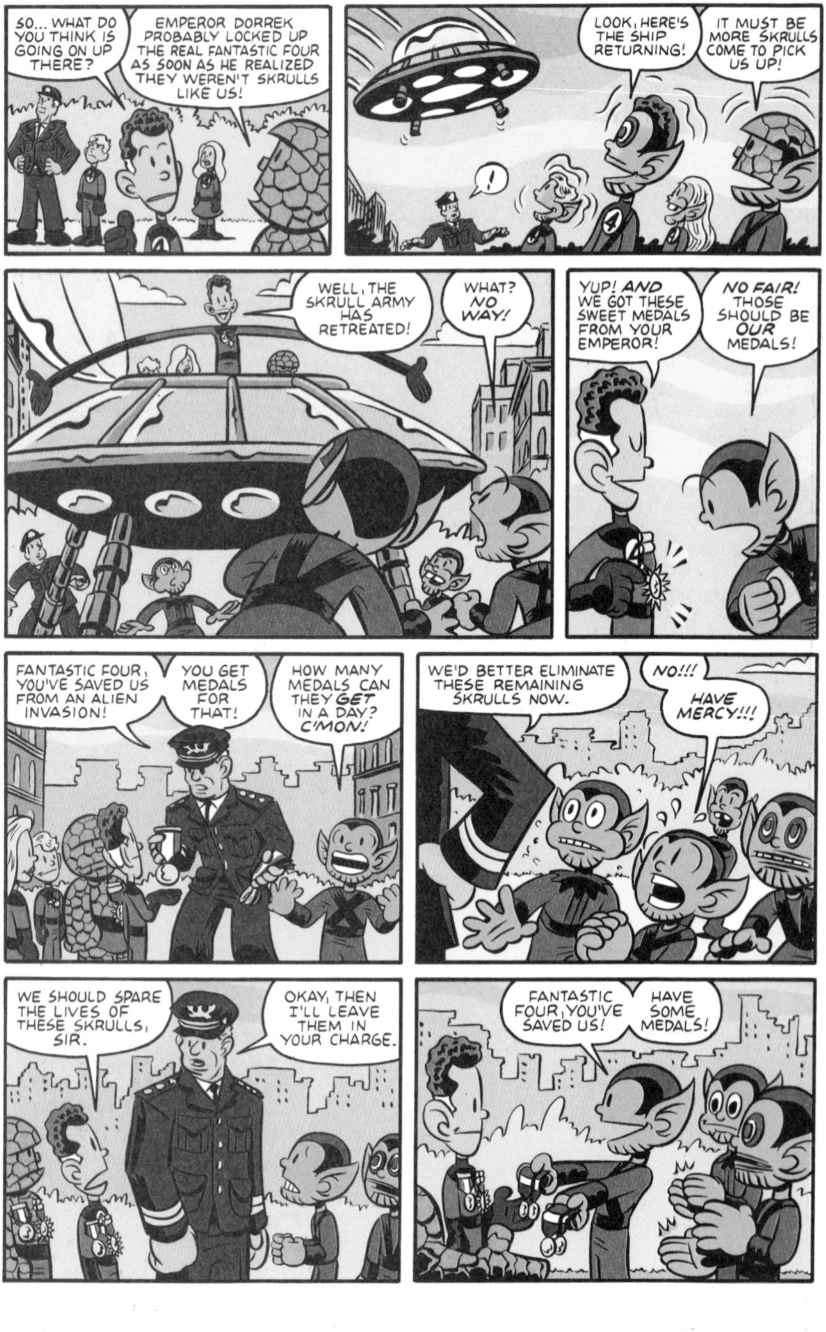
SO... WHAT DO YOU THINK IS GOING ON UP THERE?
EMPEROR DORREK PROBABLY LOCKED UP THE REAL FANTASTIC FOUR AS SOON AS HE REALIZED THEY WEREN'T SKRULLS LIKE US!
LOOK, HERE'S THE SHIP RETURNING!
IT MUST BE MORE SKRULLS COME TO PICK US UP!
!
WELL, THE SKRULL ARMY HAS RETREATED!
WHAT? NO WAY!
YUP! AND WE GOT THESE SWEET MEDALS FROM YOUR EMPEROR!
NO FAIR! THOSE SHOULD BE OUR MEDALS!
FANTASTIC FOUR, YOU'VE SAVED US FROM AN ALIEN INVASION!
YOU GET MEDALS FOR THAT!
HOW MANY MEDALS CAN THEY GET IN A DAY? C'MON!
WE'D BETTER ELIMINATE THESE REMAINING SKRULLS NOW.
NO!!!
HAVE MERCY!!!
WE SHOULD SPARE THE LIVES OF THESE SKRULLS, SIR.
OKAY, THEN I'LL LEAVE THEM IN YOUR CHARGE.
FANTASTIC FOUR, YOU'VE SAVED US!
HAVE SOME MEDALS!